D1030847

The Ukrainian Language

in the First Half of the Twentieth Century

(1900–1941)

Its State and Status

George Y. Shevelov

The Ukrainian Language in the First Half of the Twentieth Century (1900–1941)

Its State and Status

Distributed by Harvard University Press
for the
Harvard Ukrainian Research Institute

Publication of this volume was made possible by a bequest from the estate of the late John Hadzevich.

The Harvard Ukrainian Research Institute was established in 1973 as an integral part of Harvard University. It supports research associates and visiting scholars who are engaged in projects concerned with all aspects of Ukrainian studies. The Institute also works in close cooperation with the Committee on Ukrainian Studies, which supervises and coordinates the teaching of Ukrainian history, language, and literature at Harvard University.

Contents

Introduction

The history of literary languages, the Ukrainian language among them, is not a new discipline. Its study usually focuses on the written language in works of literature, less often in journalism, and quite rarely in other genres. Consequently, the main source for the characterization of a literary language in a given epoch is the writing of contemporaries. A secondary source, which can occasionally provide clues for the correct understanding of the texts, is the commentary of contemporaries on the problems of the language, especially useful if there are clashes of judgment, evaluation, and opinion. To take the closest example, such a history is my *Die ukrainische Schriftsprache, 1798–1965* (1966).

The present study includes that type of material, but intends not to be limited to or by it. A language question is not only the question of a language's internal history. It encompasses a much broader set of problems, first of all, the problem of the use of that language, both in written and oral communication, by whom it is used, in what functions, and with what legal, political, and social possibilities and limitations. For monolingual countries these are not important problems from a strictly linguistic point of view. The language of those countries is used in all the functions the given society requires and in all the circumstances that arise in that society. Therefore in that case the study of such functions and circumstances belongs to sociology rather than to linguistics.

This is not so in the case of bi- or multilingual societies. There a speaker chooses for each situation one of the languages he commands. His choice is conditioned by legal, political, historical, anthropological, and other factors. Specifically, if, as is the case with Ukrainian, the society's majority (Ukrainians) is governed by a minority or minorities (e.g., between the two World Wars, by Russians, Poles, and Romanians, as well as Czechs and Slovaks), the language question necessarily becomes not only or immediately a linguistic question, but also, and often primarily, a political, sociological and cultural question. The researcher has to show not only how, but why the language developed. This "why" is conditioned by the possibilities the language was granted and the limitations that were imposed on it, be they legal or social-historical. Hence it is necessary, in this study, to bring in such historical facts as language legislation, changes in political course, and social changes that influenced the use and form of the language and often even directly determined it, especially in the tempestuous conditions of the wars, revolutions, and social upheavals that shook Eastern and Central Europe in the twentieth century.

The problem of language choice by the bilingual speaker in various situations is especially difficult to study. To begin with, the speaker himself does not always know why, here and now, he chose one language and not the other. A large-scale investigation applying the methodologies of modern psychology and statistics could shed some light on that. But such an investigation is beyond the possibilities of a researcher who does not live in the country of his subject. Moreover, any such investigation would hardly be welcome in the present-day Ukraine, where one principle of the overall policy on language is not to draw speakers' interest and attention to such problems. Finally, this approach cannot be applied to periods of time not yet remote, but still well past, as the years 1900–1941 are. Some conclusions about the status of a language as shown by its selection or rejection for an act of communication can be drawn indirectly from extra-linguistic evidence, such as the system and the development of education, the press, book production, and cultural life. This explains why it was expedient, in this study, to use data of that kind.

As a result, each chapter of this study includes a survey of language legislation during the time under consideration as well as a survey of pertinent political development and of some characteristic features of the educational system and of cultural life. These surveys, naturally, are brief and incomplete. Even so, they often were outside of my field of specialization. So I consulted the experts and benefitted greatly from their expertise. I am much indebted to Martha Bohachevsky-Chomiak, Roman Ilnytzkyj, Sofia Janiw, Arkadii Joukovsky, Edward Kasinec, Vasyl Luciv, Ivan Majstrenko, Jaroslaw Padoch, George S. N. Luckyj, Ivan L. Rudnytsky, Myroslava Znayenko, and especially John-Paul Himka and Myroslav Prokop. Of course, they are not responsible for the simplifications necessary in so concise a presentation or for any errors resulting from my use of the information they provided. Uliana M. Pasicznyk worked conscientiously on form and style.

This study is very incomplete. It must be incomplete, due, above all, to limitation in the use of sources. The archives of the USSR and of other countries involved are not accessible to me. For instance, the proceedings of the conference on Ukrainian orthography held in Kharkiv in 1927 have never been published; there were some closed discussions of dictionaries that were never even mentioned in the Soviet press; and there must be many more materials never printed. One small consolation—if it can be called that—is that these data are not only unavailable to me, but also to researchers who work in the Ukraine—at least, certainly not in full.

The limitations do not end here. Even published materials were not all available to me. Many a Ukrainian publication, especially those of the 1920s and 1930s, has become a bibliographic item of extreme rarity. Because I limited my research basically to the resources of the American libraries on the East Coast, I cannot claim to have used all the pertinent publications, and occasionally even important ones have remained outside the scope of my research.

Two more self-imposed limitations should be brought to the attention of the reader. First, this study is limited essentially to the problems of Ukrainian in its internal development and in its relation to the languages of the nations that ruled in the Ukraine: Russian, Polish, Romanian, Hungarian, and Czech. The languages of national minorities in the Ukraine—Russians, Jews, Poles, Moldavians, Hungarians, Greeks (see the article by R. Moroz in *Sučasnist'* 1980, no. 12), Germans, Bulgarians, and others—though able to shed some light on the development of Ukrainian and on the language policy of the ruling nation, are left out of this survey. There are two main reasons for this: materials on this subject are largely unavailable; and the problems involved are not identical with those of the Ukrainian language.

Also left outside the scope of this study are problems concerning the status and character of the Ukrainian language in regions not now part of the Ukrainian SSR: in Eastern Slovakia, in postwar Poland, in the South Berestja (Brest) oblast' that by Stalin's decision became part of Belorussia in 1939, in the South Kursk, West Voronež and Kuban' areas of the Russian Soviet republic, not to speak of the Ukrainian-language enclaves in Kazakhstan and the Far East or in various countries of Western Europe, the Americas, and Australia. One reason for the omissions is that for some of these areas (particularly in postwar Poland and in Soviet Union republics other than the Ukraine, where Ukrainians are subject to systematic information blackouts) virtually no data are available. No less important is that in all these areas Ukrainians constitute a minority, whereas I have set out to investigate the status and character of the Ukrainian language in those places where Ukrainians are the majority. Practically, then, the present study concentrates on the Ukrainian language within the frontiers of the present-day Soviet Ukraine.

All these problems should be elucidated in a comprehensive work on the status and the character of the Ukrainian language in its connections with the coterritorial languages, yet to be written. Such a study can propose definitive solutions. Those offered here are, alas, too often only tentative, hardly more than material for discussion and perhaps a springboard for that integral study one can only dream of today.

It is also my hope to return to the topic of this essay to discuss, using the same approach and working within the same boundaries, the situation of the Ukrainian language after World War II (1945–1985).

CHAPTER ONE

The Standard Ukrainian Language in 1900: A Tentative Crosscut

Divided among the three states of Russia, Austria, and Hungary (of which the latter two were united in Austro-Hungary), Ukrainians lived under three different legislative systems. The functions, privileges, and restrictions of the public use of their language were delineated quite differently in each system. The status of the Ukrainian language for the ca. 85 percent of Ukrainians who lived in tsarist Russia was the worst; the ca. 13 percent of Ukrainians who lived in Eastern Galicia and in Bukovina, integrated into Austria, enjoyed relatively better conditions; the remaining ca. 2 percent in Transcarpathia lived in a situation closer to that in the Russian Ukraine.[1]

Autocratic Russia had no constitution. The source of legislation was the supreme will of the tsar. At the turn of the century the language regulations in the Ukraine were based on Tsar Alexander II's ukase signed in Ems, Germany, on 18 May 1876, as slightly modified by Tsar Alexander III on 8 October 1881.[2] The ukase of 1876 proscribed the printing of any texts, either original or translated, in Ukrainian, except for belles lettres and historical records. It also forbade any theatrical performances or public recitations in Ukrainian; the importation of any Ukrainian books published abroad; the teaching

---

[1] The number of Ukrainians in the Russian Ukraine has been calculated on the basis of the census of 1897; that for Austria and Hungary, on the basis of the census of 1900. The data are quoted in *Ukrainskij narod v ego prošlom i nastojaščem*, ed. F. Volkov [Vovk] et al.; the article on population statistics, by A. Rusov, appears in vol. 2 (Petrograd, 1916), pp. 381–406.

[2] Much earlier, Ukrainian was entirely banned from the church. No sermons were allowed in Ukrainian, and the Ukrainian pronunciation of Church Slavonic was outlawed as early as the 1720s.

of any discipline in Ukrainian in schools; and the preservation or circulation of any Ukrainian books in school libraries. School teachers and all staff were to be screened, and all persons suspect of Ukrainophilism were to be transferred to schools outside of the Ukraine; new appointees would be recruited "predominantly" from among Russians (Savčenko, 381ff). The modification of 1881 concerned basically two points: dictionaries were excepted from the prohibition, provided the Russian alphabet was used; and theatrical performances were allowed, but only by the special permission of a province's governor-general or governor for each performance and with the provision that there be no exclusively Ukrainian theatrical companies.[3] Essentially, the regulations of 1876–1881 aimed at the complete elimination of the Ukrainian language from public life. (The exclusion of Ukrainian from any court or administrative proceeding needed no formal prohibition because that practice had been in effect from the late eighteenth century.)

Neither the ukase of 1876 nor the amendments of 1881 were ever published by the Russian government. They were secret and were supposed to remain so from the public. Nevertheless, very soon their existence and even the verbatim text became known. As early as 1876 they were analyzed in the article "Ukaz proty rus'koho jazyka" published in the periodical *Pravda* in Lviv. In 1878, Myxajlo Drahomanov, who emigrated from Kiev to Geneva, deposited at the International Literary Congress in Paris the paper "La littérature ukrainienne proscrite par le gouvernement russe," which was published that same year in Geneva. Information on the ukase reached intellectual circles in Russia through foreign periodicals. For instance, the *Revue des deux mondes* published the article "La presse et la censure" by Anatol Leroy-Beaulieux in his series *L'empire des tsars et les russes* (vol. 37, p. 88). In 1880–1882 the subject of the anti-Ukrainian legislation was widely debated in the legal Russian press within the empire in at least twelve periodicals, among them the authoritative journals *Vestnik Evropy* and *Russkaja starina* (Savčenko, 175).

---

[3] This only reiterated the policy conceived of by Minister of Interior M. Loris-Melikov in 1879. He permitted concerts and theatrical shows in Ukrainian, but only on Ukrainian rural subjects; no plays could be translated and no Ukrainian plays could be performed in Kiev (Čykalenko 103, 112, 245).

A yet graver breech of the prohibition and intended absolute blackout of the Ukrainian language as a vehicle of literature and public communication was the appearance of legal Ukrainian publications—true, all of them in the Russian alphabet—after the ukase of Ems. The first major breakthrough was the publication of Ševčenko's *Kobzar* in 25,000 copies (about 1880; Čykalenko, 295). Without attempting to enumerate all such books, I can illustrate the point by noting the titles of published almanacs as listed, chronologically, in Bojko, 1967: *Rada*, 1 (Kiev, 1883), *Rada*, 2 (Kiev, 1884), edited by M. Staryc'kyj; *Nyva* (Odessa, 1885), edited by M. Borovs'kyj and D. Markovyč; *Step* (Kherson, 1886), edited by D. Markovyč a.o.; *Skladka*, 1 (Kharkiv, 1887) and 2 (Kharkiv, 1893), edited by V. Oleksandriv, 3 (Kharkiv, 1896) and 4 (Khariv, 1897), edited by K. Bilylovs'kyj; *Xutir* (Kobeljaky, 1891), edited by T. Kalenyčenko; *Prolisky* (Odessa, 1893); *Virna para* (Černihiv, 1895), edited by B. Hrinčenko; *Krynyčka* (Černihiv, 1896), edited by B. Hrinčenko; *Maty* (Kiev, 1896), edited by O. Tyško; *Bat'kove viščuvannja* (Černihiv, 1898), edited by B. Hrinčenko; *Malorossijskij sbornik* (Moscow, 1899); *Stepovi kvitky* (Černihiv, 1899), edited by B. Hrinčenko; *Ščyri sl'ozy* (Baxmut, 1899); *Vik* (Kiev, 1900), edited by S. Jefremov; *Xvylja za xvyleju* (Černihiv, 1900), edited by B. Hrinčenko; *Dubove lystja* (Kiev, 1903), edited by M. Černjavs'kyj a.o.; *Z nad xmar i z dolyn* (Odessa, 1903), edited by M. Voronyj; *Literaturnyj zbirnyk* (Kiev, 1903); *Na vičnu pamjat' Kotljarevs'komu* (Kiev, 1904), edited by S. Jefremov.

How the publishers of these almanacs managed to outmaneuver the censorship, tacking among various ministries, departments, and branches of censorship, is in itself a subject for study. It was not an easy undertaking. Sometimes it took years of effort and camouflage. For instance, it took Čykalenko five years to see his innocuous popular pamphlet designed for peasants, *Rozmovy pro sil's'ke hospodarstvo*, into print (Čykalenko, 189). Nonetheless, the plan to silence and annihilate Ukrainian literature completely had failed. There was even a Ukrainian bookstore in Kiev owned by *Kievskaja starina*, although the only one of its kind in the whole country. A society founded in Moscow under the Russian name "Blagotvoritel'noe obščestvo izdanija obščepoleznyx i deševyx knig" (Charitable Society for the Publication of Inexpensive Books for General Use) began in 1898 to publish pamphlets for the Ukrainian peasantry in Ukrainian. In 1903,

the Kiev governor-general M. Dragomirov permitted fiction in
Ukrainian, rendered in the Russian alphabet, to be published in
Kievskaja starina.

The government also failed to halt fully the importation of foreign,
mainly Galician, Ukrainian-language publications into the Russian
Empire. For instance, both M. Komar in Odessa and Je. Čykalenko at
his estate in Eastern Ukraine managed, in 1881, to subscribe to *Zorja*
and *Dzvinok* published in Lviv (Čykalenko 177). In the years 1890 to
1896 *Zorja* had over 400 subscribers in the Russian Ukraine (Žyvotko
75); *Literaturno-naukovyj vistnyk* had 155 such subscribers in 1899
(but importation became impossible in April 1901: Žyvotko 78;
Dorošenko 1949, 7). The central censorship office fought back, time
and again, reprimanding its too liberal censors (some such letters are
mentioned in *Ob otmene stesnenij malorusskogo pečatnogo slova*),
but violations continued. The Ukrainian language did not completely
lose its function as a literary language. Also the Ukrainian theater,
despite many often senseless and arbitrary restrictions, continued to
exist and to enjoy great success, even in St. Petersburg and with Russian critics.

The effect of the prohibitions of 1876–1881 is not to be underes-
timated, however. They affected human relations as well as publications. The main center of "Ukrainophilism," namely, the Kiev *Hromada* (Community), shrank from ca. 100 members before the ukase of
1876 to 14 after it; it had no more than 25 members by 1900
(Čykalenko 293, 296). Only a very small fraction of Ukrainian texts
readied for publication succeeded in getting through the censorship,
and they were exclusively belles-lettres or publications for the uneducated. There was no Ukrainian periodical press in the Russian
Ukraine. From the higher spheres of public life, as well as from spiri-
tual discussions, truly modern literature, scholarship, and science, the
Ukrainian language was excluded. It was entirely absent from education on all levels, from elementary school through university. All this,
of course, contributed to the lowering of the prestige of the Ukrainian
language (which in any case was labeled a dialect of Russian, just as
Ukrainians themselves were officially only "Little Russians"). More
and more, Ukrainian was acquiring the reputation of being the
language of the uneducated—essentially, of peasants.

The social status of peasants was low, a situation perpetuated by their lack of education. According to the census of 1897, 80 percent of the Ukrainian population was illiterate (Čykalenko 380), and the percentage would have been even higher if only peasants were considered. It is not surprising that peasants, too, were often ashamed of speaking Ukrainian and, in conversations with persons of the upper classes, inserted as many Russian words as they could. Speaking of his school comrades Čykalenko (86) says: "Characteristically enough, country boys, pupils in care of the zemstvo, spoke Ukrainian the least. . ., they were ashamed of their native tongue and tried to conceal [this fact], apparently wishing to get rid of their stigma of hill-billyism." No wonder, then, that later, in 1903, when the question of Ukrainian elementary school became topical, some parents rejected education in Ukrainian for their children. They thought that this experience would keep their children in the lower classes for good, by undermining their chances to become "teachers, priests, physicians" (349). Nonetheless, in 1905, a petition for Ukrainian elementary schooling is said to have gathered "many thousands" of signatures (403).

The official measures concerned Ukrainian as the vehicle of literature, scholarship, and public speech. Indirectly, however, they also affected how the educated spoke among themselves and within their families. The use of Ukrainian even in private was often grasped as the manifestation of a low social status; or, if used, it was considered the expression of a deliberate opposition to the Russian language as a symbol of the tsarist empire, which more often than not was simply dangerous. The memoirs of many contemporaries note this. For example, Čykalenko (343) says: "One cannot blame too sharply the use of Russian in Ukrainian families. At the time [in 1903] for the use of Ukrainian people were dismissed from their positions not only in state or zemstvo offices, but sometimes even in private enterprises." No wonder, then, that in listing families of intellectuals who nonetheless spoke Ukrainian, Čykalenko could name only eight: the Lucenko, Hrinčenko, Antonovyč, Lysenko, Staryc'kyj, Kosač, Šul'hyn, and his own (222, 298, 308). Perhaps there were a few more such families (Lotoc'kyj, in his memoirs, mentions Ukrainian being spoken by some others, e.g. 2, 98; 2, 190) but certainly they were exceptional. The Russification of the younger generation of clergy and of the upper classes in general was depicted many times and with many realistic details in belles lettres, e.g., in A. Svydnyc'kyj's *Ljuborac'ki* and in V. Mova's "Stare hnizdo i molodi ptaxy." Čykalenko speaks about these processes in his memoirs (188ff). Lotoc'kyj several times mentions students who were patriotically Ukrainian but spoke Russian (2, 102, 105).

In speaking of the devastating effects of the ukases of 1876 and 1881 and the ensuing police persecutions, one should not forget that in addition to the administrative measures another factor, perhaps just as significant, undercut the use of the Ukrainian language among the educated. Practically no one among the bourgeoisie spoke or supported the use of the Ukrainian language. Čykalenko mentions only four such families—the Symyrenko, Leontovyč, Arkas, and his own; Lotoc'kyj mentions others (2, 63; 2, 93), but the number was negligible. This fact, too, undermined the prestige of the Ukrainian language and, more directly, deprived it of economic support.

By the very nature of the phenomenon, there can be no precise statistical data about the everyday language of communication chosen in settlements throughout the Ukraine. Only on the basis of the occasional reference in fiction, in memoirs, in letters, etc., can one tentatively conclude that in the largest population centers—Kiev, Odessa, Kharkiv—in the large industrial centers of the Donec' basin, and in the most important seaports, the language was predominantly Russian or a mixture of Russian and Ukrainian. In 1900, Lesja Ukrajinka wrote "Černivci [Bukovina]. . . is interesting to Little Russians in that it is the only bigger (*značitel'nyj*) European city in which the Little Russian language is in use everywhere, in homes and on the street as *langue parlée*" (Lesja Ukrajinka 128)—an indirect testimony for the situation in Kiev, Odessa, etc. In somewhat smaller towns, like Poltava, Vinnycja, Kamjanec'-Podil's'kyj, Lysavet (now Kirovohrad), Černihiv, etc., the language was predominantly Ukrainian, although even there Russian was spreading. In Aleksandrovsk (now Zaporižžja), for instance, Ukrainian was the only language spoken until about 1870, but by 1910 "all inhabitants knew Russian and only those [nationally] conscious spoke Ukrainian" (Čykalenko II, 154b). Dorošenko (1949, 35) mentions as a historical fact that in the Komlyčenko family living in Poltava in 1903, two teen-age boys, students at the local high school, spoke with each other in Ukrainian and comments that this observation "pleasantly surprised" him because "until then I never saw such high school students (*himnazysty*)."

Ukrainian prevailed throughout the countryside, except that in their conversations with people of the upper classes peasants often mixed in Russian words, thus laying the foundation for what was later, in slang, called *suržyk*.[4] Yet it must be kept in mind that peasants spoke dialects of Ukrainian that varied from one locality to another. Thus the literary language was used more often in written than in oral speech. Yet in neither did Ukrainian encompass all aspects of modern life and thought, which in turn limited its possibilities and diminished its prestige still further. Even among those who defended and fostered the Ukrainian language this situation sometimes led to a deliberate bilingualism in which Ukrainian was assigned rural-familial-folkloric-poetic functions, but not others (e.g., by Kostomarov and Panas Myrnyj; see below, fn. 15).

The imprint of this situation can be found in the Ukrainian language itself. Its phraseology came to abound in images rooted in rural life. Sometimes this is reflected even in semantics. To give one example, the notion of "citizen," which in the West European languages (and in Russian) derives from the word for "city," in Ukrainian is based on the word meaning "(village) community" (*hromadjanyn, hromada*).

In Galicia and Bukovina—that is, in the Austrian Ukraine—the rather liberal constitution of 21 December 1867 (with later amendments that liberalized it still more, especially in 1907) was in force. Its section on citizen rights allowed for extensive local and private initiative in education (§ 17). It also stated (§ 19): "All peoples of the State, of whatever race, are equal in their rights; each race has the inviolable right to maintain and to foster its nationality and its language. The State recognizes for all the languages used in the lands of the Monarchy an equal right to be used in school and to perform the functions and diverse acts of public life," and, further on: "Everyone may receive the necessary elements of his/her education in his/her language" (Dareste 443ff.).

The Ukrainians' exercise of these rights was, however, somewhat impeded by the peculiar administrative division of the country. Ukrainians in Austria had no "land" of their own. Rather, they belonged to the "Kingdom of Galicia and Lodomeria with the Grand-

---

[4] Originally a miller's term meaning an admixture of rye or barley to wheat flour.

Duchy of Cracow,'' which Austria had inherited from Poland,[5] and to the Duchy of Bukovina, once part of Moldavia in vassalage of Turkey. In the first of these administrative units, which encompassed ethnically Ukrainian Eastern Galicia, and ethnically Polish Western Galicia, Poles were the majority in the region as a whole; in addition, the upper classes were almost entirely Polish. As a result, the Poles, profiting from the curial principle in elections, succeeded in passing laws that imposed Polish as the language of education and of the courts, in 1868, and, a little later, of administration as a whole (Dareste 430). In Bukovina Ukrainians were in the absolute majority in the region's northern part, whereas Romanians prevailed in the south. Here, too, Ukrainians belonged mostly to the lower classes, although here social and cultural domination by the other nation over Ukrainians was not as strong as in Galicia, and bilingualism among the educated was not so widespread. In fact, in Bukovina Ukrainian-German bilingualism was more typical than Ukrainian-Romanian.

In contrast to the Russian Ukraine, by 1900 the Austrian Ukraine was not denied public use of the Ukrainian language. Yet the actualization of the constitutional rights of Ukrainians was in nearly every instance the product of long and bitter strife with the Polish administration, which controlled the bureaucracy. As a result, by 1900 Ukrainians possessed their own relatively well-developed press (which frequently also published Ukrainian authors from the Russian Ukraine) and educational system, but both were insufficient in relation to the number of Ukrainians and in comparison with that of the Poles.

According to my data (collated mostly from Žyvotko, passim, and Ihnatijenko 1968, 116ff.), which may well be incomplete, in 1900 Galicia had 25 periodicals (according to Ihnatijenko [1926, 40], in Austro-Hungary as a whole the number of Ukrainian periodicals was 20). They included: four dailies (*Dilo* 1880,[6] organ of the Ukrainian National-Democratic Party; *Narodna časopys'*, 1896, semiofficial; *Ruslan*, 1897, Catholic; *Halyčanyn* 1893, Moscophile); two weeklies (*Svoboda*, 1897, organ of the Ukrainian National-Democratic Party; *Russkoe slovo*, 1890, Moscophile); nine biweeklies (*Hromads'kyj holos*, 1895, organ of the Ukrainian Radical Party; *Volja*, 1900, organ

---

[5] In 1848 the foremost demand of Ukrainian representatives was the division of Galicia into two separate lands.

[6] Years are the dates of founding.

of the Ukrainian Social-Democratic Party; *Misionar,* 1897, Catholic; *Dzvinok,* 1890, for children; *Russkaja rada,* 1871, Moscophile; *Poslannyk,* 1889, Catholic, Moscophile; *Zerkalo,* 1890, humoristic; *Komar,* 1900, humoristic; *Straxopud,* 1880, Moscophile, humoristic); five monthlies (*Literaturno-naukovyj vistnyk,* 1898; *Moloda Ukrajina,* 1900, for students; *Prapor,* 1897, for clergy; *Djakovskyj holos,* 1895; *Nauka,* 1871, Moscophile); two quarterlies (*Zapysky Naukovoho tovarystva im. Ševčenka,* scholarly; *Bohoslovskyj věstnyk,* 1900, Moscophile); and one semiannual (*Časopys' pravnyča i ekonomična,* 1900). There were also two periodicals devoted to practical economic matters—*Providnyk ril'nyčyx kružkiv* (1896) and *Hospodar'* (1898)—and two editions of the official publication *Vistnyk zakoniv,* which came out in Vienna and Lviv, respectively. It must be noted that the Moscophile publications aimed to use the standard Russian language, although in most cases they included many elements of local speech.

Six Ukrainian periodicals were being published in Bukovina in 1900: *Bukovyna,* 1885, then published three times a week, and *Ruska rada,* 1898, organs of the Ukrainian National-Democratic Party; the weekly *Bukovynsky vědomosty,* 1895; the biweekly *Pravoslavnaja Bukovyna,* 1893, and the monthly *Narodnyj věstnyk'',* 1899, both Moscophile; and *Dobri rady,* 1889, which published agricultural advice for peasants. There was also *Obščyj zakonov. . .věstnyk,* an official publication without strict periodicity.

Unfortunately, little is known about the circulation of these Galician and Bukovinian publications. *Dilo,* in the first year of publication (1880), is said to have had 600 subscribers (Žyvotko 68), among whom 173 were priests and 142, teachers (Žyvotko 68, 78); in its first year, *Literaturno-naukovyj vistnyk* had 799 subscribers, of whom 625 lived in Galicia, 32 in Bukovina, and 101 in the Russian Ukraine. Newspapers must have had somewhat more subscribers.

In sum, the development of the periodical press in Ukrainian territory under Austro-Hungary as compared to the Ukraine under tsarist Russia, where there were no Ukrainian periodicals, was impressive. But taken on its own merits, the periodical press in Galicia and especially in Bukovina was underdeveloped, its political differentiation was in only its initial stage and it was insufficiently differentiated in content and focus. Many publications were ephemeral, but some already had a certain degree of stability and authority, notably *Dilo,*

Literaturno-naukovyj vistnyk, Zapysky Naukovoho tovarystva im. Ševčenka, and *Bukovyna.* Undoubtedly their language standard exerted a certain linguistic influence in Ukrainian society. This was, however, necessarily if not programmatically regional, as is discussed below.

A factor of great influence in shaping the language of educated Ukrainians in Galicia and Bukovina was the school. The dynamics of the growth of Ukrainian elementary schools is shown by the fact that in 1881 their number in Galicia alone was 1,529 (*EU* 2, 2518), whereas on the eve of World War I—when 97 percent of Ukrainian children went to Ukrainian elementary schools despite the many bureaucratic obstacles posed by the predominantly Polish administration—it was 2,510. Some Ukrainian elementary schools were, however, incomplete (two grades out of the possible six). The number of Ukrainian vs. Polish public high schools (*himnaziji* and *real'ni školy*) was 6 to 50; in partial recompense, however, Ukrainians had 10 private high schools (1911; *EU* 1,929). The University of Lviv was entirely Polish by 1900, but it had several Ukrainian chairs: from 1894, history of the Ukraine; from 1900, Ukrainian literature; by 1914, there were 8 Ukrainian chairs vs. 72 Polish ones. Educational work among adults was carried out by the Prosvita (Enlightment) society founded in 1862. In 1900, Prosvita had 22 branches, 924 reading rooms, and 1,248 libraries (*EU* 2, 2366).

There were in Bukovina (in 1896) 131 Ukrainian and 34 bilingual (Ukrainian-German, Ukrainian-Romanian) elementary schools, out of a total of 335 (Kvitkovs'kyj 663), but only one high school: in Černivci, from 1896; the Ukrainian language was taught as a subject in other high schools. The University of Černivci was German and had Ukrainian chairs only in theology and the Church Slavonic language, as well as a chair of Ukrainian language and literature (Kvitkovs'kyj 694). The society Rus'ka besida (founded in 1869) conducted educational work among adults similar to that of Prosvita in Galicia.

Given the peculiar social structure of the Ukrainian population in Galicia and Bukovina, one of the most influential social groups was the clergy—Catholic in Galicia, Orthodox in Bukovina. In Galicia the once prevailing situation, when "the clergy willingly used the Polish language both at home and publicly, and in churches, especially in towns, preached in Polish" (Xolms'kyj 338), was overcome in the mid-nineteenth century. By the 1890s after the period when Mosco-philism was in fashion, the majority of the clergy adopted the Ukrainian orientation. In Galicia the liturgical language was always Church Slavonic with Ukrainian pronunciation. The same was true for the church in Bukovina; otherwise, however, the church there was predominantly in Romanian hands. In 1873, Ukrainian was admitted alongside Romanian as a language of a church administration (Kvitkovs'kyj 735), but Bukovina could claim not a single metropolitan or bishop having a Ukrainian political orientation; some, at best, were occasionally lenient about Ukrainian matters.

Transcarpathia, politically part of Hungary, had no legislation of its own. Hungary itself had no codified constitution, but was governed by the successive publication of individual laws, woven into a complicated and tangled pattern, new laws building on the older ones. As far as I could ascertain, none of these laws guaranteed the rights of any language other than Hungarian. Law 16 of 1791 excluded all other languages from official use, and law 2 of 1844 proclaimed Hungarian the only official language. Law 5 of 1848, by a complicated system of regulation, assured Hungarian preponderance in all elections. Only laws 38 and 44 of 1868 bespoke the rights of nationalities (Dareste 1, 467–470).

Having no legal protection or recourse, exposed from 1867 to aggressive Magyarization, and suffering from hopeless economic decline, by the turn of the century the Ukrainian population of Transcarpathia either submitted or looked for salvation to a strong, kindred (Slavic) power, which could have been only Russia. By 1900 the Ukrainian language was practically excluded from all public functions and that language was reduced to a series of local, highly differentiated dialects. The intelligentsia, small in number, either joined the ruling Hungarians—who included all the large landlords, aristocracy, high government bureaucrats, and the church hierarchy—or, the minority, became Moscophiles. Responding to developments in Galicia, the populist orientation gained some followers after 1900.

In summary, legally and factually Ukrainian was in the worst position in the Russian Ukraine (explicitly excluded from public life, education, and literature) and in the Hungarian Ukraine (de facto excluded from public life). Ukrainian was in the best position in Galicia, where it was admitted into public life. In Bukovina it had an intermediary position: legally Ukrainian was not persecuted in the

Austrian lands; practically the rights granted it were limited. In none of the four territories did Ukrainian enjoy high social prestige; it only stood relatively better in Galicia. Attempts to improve the language situation were undertaken on the cultural, economic, and political levels in Galicia and Bukovina; predominantly on the cultural level, in the Russian Ukraine; and virtually on no level in Transcarpathia. The medium of everyday communication in the major cities in the Russian Ukraine was Russian;[7] in Galicia, Polish; in Bukovina, German and/or Romanian (contrary to Lesja Ukrajinka as quoted above); in Transcarpathia, Hungarian. However, in the Austrian Ukraine there were individual and group attempts to introduce Ukrainian with that role, attempts naturally preceded by the consistent use of Ukrainian by the Ukrainian intelligentsia itself. These efforts are related in letters and other writings of Ukrainians from the Russian Ukraine who visited the Austrian Ukraine.

How much the fluent use of Ukrainian by educated Galicians impressed non-Galician Ukrainians is reflected in Olena Pčilka's partly autobiographic novella *Tovaryšky* (1887). The author's alter ego, the writer Ljuba, meets in Vienna the Galician Bučyns'kyj:

> She felt ashamed in the presence of this Ruthenian intellectual; he speaks Ukrainian so freely, without faltering on any topic, while she. . .must first think it over well and only then can she speak, as if she had first to translate it mentally from Russian. . . . She feels that this is the natural language of his speech and that it *must be* like this, that speaking to him in Russian would be improper, it would be a shame. Why, then, can he speak so and I cannot? They have adapted their language for cultural needs while we switch immediately to Russian when we discuss serious matters. This is not the way to act! (323f.)

Pavlo Hrabovs'kyj, who never visited Galicia but heard of the language situation there, expressed similar amazement and respect in a letter to Ivan Franko (1892):

> In which language do Ruthenian writers speak among themselves—

---

[7] Very often Russian was mixed with Ukrainian. In 1912, F. Korš wrote of "that 'disgusting Russian—Little Russian *volapük*' which more and more overflows in towns of our southern provinces." "K voprosu ob ukrainskoj kul'ture," *Ukrainskaja žizn'*, 1912, no. 2, p. 41.

Russian, Polish, or German? I ask this because I would like to know: In Galicia, is Ruthenian the language of literature only or also of life? Here, in the Russian Ukraine, quite a few write Ukrainian but speak Muscovite (190).

Lesja Ukrajinka recognized the same phenomenon and sought an explanation for it (1893):

I do not know how to explain it, but Galicians speak better than they write whereas [Russian] Ukrainians write better than they speak. As for the fact that [in Russia] Ukrainian families speak Russian, well, it seems that the time is not remote when Galician Ruthenian families spoke Polish. If our language had the same rights in Russia as in Galicia, I am convinced that we would not lag behind. He who likes may throw a stone at the [Russian] Ukrainians suppressed by school, government, social institutions. I cannot do that. (Simovyč 1938, 28)

Galicians were aware of the difference. Illja Kokorudz wrote (1891):

While in the [Russian] Ukraine the Ukrainian-Ruthenian language is rarely used as a spoken language among intellectuals, in Galicia it is spoken in a simple peasant cottage in the same degree as in the most elegant and highest salons. . . . In Galicia it is in this language that the Emperor is addressed, political speeches in the parliament are delivered, all subjects are taught in high schools, it is heard from university chairs, in it articles and studies are written in philosophy, philology, history, mathematics, physics, law, etc. (Kokorudz, 471 – 72)

In reconstructing the overall language picture in Galicia by 1900, it should be remembered, however, that all such testimonies—and there are many more—were drawn on the comparison of the Austrian Ukraine with the Russian Ukraine. The contrast was indeed dazzling. But one must bear in mind that in absolute terms the situation of the Ukrainian language in Galicia was far from the one normally enjoyed by a language supported and protected by the state, as, say, French in France or Swedish in Sweden. In the same year, 1892, another Galician, Ivan Verxrats'kyj, wrote: ''Our circumstances are not really joyful. We have no aristocratic patrons, no rich bourgeoisie, no well-to-do intelligentsia, no full-fledged Ruthenian university, no Ruthenian academy'' (Verxrats'kyj [pseud. Losun], in *Zorja,* 1892, no. 7). He, too, was quite right.

Yet another aspect of the language situation in Galicia must be kept in mind. It is true that in the Austrian Ukraine educated Ukrainians (and even some Moscophiles) spoke Ukrainian among themselves. But it would be an exaggeration to think that this language was the same as the literary Ukrainian used by writers in the Russian Ukraine, which theoretically was the standard language of the entire country. And how could it have been, when education, the popular press, and the very habit of speaking Ukrainian on all subjects among the educated were all of relatively recent date, and contacts with the Russian Ukraine were so tenuous? After all, even for the Russian Ukraine of that time the designation of the standard language can be made only with great reservation. There was a certain norm of usage, but it was not codified, nor even exhaustively described, and there was no authority to prescribe it. In Galicia there were several Ukrainian text-books (M. Osadca, 1862; H. Šaškevyč, 1865; P. Djačan, 1865; O. Partyc'kyj, 1873), but none had the approbation of any authority other than the author. The school grammar of S. Smal'-Stoc'kyj (*Rus'ka hramatyka,* published in Lviv in 1893, with subsequent editions published in 1907, 1914, and 1928; all were written in collaboration with F. Gartner), which was closer to the Central Ukrainian standard, especially in introducing so-called phonetic spelling (with substantial local peculiarities), was approved by the Austrian Ministry of Education after bitter and unscrupulous debate, but found its way into schools only in 1893.[8] It was preceded in lexicology by the first major Ukrainian dictionary (by E. Żelechowski), in 1886. No wonder, then, that each writer's and speaker's dialectal background manifested itself clearly throughout the Ukraine, and the more so in the Austrian Ukraine, where the dialects were more numerous and more differentiated. In these regions speaking Ukrainian essentially meant speaking one's own dialect.

---

[8] On this grammar and the conflict around it, with further bibliographic references, see V. Simovyč, "Stepan Smal'-Stoc'kyj jak pedahoh i pedahohičnyj dijač," *Šljax vyxovannja j navčannja,* 1939, no. 1; reprinted in V. Simovyč, *Ukrajins'ke movoznavstvo,* vol. 2 (Ottawa, 1984), pp. 160–76.

Contacts between educated speakers of West Ukrainian dialects were at their liveliest in Lviv. It seems that by 1900 a kind of Galician or Galician-Bukovinian koine, based on the Dniester dialect, was in the making there. The question needs further study, yet the sources for oral speech of the educated at that time are scanty. As a memoirist (a non-linguist) later correctly observed: "Lviv did not have its own Ukrainian dialect because the cultivated class (*inteligentna verstva*) spoke a more or less common literary (*pys'menna*) Galician, whereas the burghers, who were arriving from the environs and, at the last in the third generation, were being Polonized in the language melting pot of Lviv, spoke the dialect of their village contaminated with Polish" (Šax 111). If the hypothesis of a Lviv koine in the making is correct, then the large-scale and often tempermental linguistic discussion of 1891 – 1892 that B. Hrinčenko began with a vitriolic attack on the "Galician poets" was essentially a conflict between two standards in the making, that of the Russian Ukraine and that of the Austrian Ukraine.[9] The discussion ended with the general acceptance of the thesis that all Ukrainians should have the same standard literary language, and that that standard should be based on the Central Ukrainian (Kiev-Poltava region) dialects upon which the language of the most influential classical writers—T. Ševčenko, Marko Vovčok, a.o.—was built. Not in that discussion nor at any later time were there ever any partisans of establishing a standard Ukrainian language on Galician foundations, nor of creating two parallel variants of the literary language on the pattern of, say, the Serbs and Croats among the South Slavs.[10] Yet no discussions could erase the actual local differences as long as the country was divided by political (and actually cultural) boundaries. Characteristically, even the later editions of S. Smal'-Stoc'kyj's grammar never followed the Central Ukrainian standard. In 1889, the editors of *Zorja* wrote: "If a dictionary of how we should not speak and write were to be compiled, it would possibly

[9] The course of the discussion is traced and analyzed in Shevelov, 1966, pp. 61 – 68.

[10] Contrary to fact-distorting contentions of M. Žovtobrjux, 1970, 275, and, especially, 1964, 20.

be as large as that which would record our genuine, i.e., recommended words and expressions."[11] That situation certainly did not change by 1900 nor in the years that followed.

[11] Quoted after B. Hrinčenko, "Kil'ka sliv pro našu literaturnu movu," *Zorja*, 1892, no. 15, pp. 310 – 14.

CHAPTER TWO

The Years Before World War I and Revolution (1900 – 1916)

In the Austrian Ukraine the years 1900 – 1916 did not bring new forces to bear on the status of the Ukrainian language. The single exception was the brief Russian occupation of Galicia during World War I, from the autumn of 1914 through the spring of 1915, and the first occupation of Bukovina, September 1914 to June 1915, when all Ukrainian political and cultural institutions were crushed, a great number of intellectuals were persecuted and deported, and the use of the Ukrainian language for public functions was practically outlawed (this policy was not applied during the second occupation of Bukovina, June 1916 to July 1917). On the whole, then, the trends shaped by 1900 developed further and grew much stronger in the Austrian Ukraine.

There were no major changes in the legal status of the Ukrainian language in Galicia and Bukovina. The years 1900 – 1916 were characterized by attempts to use its legally granted rights to a fuller extent than before, efforts reflected in the growth of the press and the educational system.

At the outbreak of World War I (using data for 1913 – 1914) the periodicals being published in Galicia in 1900 (except for *Volja*, *Prapor*, the Moscophile *Russkaja rada*, *Poslannyk*, *Djakovskyj holos*, *Bohoslovskyj věstnyk*, and *Straxopud*) were still being published (in 1907, *Literaturno-naukovyj vistnyk* had moved to Kiev). Also, a new daily, *Nove slovo*, the organ of the National Democrats, with a circulation of 12,000 copies (*EU* 2, 1782), had been added. The Galician periodicals also began to display a new feature: diversification. About 1900, differentiation was evident only in terms of political (party) orientation. This continued, but diversity according to professional interests set in by 1914. By that time there were ten Ukrainian periodicals specializing in economics, agriculture, and trade; two juridical; three pedagogic; five student- and youth-oriented; one for women; one popular medical; two devoted to sports; one artistic; one on history and arts; two ecclesiastic; and one devoted to humor and satire. There also appeared many local and regional periodicals. In Bukovina a substantial diversification in the political orientation of publications occurred (there were seven such periodicals, one of them Moscophile). Diversification according to profession lagged behind (one theatrical, two economic), but Bukovinians had easy access to Galician professional (and other) publications. Žyvotko (129) estimates the general number of "West Ukrainian" periodicals (i.e., including Transcarpathia; see below) to have been 80, whereas Ihnatijenko's data (1968, 197ff.) yields 84.

A closer analysis of the periodicals appearing in Galicia and Bukovina in 1913–1914 as compared to those of 1900 reveals an unquestionably rapid growth of the periodical press and thus reflects an increasingly complex social structure. The analysis also reveals, however, that this society was still not modern and harmoniously developed. Other than for the publications of the Shevchenko Scientific Society, the number of publications in the industrial and technological areas was strikingly low while the proportion of agricultural publications was exceedingly high. The distribution of periodicals mirrored the fact that the Ukrainian society in Galicia and Bukovina of this time still consisted primarily of peasants and of intelligentsia that originated from the peasantry and served it, namely, clergy and teachers and to a smaller degree lawyers and physicians. A Ukrainian aristocracy, wealthy bourgeoisie, and technological intelligentsia were virtually nonexistent, and the working class was small and underdeveloped.

All this had a bearing on the language. Scholarly abstract terminology and technological terminology were at best *in statu nascendi*. Rudimentary technical terms were used in everyday life, but the use of specialized terms in periodicals was very limited; their low representation in the press, in turn, did not foster their development, creating a vicious circle. Another feature generated by the overall social situation was the extremely strong influence of dialects on the language of intellectuals. The periodical press, though making some effort to use a common Ukrainian standard language, at best cultivated a Galician koine which was actively taking shape primarily on the basis of the Lviv region dialects. Often periodicals slipped into what were—

theoretically inadmissible—dialectal forms, words, and constructions. Because of its deficiencies and underdevelopment the Ukrainian culture and language were supplemented by borrowings from the more fully developed cultures and languages of the area: virtually all intellectuals were bilingual (Ukrainian and Polish) or trilingual (Ukrainian, Polish, German). This situation could not but leave its imprint on the very character of the local Ukrainian literary language, vulnerable to borrowings from and patterning on the coterritorial languages.

This state of affairs was reinforced and perpetuated by the situation in education. As the data presented above (chap. 2) show, the education of Ukrainian children in Galicia between 1900–1914 consistently though slowly improved. Yet successes were substantial only on the lower levels. They were inadequate on the high school level (*himnaziji*), and on the university level there were Ukrainian chairs only in the purely Ukrainian subjects; in other words, there was no education in Ukrainian in any field of technology, medical science, law, etc. The existence of ten teachers seminaries, with parallel classes in Polish and Ukrainian, did not, of course, change the situation. The struggle for a Ukrainian university sometimes took on aggressive forms, including political demonstrations and even an assassination, but this did not bring about any change. Moreover, even on the high school level, Poles were granted, besides *Gymnasien* (i.e.,*himnaziji*), eleven *Realschulen* (technical high schools), whereas Ukrainians had none of the latter (which they referred to as *real'ni školy*). The system of education, though preventing the Ukrainian nation's denationalization, constantly reinforced and recreated its archaic, insufficiently differentiated social structure.

In Bukovina the number of Ukrainian elementary schools grew from 131 to 216, plus 17 bilingual schools (Kvitkovs'kyj 668), but Ukrainians had only one high school, plus two Ukrainian-German ones. The only Ukrainian technical high school was a private institution. The Černivci teachers seminary, originally only German, was in 1910 reorganized into three parallel sections—Ukrainian, German, and Romanian. The University of Černivci, except for a few Ukrainian chairs (see chap. 2), remained German. Thus, in terms of the requirements of a modern, industrial, and professionally differentiated society, eduction in Bukovina was as outmoded and inadequate as in Galicia. As in Galicia, the educational system in Bukovina both reflected and perpetuated the lopsided structure of Ukrainian society and of its language.

As if symbolically, this state of affairs found its bureaucratic reflection in the official name of Ukrainians in Austro-Hungary. Despite the rights Ukrainians enjoyed in Austria, their official name continued to be "Ruthenians." In 1915 a group of Ukrainian delegates to the Austrian parliament moved that the term should be replaced by "Ukrainians." The government nominated two experts to give their opinions. One of them, Vatroslav Jagić, a respected authority in matters Slavic who was relatively unbiased (he was of Croat descent), suggested that it would be prudent to retain the traditional label, that of "Ruthenians," because it was not loaded with modern nationalist sentiment.[1] The problem remained unresolved up to the time of the final disintegration of Austro-Hungary, in 1918.

One implication of the name "Ruthenian" was a certain degree of non-identification of Austrian Ukrainians with Russian Ukrainians. In the literary language this provided some authorization for the preservation of local linguistic peculiarities—which reflected the actual state of affairs, that is, the broad influence of local dialects—and for the development of a Ukrainian koine within Austria. On the other hand, the spreading acceptance among Austrian Ukrainians of the self-identification "Ukrainians" was, in fact, precluding any attempt to create a separate "Ruthenian" language. Practically, it fostered the desire to establish a common language, while preserving some features of the Galician sub-standard.

That attitude marked language regulations which were being elaborated in Galicia. The first step in language regulation was the approval of Smal'-Stoc'kyj and Gartner's *Rus'ka hramatyka* for school use by the Vienna government. Then came the first attempt at language normalization by a Ukrainian organization. In 1904 the Shevchenko Scientific Society published *Ruska pravopys' zi slovarcem* (152 pages). While making some concessions to the language usage in the Russian Ukraine (e.g., accepting the feminine forms *drama, poema, systema, tema,* rather than *dramat, poemat, system, temat,* etc.; renouncing forms in *-a* for such words as *artyst, arxitekt, mytropolyt,*

---

[1] Published and commented by D. Dorošenko in *Zapysky istoryčno-filolohičnoho viddilu* of the Ukrainian Academy of Sciences, 10, 1927. For the original text in German, see pp. 268–74.

poet—Tymošenko 2, 342ff.) the booklet kept intact such striking peculiarities of Galician orthography as the use of *ï < ě, e* (дїд 'old man'), the spelling of the postfix *sja* separately from verbs, the use of the soft sign between two palatalized dentals (*s'vit* 'world'), in morphology the ending -*yj* in the genitive plural of substantives in a consonant (*kónyj* 'horses', *hrudýj* 'breasts'), and especially in the rendition of *g* and *l* in foreign words (*biol'ogija* 'biology') (Tymošenko 2, 336, 338, 343). Characteristically, the title of these rules contained the word "Ruthenian" (*ruska*), and not "Ukrainian," which, it is true, may have been motivated by Austrian official regulations.

The smallest and the most backward Ukrainian land, Transcarpathia, made no contribution to the standard Ukrainian language—in fact, Ukrainians there were little acquainted with it. The underdeveloped school network was entirely Magyarized after the introduction of the so-called A. Apponyi laws (36 and 37 of 1907), which made every elementary school a stronghold of Hungarianism. By article 23 of law 36 and article 32 of law 37, all teachers, whether in public or private schools, became civil servants who were obliged to swear an oath of loyalty to, and zeal for, all things Hungarian (*Törvénytár* 368, 392; an English translation of one passage appears in Magocsi 65; cf. his fn. 116, p. 380). Article 18 of law 37 (*Törvénytár* 383) prescribed the use of Hungarian as the language of instruction in every school in which the parents of 20 children (or, if less, 20 percent of the children) wanted it. As a result, by 1915 there were no entirely Ukrainian (Slavic) schools in Hungary and only 18 mixed Ukrainian-Hungarian ones (*EU* 2, 55). The influential newspapers and magazines were also in Hungarian. Some periodicals were published by Moscophiles in Russian with varying admixtures of elements of local speech. There was only one Ukrainian periodical: a weekly which in 1912–1914 became a monthly, published by the St. Basil Society; its language was a peculiar brand of standard Ukrainian, with a strong admixture of Church Slavonic and local elements, rendered in an etymological spelling. The spoken language of most Ukrainians in Hungary was dialectal, varying from one locality to the other; the intelligentsia most often spoke Hungarian. Characteristically, A. Vološyn published a grammar of the Transcarpathian variant of the Ukrainian language in Hungarian: *Gyakorlati kis-orosz (rutén) nyelvtan* (1907) (Gerovskij 1934, 508). Among other things it was intended to serve as a textbook for Ukrainians educated in Hungarian who wanted to have a look at their native language.

In discussing the language situation in the Russian Ukraine it is expedient to divide the period 1900–1916 into three subdivisions: 1900–1905, 1905–1914, and 1914–1916. In the years up to 1905 the same circumstances obtained and the same trends continued that had marked the last decade of the nineteenth century. To recapitulate them briefly, they included: the complete lack of any Ukrainian schooling,[2] church, or press; only delayed and sporadic publication of Ukrainian belles lettres and poetry, with almost no translations from foreign languages; a successful Ukrainian theater which was permitted to depict in domestic repertory only peasant life; the exclusion of Ukrainian speech from public life, and its only exceptional use in intelligentsia families. The non-denationalized intelligentsia were, by profession, writers and teachers, with some exceptions; the Ukrainian language had low prestige even among the peasantry, who nonetheless among themselves spoke their original dialects.

It was in comparison with this situation that the prestige of the Galician variant of the standard Ukrainian language stood high in the eyes of many contemporaries. In their meetings with Austrian Ukrainians, Russian Ukrainians continued to be impressed, inadvertently, by the Austrian Ukrainians' language, with what they perceived as its elaborateness, its culture, and its topical scope. Some activists of Ukrainian political parties existing in the Russian Ukraine settled in Galicia or Bukovina so as to publish political literature that could be smuggled into the Russian Ukraine. They often came under the spell of Galician political life and transferred this fascination to the language of the Austrian Ukrainians. Such attitudes and occurrences were mirrored in works of literature, e.g. in N. Romanovyč-Tkačenko's novel *Manivcjamy* (On the Byways). This is how the author describes the impressions of her characters, young revolutionaries from the Russian Ukraine who are participating at a rally in Lviv:

> Here, amidst this splendid crowd, in a hall flooded with light he hears the language of his steppes, of his fields, the language spoken by those brothers of his who live in narrow shanties without light and fresh air.

---

[2] In 1904 a request that a partially Ukrainian school in memory of I. Kotljarevs'kyj be opened in Poltava was denied (Lotoc'kyj 2, 283ff.).

True, the language here seems to be slightly different, but this is a natural alteration as is that which happened to him: he is the same, born under a peasant's thatch—and not quite the same now: not in a villager's shirt, not in a villager's tunic (*svyta*), but in a "German" suit. And yet he is the same (145).

Some generalizations are made:

Then he heard the Ukrainian language of the speakers. Not that language of wide steppes, of boundless fields, slow, colorful, sonorous, no, but a fast language, monotonous but elaborate and cultured. . . (531).

The wish appears to stay in this atmosphere, where these Europeans speak the language of his far-away native villages (147).

That attitude was also imported to cities of the Russian Ukraine. There youth groups were occasionally visited by renowned politicians, members of the Revolutionary Ukrainian Party and other parties, who brought back with them elements of language picked up in the Austrian Ukraine. The young audience willingly and eagerly adopted the words and expressions of those they considered to be revolutionary heroes, even though these language peculiarities often had nothing to do with revolutionary activity. A noted Ukrainian bibliographer, V. Dorošenko, relates an episode from the time when he was a *himnazija* student in Pryluka (now in Černihiv oblast'):

We did not know the [Ukrainian] language well, so we were keen to adopt all sorts of [language] monstrosities which we happened to hear from Galician politicians. We deemed them—because they were so unusual to us—something very special. I remember that we fell greatly in love with the word *pozajak* 'because' as a beautiful Galician novelty. It was brought to us by a member of the *hromada* from Lubni [now in the Poltava oblast']. (V. Dorošenko)

Particularly interesting in this reminiscence is that the Galician word was adopted not directly, from a Galician, but indirectly, from a Poltavan. The memoir illustrates how the use of "contagious," "urbane" Galician words and expressions expanded. The mediating role played by Ukrainian circles in *himnaziji* (as well as at universities) is indisputable. Such circles are known to have existed not only in Pryluka, but in Lubni, Nižen (now Černihiv oblast'), and Kiev

(Dorošenko 1949, 17) and there were probably others. It can be noted that the word *pozajak*, rather a misnomer from the linguistic point of view, found its way not only into the vocabulary of a young and inexperienced student, but also into the writings of an outstanding linguist of the time, K. Myxal'čuk (p. xv). I. Nečuj-Levyc'kyj, a bitter enemy of all things Galician, summarized the trend thus: "Our young men have read so much of Galician newspapers that their language has Galicianized, as if they had so busied themselves with that [stuff] that they learned those newspapers and journals by heart" (1907, 8). An exaggeration, but certainly one with a grain of truth.

The impact of Galicia and the Ukrainian language there was one of the new and to some extent subversive processes that percolated behind the façade of the Russian Empire's apparent stability. Another was the activization of Ukrainian intellectuals in their own right, which became possible because of the growing social and political unrest in the Russian Empire. In the Ukraine there were widespread peasant mutinies in 1902–1903, centered in the Poltava region but radiating far beyond it. Their impact was substantial, even though they had no national slogans and were aimed exclusively at economic and social revindication. Ukrainian *hromady*, which had shrunk in size after the law of 1876, were reactivated and, in 1897, united in the General Ukraine Non-Partisan Democratic Organization; affiliated with it was the publishing company Vik (1895–1918). The organization's activities included the exploitation of all legal avenues for promoting Ukrainian as a vehicle of public communication. This was easier to do from outside the Ukraine. In the spring of 1902, D. Mordovec' gave a public speech in Ukrainian in memory of T. Ševčenko at the Blagorodnoe sobranie (House of Nobility) in St. Petersburg, an act unthinkable in Kiev or Odessa. In the Ukraine, at the archaeological congress convened in Kiev in 1899, scholars from the Austrian Ukraine wanted to deliver their papers in Ukrainian (Slavic languages were generally admitted at such congresses). When the authorities vetoed the use of Ukrainian, the Austrian Ukrainians demonstratively withdrew from the congress. The defiant act did not spread to speakers from the Russian Ukraine, who submissively used Russian. Another incident occurred on 30–31 August 1903, at the unveiling of the monument to Kotljarevs'kyj in Poltava. Here the authorities relaxed, and the Austrian-Ukrainian participants were allowed to speak Ukrainian. They were followed by speakers from the Russian Ukraine; but the very first address to be delivered in Ukrainian by an imperial subject was interrupted by the mayor of Poltava, who forbade it according to the directives of the Ministry of Interior; several speakers reneged their right to speak and lodged protests (Čykalenko 337, 340; Lotoc'kyj 2, 278–280; Pypin 398–402). V. Korolenko related this episode as demonstrating that Ukrainians enjoyed rights in Austria and not in Russia (Korolenko 376). Later the tsarist senate would reprimand the Ministry of Interior and overturn its decision, but this happened in 1906, after the Revolution of 1905.

Anniversaries of M. Lysenko and I. Nečuj-Levyc'kyj in 1904 were occasions for similar manifestations, and protests occurred at archaeological congresses held in Kharkiv in 1902 and in Katerynoslav in 1905. Such public demonstrations would hardly have been possible a decade earlier.

Despite the laws prohibiting their appearance, the number of popular pamphlets in Ukrainian on agriculture and medicine began to grow. These were published by the Blagotvoritel'noe obščestvo izdanija obščepoleznyx i deševyx knig, a spuriously Russian charitable society founded in 1898 in St. Petersburg, having more than a thousand members, which produced 6–8 items annually (Lotoc'kyj 2, 253); by B. Hrinčenko in Černihiv, averaging 7 or 8 pamphlets per year; and by the publishing house Vik in Kiev (from 1895) and Hurt in Kharkiv (Lotoc'kyj 2, 97). These organizations capitalized on the contradictions between the Main Office on Press Affairs, which supervised the enforcement of the regulations on censorship, and the ministries of agriculture, health, etc., which were interested in the improvement of rural economy and sanitation. True, to avoid censorial restrictions, these pamphlets were written as a thinly-disguised narrative or dialogue. Yet, they were, in fact, a breach in the enforcement of censorship laws. The society published pamphlets such as "Why Did Melasja Die" (on diphtheria), "Good Advice" (on rabies), "Adventure on the Farm" (on meteorology), etc. (Lotoc'kyj 2, 256). But pamphlets on Socrates and on the life of Ševčenko also appeared. Of course the number of texts buried in the censorship offices was many times higher; for instance Lotoc'kyj (2, 238ff.), in an incomplete list, names 76 items. All the published pamphlets were designed to be understandable to a barely literate peasantry. Nevertheless, they promoted the idea of a Ukrainian scholarly language and applied some

rudimentary terminology. Thus the movement of Ukrainian into public speech and into print, very modest though it was, began even
before the revolution of 1905.

Political parties added to the cultural activities usually conducted,
directly or indirectly, by *hromady*. The first political party in the Russian Ukraine, the Revolutionary Ukrainian Party (RUP)—which was,
of course, illegal—was organized in 1900 in Kharkiv. Linguistically,
the activity of RUP is significant for two reasons. It distributed political pamphlets and newspapers, the first of that kind in the Russian
Ukraine (the monthly *Haslo*, 1902 – 1903;[3] *Seljanyn*, 1903 – 1905; and
Pracja, 1904 – 1905), thus laying the foundations for the journalistic
variant of the standard Ukrainian language. RUP published these
materials in the Austrian Ukraine (Černivci and Lviv), with the help
of local people, thus contributing to the Galician influence on the standard Ukrainian language.

These events, though sporadic and modest in scope, evidenced the
rise of the Ukrainian intelligentsia and its wish to cooperate with the
peasantry and, partly, the working class. This development, in turn,
brought about a change in the general attitude towards the very nature
of the standard Ukrainian language—a change whose importance cannot be overestimated. Until that time the *raison d'être* of Ukrainian
was based on one of two arguments. The older one, rooted in Romanticism, maintained that any language, Ukrainian included, is the
unique manifestation of the unique soul of a nation and therefore must
be preserved at any cost. This view, emanating from general Romantic philosophy (its expression in the Ukraine began with A.
Pavlovs'kyj's "Grammar" of 1805 – 1818), survived into the early
twentieth century, as manifested, for example, in the declarations of
1901 and 1906: "The greatest and the dearest good of every nation is
the language, because it is nothing else but a live depository of the
human spirit, the rich treasure chamber in which the nation deposits
her ancient life, her hopes, mind, experience, and feelings. . . ." "The
people's language is the expression of the popular soul, of the popular
world view" (Myrnyj 371, 374). It survives as a *gesunkenes Kultur-
gut* even today.

---

[3] *Haslo* had a circulation of 4,000, according to the Russian Minister of Education
V. Glazov (quoted in Lotoc'kyj 2, 378).

The second argument for the preservation of the Ukrainian language arose in the Positivist period. In simplified form, it usually ran as follows: peasants and their children cannot be properly educated if school is taught in a foreign language. The low level of education and even literacy in the Ukraine is perpetuated by the lack of Ukrainian schools. In the same vein, literature must serve peasants; therefore, its language must be generally understandable. As Drahomanov put it (1891 – 1892): "Language is not a sacred thing, not the master of a man or of a people, but their servant. Literature must bring education to the masses of people in the easiest possible way" (Drahomanov 322).

The two points of view seem quite different, and yet their practical programs coalesce: the literary language should never break its ties with the language of the peasants (Romanticists); it should be entirely understandable to peasants (Positivists). The often ridiculed motto Nečuj-Levyc'kyj formulated in 1878—"The model of the literary language should be drawn exactly from the language of a countryside woman, with her syntax" (*Pravda* 1878, p 26)—simply and honestly defined this program. In less direct form the same idea was expressed by nearly every Ukrainian writer of the time. "This is the way it is said among our people, and, since this is neither a Polonism nor a Russianism, why should we not write it like this?," asked V. Samijlenko (437); "I only say that the language must be genuinely popular," asserted P. Hrabovs'kyj (1891, 185); representing this attitude as a historical fact, Ivan Franko in 1907 wrote, "A Ukrainian intellectual and semi-intellectual never heard nor saw a grammar of Ukrainian; he drew models for his language directly from the live source" (338); and, reverting to the straightforwardness of Nečuj-Levyc'kyj, A. Kryms'kyj as late as 1922 declared, "As common people speak in the Ukraine, exactly so one must write, making no concessions by abandoning any specific features of that language, without sacrificing them to common-Slavic mutual understandability" (274). In fact, such argumentation was broadly used in the memorandum seeking the abrogation of restrictions against Ukrainian by a commission of the Russian Academy of Sciences in 1905.[4]

---

[4] Those who defended the Ukrainian language with this argument did not recognize that it led to the denial of higher levels for the Ukrainian standard language, to its restriction to domestic use (*dlja domašn'oho vžytku*), and to its eventual extinction.

In these conditions, it was a revolutionary idea indeed to publish an almanac devoted entirely to the intelligentsia, to their way of life, and to cosmopolitan topics. The idea came to the writers M. Kocjubyns'kyj, M. Černjavs'kyj, and M. Voronyj (1903). It materialized in the almanacs *Dubove lystja* (Kiev, 1903) and *Z potoku žyttja* (Kherson 1905), to the objection of some authors of the older generation. Panas Myrnyj defended rural topics, saying that they "shaped our life since long ago. . . and still provide, live and original, our own types." "As for our intelligentsia," he continued, "it did not exist up to now; it is only beginning to shape itself and, even then, educated by an alien (*inšoju*) school, it has not created such vivid images that can be called our own and original" (30 March 1903, p. 503). To which Kocjubyns'kyj answered (3 July 1903): "I cannot agree that we should not treat topics taken from the life of the intelligentsia because we do not have one. We do have an intelligentsia. . . . The shaping of a cultural type, as is well known, does not depend on national or political consciousness alone. . . . Literature should not be confined to

---

Well aware of this were Russian defenders of the rights of Ukrainian, such as A. Pypin and A. Šaxmatov.

Among Ukrainians the argumentation was most fully developed by M. Kostomarov in his article "Malorusskoe slovo" (*Vestnik Evropy*, 1881, 1, pp. 401 – 407) and in his review of the almanac *Luna* (*Vestnik Evropy*, 1882, 2). Kostomarov opposed neologisms in language as well as translations in literature (1882, pp. 892ff., 897, 900); he said that Ukrainian literature should be "exclusively for peasants (*isključitel'no mužickaja*)" (896); Russian should be reserved for all higher cultural needs (888). If under such conditions Ukrainian withers away, that is wholly acceptable, provided it happens from Ukrainians' free will and not under duress (897).

We do not know to what extent these were the actual views of the aging Kostomarov (Lotoc'kyj 2, 139 denies the sincerity of his statements), or whether they were a tactic for achieving the cancellation of the Ems ukase; the former assumption is the more likely. But similar views, except for the conclusion about the withering away of Ukrainian, were expressed sincerely by Panas Myrnyj, in private letters not designed for publication.

Myrnyj was against any non-Ukrainian subjects in literature (e.g., he objected to the Crimean short stories by M. Kocjubyns'kyj), against translations (although he himself translated *King Lear*, he never published the translation), against any non-peasant words, including loanwords ("words which the peasants [*narod*] do not use, such as *nervy, energija*"), and for the consistent purity of the rural language in literature (Myrnyj, 491, 461). The reason behind Myrnyj's views, however, was primarily practical, namely, the absence of a Ukrainian intelligentsia. He admitted the possibility of later change, "as life would create [our] intelligentsia" (503).

peasants' everyday life; it must reflect the real way of life of all layers of the society'' (Kocjubyns'kyj 294). Myrnyj had not noticed that in his own critique, composed as a letter to Kocjubyns'kyj, he had used such words as *psyxolohičnyj, inteligencija, typ*, and even *literatura* — thereby defeating his own thesis, because these words and similar ones did not originate from peasants' speech. Unwillingly, in Myrnyj's own use, they manifested the existence of a Ukrainian intelligentsia.

The linguistic ramifications of these literary polemics are obvious. Even though limited by official prohibitions to belles lettres, the literary language followed the dialectics of every standard language. At the outset, it might be attached most strongly to one (rural) dialect. As soon as it becomes the tool of the educated, however, that language breaks through its original boundaries, absorbs elements alien to the underlying dialect, and acquires its own propelling forces of development. This trend did not, of course, begin with *Dubove lystja*, in which Kocjubyns'kyj wrote about Ukrainian intellectuals, Lesja Ukrajinka dealt with topics of ancient Egypt and ancient Scotland, and Kryms'kyj published his variations on Old Iranian motifs—all topics blatantly remote from the interests of the Ukrainian peasant and requiring a vocabulary to a great extent unfamiliar to that supposed consumer of literature. As early as the 1870s an ardent discussion had flared up around the non-peasant words (either borrowed or newly created) then being introduced by M. Staryc'kyj—the opponents ironically called them ''forged words'' (*kovani slova*). Even in the 1850s, under the pen of the masters and creators of Modern Ukrainian T. Ševčenko and P. Kuliš, words unknown in the everyday spoken language of the countryside were introduced and used lavishly in Ukrainian literature.

The novelty of the time around 1903 was that these problems were raised not only by language practice, but as a programmatic statement. Inescapably, a reassessment of the *raison d'être* of the standard Ukrainian language had to be made. Now losing at an increasing rate its understandability to peasants, the language was in need of a new justification, of a complete revision of the old arguments presented in its defense. And defense it needed, because, as we have seen, its social status was different from that of a sole or official language within a state. Such languages needed no theoretical support, for they were the only means of communication in their respective countries. If one day, say, French suddenly disappeared in France, the entire life of the country would be paralyzed. This was not the case of Ukrainian in the then Russian Ukraine, where all higher communication was conducted in Russian and the intelligentsia either did not use Ukrainian or, at best, could switch to Russian at any time. These problems, although never clearly articulated as has been presented here, came to the fore after 1905.

The Revolution of 1905 swept away the ukase of 1876 and its revised version of 1881, although, characteristically, they never were officially repealed and thus, in purely legal terms, could have been reinstituted at any time. Numerous petitions and recommendations to revoke these decrees were made before 1905. For instance, in 1880 such appeals were made by the Kherson zemstvo and the Černihiv zemstvo, and in 1890, by Oleksander Konys'kyj. In 1900 Konstantin Voenskij, a Russian functionary of the St. Petersburg Censorship Committee, submitted such a petition (reprinted in full in Lotoc'kyj 2, 246ff.). In 1902 one was made by the Kharkiv Society for Literacy; in 1902, by the Economic Council of the Černihiv zemstvo; in December of 1904, by Ukrainians gathered at the celebration of the anniversary of I. Nečuj-Levyc'kyj; in 1901, at the Agricultural Congress in Moscow; in 1902, at the Congress of Handimen in Poltava (cf. Lotoc'kyj 2, 239ff., 285, 292, 371).

On 12 December 1904, the tsarist government (then headed by S. Witte) initiated a reconsideration of the special laws on the censorship of non-Russian (*inorodčeskix*) publications in the empire (Lotoc'kyj 2, 287). In its meetings of 26 and 31 December 1904, the Committee of Ministers resolved to initiate a revision of the laws on Ukrainian publications, provided committees of experts recommended such a measure. Such committees were to be nominated at the Russian Academy of Sciences and at the Universities of Kiev and Kharkiv; the governor-general of the provinces of Kiev, Podolia, and Volhynia was to be consulted, as well.

The Academy's committee, nominated on 5 February 1905, consisted of six academy members, headed by F. Korš, a sympathizer of Ukrainian cultural aspirations. Characteristically enough, the committee coopted six prominent Ukrainians who belonged to the St. Petersburg *hromada* (listed in Lotoc'kyj 2, 365). The resulting memorandum (its general and literary section was compiled by Korš, and the philological section, by A. Šaxmatov), entitled "On the Revocation of the Restriction of Little Russian Publications," recommended the abrogation of the laws of 1876 and 1881. The memo was adapted by the Academy as a whole on 18 February 1905. It was published in March for "internal use" only (150 copies), but the text was leaked and appeared in Galicia, in the *Literaturno-naukovyj vistnyk* (vol. 30, 1905, in the translation of V. Hnatjuk; pp. 164–81, 218–30), and as an offprint. It was published in Russia, by an unnamed private publisher (but with permission of the academy) only in 1910, when it had only historical significance.

The Kharkiv committee comprised eleven professors, chaired by M. Sumcov; nine of its members were Ukrainians. The Kiev committee included eight professors, six of them Ukrainians. Both committees opted for the revocation of the anti-Ukrainian decrees. The administration in Kiev did not object to that. The governor-general's reply (written by N. Molčanovs'kyj, director of his chancery—Čykalenko 368) favored the cancellation of the law of 1876.

The Kharkiv resolution (written by M. Sumcov—Čykalenko 368) derived primarily from a concern for the interests of the Ukrainian people, whereas the academy memo sprang clearly from a concern for the integrity and the interests of the Russian Empire. Permission to publish in Ukrainian was being recommended by the academy on the premise that Ukrainians posed no threat to the unity of the Russian Empire, whereas discontent brought about by the blossoming of such publications in Galicia while they were banned in the empire might be a potential danger. The other premises of the Academy's memo were that Ukrainian publications would benefit the uneducated or little-educated peasants, that Ukrainian literature would by its very nature remain regional and "in its entire make-up would remain Russian," and that Ukrainians would remain "faithful and tried sons of the Russian nation" (Tymošenko, 328). No wonder that in 1917, when the political aspects of the Ukrainian liberation movement became obvious, Šaxmatov radically changed his attitude (see Lotoc'kyj 2, 359).

The Kiev committee took a position close to that of the academy in St. Petersburg. In his preliminary draft of the Kiev memo V. Antonovyč went so far as to say that the Little Russian nationality "is entirely devoid of the instinct for statehood; not only did it never constitute a separate state, but it voluntarily declined the formation of such even when historical circumstances provided such a possibility" (Antonovyč 283). All three committee reports emphasized the importance of Ukrainian publications for the un- and little-educated; none suggested the free, full-fledged development of Ukrainian literature.[5]

On the basis of these recommendations, the minister of education, V. Glazov, reported to the Committee of Ministers that the laws of 1876 and 1881 should be revoked, while emphasizing that in the church, schools, courts, and administration, Ukrainian must remain inadmissible.[6] Measures taken must agree with § 1.3 of the "Fundamental Law of the Empire," which stated: "The Russian language is the official language and [it is] obligatory in the army, the navy, and all governmental and public institutions" (Dareste 2, 151; the text is from 1906); and with the programmatic slogan of the Russian nationalists: "Russia can be great, united, and indivisible only if she is well bound by one cement, that of the one and only Russian official language" (*Nacionalisty*, 259). By the time of Glazov's report, however, the entire procedure had become pointless: "Provisional regulations for censorship," compiled by 24 November 1905, and accepted on 26 April 1906 (Lotoc'kyj 2, 381; Jefremov 76), virtually abolished any preliminary censorship.

The repercussions of these measures, together with the general turmoil of 1905, were far reaching. First of all, they brought about the rebirth of the Ukrainian periodical press and the inauguration of legal political newspapers in the Russian Ukraine. After the tsar's manifesto of 17 October (which, in the words of a contemporary, "promised all liberties and granted none") and before the appearance of the new press regulations a month later, *Xliborob*, a newspaper for peasants, started appearing in Lubni (Poltava region), without having received any preliminary authorization. Appearing in a circulation of 5,000, it succeeded in publishing five issues, after which it was closed. *Xliborob* was followed, beginning on 24 December 1905, by the weekly *Ridnyj kraj*, published in Poltava; after its sixteenth issue appeared, it was closed and then transferred to Kiev, where it continued to appear through July of 1910 (Žyvotko 104). In the wake of the revolution Ukrainian periodicals appeared in other places, but they were all ephemeral due to the interference of the authorities (Jefremov

---

[5] The essential passages of the Kiev and Kharkiv memos are reprinted in Lotoc'kyj 2, 375ff. The St. Petersburg memo is reprinted in Tymošenko 2, 297ff., but without the appendices compiled by the Ukrainian members of the committee (they are listed in Lotoc'kyj 2, 373).

[6] The text is partly reproduced in Lotoc'kyj 2, 378ff.

78): the bilingual Ukrainian-Russian *Narodnoe delo* (one issue), *Narodnja sprava* (one issue), and *Visty* (five issues) in Odessa; *Dobra porada* (four issues) and *Zaporožžja* (one issue) in Kharkiv; *Zorja* (four fascicles) in Moscow; and *Vil'na Ukrajina* (six issues) in St. Petersburg (Žyvotko 110ff.). The most important was the daily *Hromads'ka dumka* which was designed primarily for the rural intelligentsia. It began to appear in Kiev on 1 January 1906, and was shut down by the censorship on 18 August 1906 (Čykalenko 440).

Having been encouraged by the sweep of revolution, all the periodicals fell victims to the reaction that immediately followed the manifesto of 17 October 1905. The reaction became overpowering after the dispersal of the 72-day-old First Duma, on 21 July 1906, and became even greater after the dissolution of the 71-day-old Second Duma, on 15 June 1907, and the introduction on 16 June 1907 of a new electoral law which secured a pro-government majority in all subsequent dumas (so that the Third Duma existed for the normal five years: 14 November 1907 to 22 June 1912). Under the governments headed by, in sequence, Goremykin, Stolypin, and Kokovcev, when through courts-martial thousands of people were either hanged or banished and the Black Hundred ran wild, the situation of the Ukrainian press was precarious. In the provinces it was almost non-existent.

Yet there was no total blackout of Ukrainian publications, as before 1905. In Kiev, some periodicals managed to survive even in the worst conditions. The shut-down *Hromads'ka dumka* was reborn in 1907 as *Rada*, which became the leader among Ukrainian publications within the Russian Empire and survived until 1914. The literary and political monthly *Nova hromada* was published through 1906. In 1907 M. Hruševs'kyj transferred the publication offices of *Literaturno-naukovyj vistnyk* from Lviv to Kiev, where it merged with *Nova hromada*. The Russian language *Kievskaja starina* was transformed into the Ukrainian-language *Ukrajina* in 1907; when that ceased publication, the *Zapysky Ukrajins'koho naukovoho tovarystva v Kyjevi*, a strictly scholarly publication, began to appear, in 1908 (through 1918 with wartime interruption). By 1908 the list of Ukrainian periodicals grew to include the Social-Democrats' *Slovo* (Kiev, 1907–1909) and, as the only Ukrainian periodical published outside Kiev, *Svitova zirnycja*, a weekly designed by conservative Poles for the peasantry that was published in Podolia. In 1909, Hruševs'kyj began to publish *Selo*, a weekly for peasants, which was superseded in 1911 by *Zasiv* and in

1912 by *Majak*. From 1910 through 1913 the weekly *Dniprovi xvyli* appeared in Katerynoslav. Two new literary monthlies, *Ukrajins'ka xata*, a forum for modernism in literature and nationalism in politics, and *Dzvin*, a Marxist publication, were inaugurated in 1909 and 1913, respectively. The art magazine *Sjajvo* started to appear in Kiev in 1913. The Russian Ukraine got its first Ukrainian monthly for children, *Moloda Ukrajina*, in 1906; for students, *Ukrajins'kyj student*, in 1913; for pedagogues, *Svitlo*, in 1910. There were also agricultural and household periodicals such as *Rillja*, *Ukrajins'ke bdžil'nyctvo*, *Žyttje i znannje*, *Naša kooperacija* (Žyvotko 121ff.).

The growth of the Ukrainian periodical press was unprecedented and certainly impressive. After so many dormant years there suddenly proved to be Ukrainian publishers, editors, authors, and, most important, Ukrainian readers. Yet, that sudden flourishing, in heavily unfavorable conditions, should be examined not only for its achievements but also for its shortcomings. The most obvious of these was the low circulation of virtually all the new Ukrainian periodicals. Only a few had a circulation of more than 1,000 copies, and probably none were published at a profit. Therefore they were financially strapped and permanently relied on monetary support from a very limited number of benefactors.

Rada, the most popular periodical, was supported financially by, among others, Vasyl' Symyrenko, V. Leontovyč, M. Arkas, and, especially, Je. Čykalenko. It is Čykalenko who in his memoirs provides details about the newspaper's situation. *Hromads'ka dumka/Rada* was planned to have 5,000 subscribers. In the first half of 1906, it had 4,093; by the second half of the year, subscribers fell to 1,509 (Čykalenko 466); no data on newstand sales are provided.

Among provincial periodicals, there are some data on *Dniprovi xvyli*, which was edited by D. Drošenko and was published in Katerynoslav (now Dnipropetrovs'k). It had "several hundred" subscribers, mostly peasants, and subscription income covered the expenses of publication, but only because neither the editors nor the authors were paid (Drošenko 1949, 143).

The most important reason for the decline in subscriptions was the persecution of subscribers: harassment by police, searches, firing from government jobs, blacklisting, and confiscations (Čykalenko 425, 465; II, 18 passim; *Rada* subsequently partly recouped its subscribers: in 1908 there were 1400, in 1909 there were 2500, in 1911

there were 3300—ibid., II, 3a, 30b, 75c). At the instigation of the police, some provincial post offices refused to accept subscriptions.
Cases of the harassment of subscribers and readers of the Ukrainian
press are described by Jefremov (78ff.). A second reason for low circulation was the low level of literacy. A third was the lack of
Ukrainian journalists of high caliber, due to the lack of professional
education.[7]

Contemporaries mentioned language difficulties as another reason
for the low circulation of the Ukrainian press. Mastery of a literary
language spreads through education in schools and through its use by
the intelligentsia. Neither situation obtained for the recently de-
ruralized (or now de-ruralizing) Ukrainian literary language.
Čykalenko describes the attitude of various strata of the Ukrainian
society: the peasantry "is either illiterate or [their language] is
maimed by the Russian school, or else they do not want to read a
Ukrainian newspaper which is written in a language shaped by a small
circle of intelligentsia, true, on the foundation of the people['s
language] but with a host of words and expressions which do not
[come from] people and are alien to them because they do not hear
them in the school, in the court, in [everyday] life" (II, 18a); in cities
"a regular city dweller who for better or worse can speak in the rural
Ukrainian language will not subscribe to our newspaper, for he understands the Russian language better" (II, 18a). Finally, a Ukrainian
landowner "loathes the standard Ukrainian language [and] considers
it injurious to the people's speech that is dear to his heart; he would
like a newspaper written in the language of Ševčenko [and]
Kotljarevs'kyj, and, if native [Ukrainian] words are lacking, one
should, in his opinion, adopt the now generally known Russian
words" (II, 33a).

In Galicia, where a Ukrainian school and the tradition of a
Ukrainian-speaking intelligentsia did exist, these problems did not
arise. Therefore the regional Ukrainian press could appear in a
language elevated above the vernacular of the lower classes. This
added to the linguistic differences between the Ukrainian press in Galicia and in Kiev. The situation is well represented in a description of a

---

[7] S. Petljura complained about this in 1908 and again in 1912 (Petljura 2, 125,
248).

visit by the editor of the Lviv *Dilo* to the offices of the Kiev *Rada*, where these observations were made to him:

> The Lviv *Dilo* is published in such a mixed language that reading it is difficult and disagreeable: the many Latin, German, Polish, and even Muscovite words, and the purely Polish sentence structure, make this language entirely alien to us. Likewise, to Galicians the language of *Rada* seems unusual. Once there came here [to visit us] the *Dilo*'s editor, Panejko. He said that *Rada* is published in a very primitive peasant language, adapted to the understanding of a *muzhik*; *Dilo*, by contrast, is designed for the intelligentsia, whereas for peasants they have special newspapers that are published in a peasant language similar to that of *Rada*. (Čykalenko II, 140d ff.; cf. also II, 52c and 71bc).

In December 1906, M. Hruševs'kyj brought three Galicians—M. Lozyns'kyj, I. Krevec'kyj, and I. Džydžora—to the editorial staff of *Rada*, but they left after a few months (Dorošenko 1949, 93). Whatever the reasons, the existence in, say, 1908, of some nine periodicals published in Ukrainian with a total circulation of at best 20,000 copies (actually probably less) for a population of 30,000,000 is telling. Each of four leading Russian newspapers published in the Ukraine— *Kievskaja mysl'* in Kiev, *Južnyj kraj* in Kharkiv, *Odesskij listok* in Odessa, and *Pridneprovskij kraj* in Katerynoslav—had a much higher circulation. According to the bibliography compiled by L. Beljaeva, in 1908 Kiev had a total of 13 Russian newspapers, Kharkiv had 8, and Odessa had 20; these were certainly widely read by Ukrainians. The circulation of *Kievskaja mysl'*, which was only a local newspaper, vacillated between 25,000 and 80,000. In addition, the Ukraine absorbed an impressive number of papers and other periodicals published in St. Petersburg and Moscow. So whereas the tempo and the scope of the growth of the Ukrainian press were breathtaking, its absolute achievements were very limited.[8]

---

[8] At this junction it is of interest to mention that the agricultural booklets by Je. Čykalenko sold in 500,000 copies. Ihnatijenko (1926, 50) summarizes the state of the Ukrainian press after 1905 in the following table:

The characteristics of the growth of the Ukrainian press also apply to the book trade. Before 1905 there appears to have been only one Ukrainian bookstore in the entire Russian Empire, in Kiev (owned by *Kievskaja starina*). By 1908 there were three in Kiev (the two new ones were opened by *Literaturno-naukovyj vistnyk* and by Je. Čerepovs'kyj), and one each in Poltava, Kremenčuk, Kharkiv, Katerynoslav, Odessa, and Katerynodar, as well as one in St. Petersburg, representing an increase of 400 percent. But the total of nine Ukrainian bookstores for the whole Russian Ukraine and an additional one in St. Petersburg only testifies to the underdevelopment of Ukrainian-language publishing.

The same can be said about publication of books. Petljura made a survey of the exhibition in 1912 of books published in the Russian Empire during the previous year. The number of books published in Ukrainian was 242, against 25,526 items in Russian, 1,664 in Polish, 965 in Yiddish and Hebrew, 920 in German, 608 in Lettish, 519 in Estonian, 372 in Tatar, and 266 in Armenian (Petljura 2, 244). Ukrainians, second in population, occupied eighth place, and a low eighth place at that. In addition, the Ukrainian items included a disproportionately high number of pamphlets and popular editions.

The events of 1905 awoke hopes that there would be Ukrainian schools. Letters sent to *Rada* in favor of Ukrainian courses at the universities carried up to 10,000 signatures (Dorošenko 1949, 91). In 1906–1907, M. Sumcov at the University of Kharkiv and O. Hruševs'kyj at the University of Odessa began to teach courses on Ukrainian subjects in Ukrainian (A. Loboda and V. Peretc announced similar courses in Kiev, but these were to be conducted in Russian;

	Total number of Ukrainian periodicals	Number of Ukrainian periodicals in the Russian Ukraine	Number of Ukrainian periodicals in the Austrian Ukraine
1905	39	7	28
1906	81	32	37
1907	51	11	34
1908	47	9	33
1909	59	11	37
1910	84	14	49
1911	104	16	59
1912	95	16	51
1913	48	17	21
1914	42	16	16

Jefremov 101). Almost immediately the university administrations intervened, and the courses were stopped. Not the slightest possibility was allowed for education in Ukrainian, not even in the elementary schools. The most liberal Russian party in this respect, the Constitutional Democrats, who in the First Duma held 153 seats out of 524 and in the Second Duma 98 seats out of 518, reluctantly included instruction in Ukrainian in rural elementary schools and teaching Ukrainian as a subject in high schools in their demands (Čykalenko 387; Petljura 2, 256; Giterman 425, 440). But the party was actually split on this issue and certainly had no desire to fight for Ukrainian education.

Not a single Ukrainian school opened in 1905 – 1914. Several private *himnaziji* sought to introduce the Ukrainian language in their curriculums. The authorities consented, on the condition that teachers of the subject have diplomas for teaching Ukrainian, knowing full well that no such diplomas could have been granted anywhere in the Russian Empire (Jefremov 105). In Podolia there was an attempt to Ukrainianize instruction in parochial elementary schools. The Holy Synod, on 12 October 1907, authorized the undertaking, probably in an effort to counteract the influence of Catholicism and of the Poles. The move brought no results because several teachers who taught in Ukrainian were severely harassed by local authorities (Jefremov 103).

A spark of hope for Ukrainian education were the several Ukrainian grammars published in those years. Those most resembling school grammars were P. Zaloznyj's *Korotka hramatyka ukrajins'koji movy*, part 1 (Kiev, 1906 and 1912), and part 2, *Syntax* (Kiev, 1913); and H. Šerstjuk's (managing editor of *Rada*—Čykalenko II, 47a) *Ukrajins'ka hramatyka*, part 1 (Poltava 1907, and Kiev 1912), and part 2, *Skladnja* (Kiev, 1909 and 1913). Šerstjuk's second edition even included exercises for students. More detailed and sophisticated were Je. Tymčenko's *Ukrajins'ka hramatyka*, part 1 (Kiev, 1907), which treated some dialectal elements, and A. Kryms'kyj's never completed *Ukrainskaja grammatika* (Moscow 1907 – 1908: vol. 1, fascicles 1, 2, 6; vol. 2, fascicle 1), with a lengthy historical commentary. In the preface to the second edition of his grammar, Zaloznyj characteristically wrote that the reviewers of the first edition "say... that... my grammar does not fit schools. This is true. But where are they—the schools?"[9] Some of the grammars were republished repeat-

---

[9] Quoted after V. Vaščenko, "Perši pidručnyky z ukrajins'koji movy,"

edly. Obviously, they were used for self-education.[10] They may have contributed to the normalization of the written language, which a contemporary characterized thus: "As a consequence of the lack of authorization and the absence of a periodical press [before 1906], every author wrote in his own orthography and even in his personal language" (Lotoc'kyj 3, 167).

Some of these grammars may have been used in the Prosvita society. This organization for adult education was patterned on the institution of the same name in the Austrian Ukraine. Branches of Prosvita started to spring up in the Russian Ukraine in 1905. In Katerynoslav, this happened on October 8, i.e., even before the manifesto of October 17, with village branches opening thereafter. The example of Katerynoslav was followed by Odessa, Kiev, and many other localities in and outside the Ukraine. A total of about 40 Prosvita societies are known to have existed. From the very outset they were allowed in some provinces (Kharkiv and Poltava) and in 1908–1910, during Stolypin's regime, virtually all of them, except in Katerynoslav gubernia, were closed (Stolypin's circular order was dated 20 January 1910: *EU* 2, 2370; Čykalenko II, 40a, 47d, 153d; Lotoc'kyj 2, 126; 3, 87).[11] Prosvita's activity helped to revivify Ukrainian cultural life. Petljura characterized its branches as "the only centers of a more or less visible [social] life." Certainly they were places where the public use of Ukrainian was normal. Petljura also criticized the society, stating in the social-democratic jargon of the time (1908) that its branches mostly united the "Ukrainian bourgeois intelligentsia" (Petljura 121) and not the workers, partly because of the relatively high membership dues and partly as a result of administrative persecutions. Some bridges between intellectuals and peasants were built, however, during the short period the Prosvita branches existed.

Ukrajins'ka mova i literatura v školi, 1961, no. 5, p. 84.

[10] The fifth grammar, I. Nečuj-Levyc'kyj's *Hramatyka ukrajins'koji movy*, pt. 1: *Etymolohija* (Kiev, 1914) and pt. 2: *Syntaksys* (Kiev, 1914), was actually more of a discussion about the nature of standard Ukrainian.

[11] In justifying this act, Stolypin reported to the Senate that the cultural activity of Ukrainians was undesirable because "the three principal branches of the Eastern Slavdom by their origin and by their language cannot but constitute a unity" (quoted in Lotoc'kyj 3, 87).

The Orthodox church remained Russian. Yet here, too, there was a minor innovation, that is, the publication of the Gospel in Ukrainian translation. As late as June 1904, the imperial minister of interior affairs, V. Pleve, refused permission for such a publication, because of "the extreme paucity of the Little Russian language [making it] entirely unfit to express abstract notions in general and the lofty truths of the Revelation in particular," and because of "the quite satisfactory knowledge by the local Little Russian population of the Russian language" (Lotoc'kyj 2, 390). Yet in 1905, responding to a request by the Russian Academy of Sciences, the new minister, P. Svjatopolk-Mirskij, stated that "for the publication of the Gospel in the Little Russian dialect, there are, on my part, no objections" (18 October 1905: Lotoc'kyj 2, 396). A translation by P. Moračevs'kyj (1806 – 1879) that was made in 1860 went under thorough revision by a committee of the Academy of Sciences comprising four academicians (Korš, Šaxmatov, Fortunatov, Kokovcev) and seven members of the Ukrainian community of St. Petersburg, and then by another committee, headed by the archbishop of Podolia, Parfenij Levyc'kyj, in Kamjanec'-Podil's'kyj (later in Tula). Moračevs'kyj's translation was finally published in 1906 – 1911, more than forty-five years after its completion. It was never used in any church service. The Orthodox church in the Ukraine as an institution remained Russian from the lowest to the highest levels. Nevertheless, the Ukrainian translation of the Gospel of St. Matthew was a first breach in the solid edifice. In one year 100,000 copies were sold (Kistjakivs'kyj 139).[12]

A novelty of the period 1905 – 1914 was the de facto legalization of the Ukrainian language for scholarly use, primarily in the humanities. The Ukrainian Scholarly Society in Kiev founded by M. Hruševs'kyj in 1908 organized Ukrainian public lectures, conferences, and panels, mainly on subjects of Ukrainian history (cf. Petljura 2, 278ff.). From 1908 it published a series of *Zapysky* with scholarly materials, and in 1914 the society began to publish the quarterly *Ukrajina*. Topically,

---

[12] At about the same time teaching in Ukrainian was allowed at the two-year parochial schools of the Podolia diocese, where the community wanted it; this entailed teaching Ukrainian as a subject in the Vinnycja parochial teachers school. (The ukase of the Holy Synod is published in *Ukrajina*, 1907, 12, 78ff.) Granted on 12 October 1910, this permission was withdrawn in 1912 (Lotoc'kyj 3, 102). In the years of reaction the same Parfenij hampered the publication of the Acts and Epistles in Ukrainian.

however, these publications focused almost entirely on Ukrainian historical subjects. Outside the confines of the society Ukrainian was still excluded from scholarly usage, e.g., from the Archaeological Congress of 1912 in Černihiv (Lotoc'kyj 2, 147). A Ukrainian university remained a dream. In 1914 a clandestine institution having such a name arose in St. Petersburg; it functioned until 1917, but in fact it constituted but several courses on Ukrainian topics conducted at private homes (Lotoc'kyj 2, 325ff.).

Substantial developments took place in Ukrainian lexicography. Preceded by the Russian-Ukrainian dictionaries of M. Umanec' and A. Spilka (pseudonyms for M. Komarov and the Odessa Hromada) published in Lviv, 1893–1898 (but compiled in Odessa) and of Je. Tymčenko published in Kiev 1897–1899, the Ukrainian-Russian dictionary by V. Dubrovs'kyj appeared in Kiev in 1909. To establish technological terminology, publications such as dictionaries of various handicrafts and popular technology were important; e.g., those by V. Vasilenko (Kharkiv, 1902) and by a Kievan group published in the *Zapysky* of the Ukrainian Scholarly Society (1911–1915).

Of crucial importance was the four-volume Ukrainian-Russian dictionary edited by B. Hrinčenko (Kiev, 1909). This dictionary was initiated in 1861 by P. Kuliš. Its preparation continued under the patronage of the Kiev Hromada by such luminaries as P. Žytec'kyj, V. Naumenko, and Je. Tymčenko, who were successively chief editors. In 1902 Hrinčenko was engaged to give final form to the dictionary. P. Žytec'kyj and K. Myxal'čuk served as his consultants. The tenor of the whole work was to present an undiluted popular language while avoiding all the "forged" (*kovani*) words which had infiltrated it since the 1870s. Accordingly, the sources of the dictionary included ethnographic records, literary works published before 1870 or by writers working before that date, and selected materials drawn from earlier dictionaries or recorded in rural speech. Thus the chronological framework of the dictionary was 1798–1870, although the latter date was often transgressed. Popular technological terminology was given much attention, whereas loanwords of recent date were more often than not excluded. Although it was essentially a collection of vocabulary actually used by primarily rural speakers, the dictionary managed to avoid excessive regionalization, in fact, for most words it marked the locality of use and normalized the material phonetically, accentually, and morphologically. Thanks to these techniques, it became a

sui generis summary of the Ukrainian literary language before that
language transferred from the peasantry to the intelligentsia. At the
same time, it projected some principles and bases for the Ukrainian
language's future standardization. The impact of Hrinčenko's dictionary, with its 68,000 entries, can thus hardly be overestimated.[13]

The rapid and remarkable growth of manifestations of Ukrainian
culture in the Ukrainian language brought the question of the
Ukrainian language into the political arena. Here the Ukrainian position was very weak—as B. Kistjakivs'kyj put it, "in the political
sense the Ukrainians are so far a *quantité négligeable*; nobody can put
this in doubt" (136)—but the very appearance of Ukrainians in a political context stirred concern. In the elections to the First Duma,
Ukrainians knew they would probably not win seats on their own, and
in fact only one deputy from the Ukrainian list was elected, V. Šemet,
from Poltava (Čykalenko 421). Ukrainians regularly supported one of
the Russian parties, most frequently the Kadets, although their
Ukrainian program was very moderate—no more than the establishment of Ukrainian elementary schools in villages.[14] Once the Duma
had been elected, however, it proved to include a relatively large
group of Ukrainian deputies, and they soon formed a Ukrainian faction. The Second Duma had a Ukrainian faction of 47 deputies
(Čykalenko 422ff.); their demands were quite moderate: generally
speaking, they sought the establishment of Ukrainian elementary
schools in villages. A plan for the project was submitted in March of
1908 by 38 deputies of the Third Duma (Hruševs'kyj 4); this Duma
established a special commission on education in the native
languages, but Ukrainian was excluded from its agenda (Hruševs'kyj
10).

---

[13] More information about the engagement of Hrinčenko to work on the dictionary
can be found in Čykalenko 302ff. From a letter by his widow Maria to A. Šaxmatov
dated 19 October 1910, we know that Hrinčenko was unhappy with the Ukrainian-
Russian character of his dictionary and planned a thoroughly Ukrainian explanatory
one (Dzendzelivs'kyj 80). His untimely death, at the age of forty-six, precluded practical work on that project.

[14] Cf. the program of the Ukrainian Democratic-Radical Party, which sought autonomy for the Ukraine and for recognition of Ukrainian as a state language, to be used
on all levels of education (Čykalenko 416, 418f.).

This was a far cry from real political demands, but it was enough to disturb advocates of the idea of a Great Russia and a Great Russian culture. They feared that behind the modest groupings and even more modest demands might exist the dynamics for the cultural separatism of the Ukraine, to be followed, who could know, by political independence, which would be tantamount to the destruction of Russia as an empire. One Russian of such mind was P. Struve. In 1911, he deemed it appropriate to initiate a discussion on the Ukrainian problem. Having launched the idea that Russian culture encompasses "Great Russian," "Little Russian," and "Belorussian," he insisted that Ukrainian culture does not exist and that its partisans are attempting to create it artificially. He concluded, "I am deeply convinced that, for instance, the introduction in high (*srednej i vysšej*) school of the Little Russian language would be an artificial and unjustifiable waste of the psychological force of the population" (Struve 1911, 187). The growth of Ukrainian culture was to him but a "nationalistic multiplication of cultures."

Attacking Ukrainians and the Ukrainian language was nothing new by this time. But the attacks were usually waged by extreme Russian nationalists such as T. Florinskij or I. Filevič, who espoused the official view of *triedinyj russkij narod* (one tripartite Russian people) and whose writings bordered on political denunciations.[15] Of like mind was I. Sikorskij, a Kiev psychologist. In a paper read at the Club of Russian Nationalists in Kiev (7 February 1913) and published as the pamphlet *Russkie i ukraincy* the same year, he tried to prove that there is no psychological difference between Ukrainians and Russians and that therefore Ukrainian and Russian are two parallel languages different in sound ("phonetics") but identical in spirit ("psychology"). The existence of such languages, he proclaimed, was "a luxury which nature usually does not tolerate" (quoted from

---

[15] This boundary was actually transgressed by a "monograph": S. Ščegolev's *Ukrainskoe dviženie kak sovremennyj ètap južnorusskogo separatizma* (Kiev, 1912), 558 pp., and the abridged version, *Sovremennoe ukrainstvo, ego proisxoždenie, rost i zadači* (Kiev, 1914), 158 pp. For a characterization of Ščegolev's writings see S. Jefremov in *Ukrainskaja žizn'*, 1912, no. 4, pp. 7–8, and 1913, no. 1, p. 2; also see S. Petljura in *Ukrainskaja žizn'*, 1913, no. 11. Lenin, 1912, no. 10 labeled them "the *Zitatensack* of a police spy."

F. Korš, "Nacionalističeskaja nauka," *Ukrainskaja žizn'*, 1913, no. 7/8, p. 20).

Russian conservative and nationalist newspapers, especially from 1911, abounded in aggressive and violent attacks against the Ukrainian movement and against the use of the Ukrainian language. To note one example, in *Kievljanin* for 17 November 1911, in an article entitled "Where is the principal enemy?," A. Savenko wrote: "The Mazepinist question hits Russia at the very foundation of her ability to be a great power (*osnova ee velikoderžavija*). . . . The self-preservation of the great Russian people as a nation and as a state imperatively points to the necessity of a resolute struggle with Mazepinism."

As a second example, in St. Petersburg's *Novoe vremja* for 12 December 1911 M. Men'šikov declared: "The fanatics of Mazepinism speak louder and louder in preparing the break-away of giant Little Russia from Russia. . . . The most frightening portent for the disintegration of the Empire is so-called Mazepinism, i.e., the fervent preparation of a mutiny in Little Russia. . . . A common language must be considered the foremost national task. No obstacles should stand in the way of its materialization. . . . Not only the official language (that of law, of administration, and of the courts), but also the social language of a nation should be one. The supremacy of the official language should be defended by us Russians with the same energy as our own lives." Men'šikov concluded: "Under the name of Ukrainian *hromady*, numerous Little Russian–Polish–Jewish circles act to corrupt students and teachers of public schools, to inculcate in them, and through them also to common people, the most ferocious hatred of the Russian people and state. It is high time not only to take notice of this development—it has been noticed since long ago—but also to fight it to the death." Men'šikov titled his article "Nacionalnaja treščina" (The crack in the nation).

The aim of such articles was to incite a panic in conservative Russian circles which could lead to the destruction of Ukrainian institutions and personalities, be it by the government or public reaction. That aim was achieved. When Savenko came to St. Petersburg to lecture on "The Mazepinist movement in the South of Russia," the public attracted to the All-Russian National Club was so numerous that the auditorium was "full to overflowing" (*bitkom nabityj*), as *Novoe vremja* of 12 December 1911 reported.

In comparison to such adversaries, Struve's statements against Ukrainian culture and language sounded moderate. But as Petljura appropriately put it: "We observe in the making the shift (*sdvig*) of Russian liberalism towards Great Russian nationalism, which without any subterfuge vents a clearly zoological hatred" (*Ukrainskaja žizn'*, 1913, 3, 74). By contrast, B. Kistjakivs'kyj (under the pen name Ukrainec) urged "a further development of the Ukrainian people... in a bond with and in a close, all-faceted solidarity" with the Russians (132), but protected against "the basic feature characterizing the attitude of the Russian society to Ukrainians—its distinctly expressed selfishness" (133); he did not exclude the development of a complete Ukrainian language.

Struve presented his *profession de foi* in the programmatic article "Obščerusskaja kul'tura i ukrainskij partikuljarizm" in 1912. Struve observed that by then the Ukrainian liberation movement engaged primarily intellectuals but had but little urban support. But he also envisaged that a union between the intellectuals and masses was not impossible, and that such a development would mean the end of the Russian Empire. Struve stated: "If the 'Ukrainian' idea of the intellectuals strikes the people's earth and sets it afire, this is fraught with a gigantic and unprecedented split of the Russian nation" (85). Frightened by any such prospect Struve comforts himself that "capitalism speaks and will speak Russian" and that the dominance of the Russian language in the Ukraine's large cities is irreversible, so that a switch to Ukrainian there would be as unthinkable as a switch of Hamburg capitalists from High to Low German (81) (he forgot that in Prague, for example, capitalists did switch from speaking German to speaking Czech). But his fear does not desist. The conclusion he arrives at is that Ukrainian should be limited to being a regional idiom, while all national, cultural, and political functions are to be conducted and expressed solely in Russian for the entire area of the tripartite Russian nation (he does not use this Black Hundred expression, but comes right up to it).

This evolution of Struve's views led the Kadet (Constitutional-Democratic) party, of which he had once been a leader, to dissociate from him in the spring of 1912. A wide discussion on related topics shook the Kadet party in 1914, but Struve held fast to his views. After the outbreak of war and the Russian occupation of Galicia, he quite consistently called for "a deep and broad Russification of Galicia" (quoted from Pipes 679ff., who also provides a bibliography of these polemics; see also Lotoc'kyj 2, 409, 411, who also refers to F. Korš's articles in these discussions, pp. 335, 345). For the politician, this situation reflects the confluence of Russian liberalism with Russian chauvinism, but for the linguist it shows that the Ukrainian language at that time was attaining a position competitive with Russian, at least programmatically. The very fact that discussions on the function and maturity of the Ukrainian language took place was a manifestation of the language's development, of its coming of age. Followed with great curiosity by many Russianized Ukrainians, these discussions helped them to clarify their positions and to choose whether to convert to speaking Ukrainian.[16]

The problem of the Ukraine and the Ukrainian language also attracted attention on the left pole of Russian political thought. True, among the Social-Democrats/Bolsheviks the Ukrainian issue was treated within a more general discussion of the party program on the nationalities question; but an analysis of Lenin's notes clearly shows that a keen interest in the Ukrainian question sparked his work on the nationalities. Lenin began by reading and quoting from Struve's and Kistjakivs'kyj's articles in *Russkaja mysl'*, went on to study Ščegolev's notorious book on the Ukrainian movement, and then proceeded to M. Hruševs'kyj's *Ukrainstvo v Rossii: Ego zaprosy i nuždy* and to M. Slavyns'kyj's article "Formy nacional'nogo dviženija." Not included in Lenin's *Polnoe* (sic!) *sobranie sočinenij*, these notes were published in *Leninskij sbornik*, vol. 30 (Moscow: Partizdat, 1937), pp. 8–29. Lenin twice labelled Hruševs'kyj's views "reactionary" (pp. 11, 26).

Interest in the Ukrainian issue was also aroused by discussions of the Ukrainian language question in the Duma and by the activities of Ukrainian representatives there. The abortive First Duma (1906) did

---

[16] A typical illustration of these developments is given in Fedenko's reminiscences, where he describes a circle of young people in the small Ukrainian town of Oleksandrija, near Kirovohrad (pp. 12–15). The circle, whose members were mostly students of the local *himnazija*, used Russian as the language of their discussions. In 1912 the first Ukrainian circle of that type was founded, and some students switched to using Ukrainian in their private conversations. Fedenko mentions these developments in connection with the debates in the *Duma* that same year (see below); they could also have been connected to the Struve-Kistjakivs'kyj discussion. In any case the timing of the "Oleksandrian breakthrough" was not accidental.

not exist long enough to pursue any broad discussion of the Ukrainian question. But the rise of a Ukrainian faction there, forty-four persons strong, led by I. Šrah, and its publication of the periodical *Ukrainskij vestnik* (in Russian) were telling. Characteristically, the majority of the faction were peasants, some even illiterate; in fact, many of them learned of the national aspects of the Ukrainian issue only at the Duma (Lotoc'kyj 3, 7, 12).[17] Two of these representatives, A. Hrabovec'kyj from the Kiev and M. Onac'kyj from the Poltava province, delivered speeches at the Duma in Ukrainian (Lotoc'kyj 3, 17, 49), perhaps because their Russian was faulty, although Dorošenko maintained (1949, 83) that they spoke Russian well and used Ukrainian out of principle. Presumably the Ukrainian activities in the Duma could not have failed to impress many, but the low percentage of participating intellectuals—which reflected the actual situation in the country— could hardly have enhanced the prestige of the Ukrainian language.

Of the forty-seven members of the Ukrainian faction in the Second Duma (1907), six belonged to the intelligentsia, and the remaining forty-one were peasants (Lotoc'kyj 3, 22). The political program of the faction rejected secession but demanded the "resolute and irrevocable reorganization of the [regional] government in the sense of national and territorial autonomy" (Lotoc'kyj 3, 25). The faction's organ, *Ridna sprava*, was published in Ukrainian.

The Third Duma (1907 – 1912) was elected under controls designed to yield as docile a body as possible. Having but a minimal oppositional group, it was not an institution capable of conceding to even the most moderate Ukrainian demands. The Third Duma had no Ukrainian faction, and Ukrainian interests were at best represented by one intellectual, Professor I. Lučyc'kyj (according to Čykalenko II, 41c, d, only lukewarmly), and by several priests. Nonetheless the opposition did try to propagate independent views. The demand for Ukrainian elementary schools was raised virtually every year, especially when the budget of the Ministry of Education was debated,

---

[17] In 1910, a representative to the Third Duma from Podolia, M. Senderko, an advocate of the use of Ukrainian in the elementary school, reported about reading a Ukrainian text to peasants in his village: "The news that a Ukrainian literature existed was a pleasant surprise to my listeners, and the reading, in Ukrainian, of the Gospel, newspapers, and [an agricultural pamphlet by] Čykalenko enraptured them." (*Stenogr.* 1910, 1252.)

along with similar demands of the other non-Russian nationalities of the empire. On the agenda of the Third Duma it was a marginal question. In a summary of that Duma's activities (*Nacionalisty v 3-ej Gosudarstvennoj Dume*), the Russian Nationalists devoted 146 pages out of the total of 325 to national problems, yet Ukrainian matters occupy only some scant four pages of that 146.

In the fall of 1910 the government submitted to the Duma a plan for general elementary education throughout the empire. The project caused a prolonged and passionate discussion, especially on the question of whether the language of instruction should be Russian or the native languages of the children. In the stenographic record of the sessions, these matters cover 1,260 pages, but the Ukrainian aspects of them, barely 21 pages.[18] The question was explicitly raised in speeches by N. Čxeidze, A. Bulat, Lučyc'kyj, F. Rodičev, M. Senderko, P. Miljukov, and K. Zaviša (*Stenogr.* 1910, pp. 682, 899, 1106ff., 1226, 1250, 1263, 1322, 1799), not to mention the times when Ukrainian was meant implicitly although non-Russian languages in general were being spoken of. The outcome of the discussion was predetermined by the makeup of the Duma. Amendments to the government's plan were defeated by 178 votes to 102 (*Stenogr.* 1910, 1278). But public interest in the problem had been aroused. It may be that the public discussion of the Ukrainian question in the press initiated by Struve was to some extent promoted by these debates. In the Duma itself, the conservative deputy V. Aleksandrov summarized the importance of the problem of national languages in school as follows: "We are convinced that on the solution of this question will depend whether Russia will be the one and indivisible nation or it will head toward autonomy, union, and federation" (*Stenogr.* 1910, 437).[19]

---

[18] This figure is not quite fair as an indicator, because the discussion encompassed a whole gamut of problems—including ones as important as the transference of church schools to the secular administration and universal compulsory education—that concerned the whole empire, including the Ukraine.

[19] As for the schools, the total exclusion of Ukrainian that was the common practice was to be formulated into law according to the proposal of D. Pixno, a member of the State Council. On 4 April 1912 he suggested that the following statement be included in the school legislation: "The Little Russian and Belorussian population is not considered to speak other languages (*inojazyčnym*)" (Gosudarstvennyj Sovet, *Stenografičeskie otčety*, for 1911–1912, 7th session, meetings 1–81 [St. Petersburg, 1912], p. 2924). On April 6, Pixno withdrew this rather naive pronouncement

In the slightly less conservative Fourth Duma (1912 – 1917) Ukrainians put forward a program for Ukrainian to be used in elementary and (as a subject) in other schools, as well as in church, in courts, and public offices, which was supported by the factions of the Kadets and the *trudoviki* (Lotoc'kyj 3, 64). Discussion of these problems, again in the context of the other non-Russian languages, arose at debates of the budget of the Ministry of Education. This occurred especially in 1913, when the issue figured in the speeches of A. Šingarev, V. Bobrinskij, V. Dzjubinskij, V. Gelovani, A. Aleksandrov, P. Miljukov, A. Kerenskij, and H. Petrovs'kyj.[20]

As a separate problem the Ukrainian question first came to the fore in February 1914, when the Minister of Interior M. Maklakov prohibited any celebration of the centenary of Taras Ševčenko's birth. A similar prohibition had been made in 1911, the fiftieth year after the poet's death, but then it had passed virtually unnoticed. That was not the case in 1914.

In the Duma debate, various parties attempted to use the government measures in their own interest. The left was not interested in the national aspects of the event. To them, Ševčenko was "a great Russian poet" (Gelovani, *Stenogr.* 1914, 707), "a remarkable Russian man" (Čxeidze, 1165), and the interpellation was but another means to incite the people against the government.[21] For the Kadets (led by Miljukov), any grand-scale commemoration of the event was objectionable, for it nourished nationalistic feelings among the Ukrainians and weakened "the medium attitude which fortunately still prevails in the Ukraine" (*Stenogr.* 1914, 905). The militant Russian nationalists approved of the government measures because, in their opinion, they precluded the spread of separatism ("the movement that is now developing so broadly in Austria and that has spread and contam-

---

(p. 2924) in order to replace it, on April 7, with the following: "In localities with a Little Russian and Belorussian population, all subjects shall be taught in the Russian language starting from the first grade" (p. 3050). This amendment was adopted by a vote of 73 vs. 51 (3051). A special commission (*soglasitel'naja kommissija*) comprising seven members from the State Council and seven from the Duma was formed (p. 3864). For the reaction of Ukrainian politicians, see O. Belousenko [O. Lotoc'kyj], "Lex Pichniana," *Ukrainskaja žizn'*, 1912, no. 5, p. 30ff.

[20] *Stenogr.* 1913, pp. 1007, 1010, 1074ff., 1142, 1333, 1513, 1678, 1695, 1778ff.

[21] This was also the position of the Central Committee of the Russian Social-Democrats (Bolsheviks) in 1913. See Tymošenko 1, 243ff.

inated, to our horror, part of the masses in Russia''; V. Puriškevič, 721). But there were also voices that referred to Ukrainian strivings for autonomy (V. Dzjubinskij, 900) and to the lost Ukrainian liberties (F. Rodičev, 716). All in all, despite all the misuses and misunderstandings, it was the first time that the whole question of the Ukraine and the Ukrainian language had been taken up by the most resonant forum the Russian Empire had. The discussion in the Duma ended with its condemnation of the Ministry of Interior for unlawful acts in a vote of 161 to 115; *Stenogr.* 1914, 1206). The Ukraine reacted with demonstrations in the streets of many cities.[22] Perhaps most telling about the changing role of the Ukrainian language was that in Odessa the reactionary Sojuz russkogo naroda (Union of Russian Nationalists), published its program in Ukrainian translation (according to A. Bur'janov, *Stenogr.* 1914, 1182)!

Yet the actual position of the Ukrainian language remained essentially unchanged in 1906–1914, except for the demise of the ban on publications: there were no Ukrainian schools, and Ukrainian was continuously excluded from public life. The propaganda machine of the regime, of the Black Hundred, and of the Russianized upper classes in the Ukraine was much more powerful than that of the Ukrainians and their supporters. The prestige of the Ukrainian language remained low in Russia and in the Ukraine's large cities. Ukrainian was not only officially misrepresented as a dialect of Russian, but it was also used, alongside Russian dialects, to indicate colloquial speech by virtually all Russian writers, from Bunin to Gor'kij. This usage promoted an irate protest by V. Vynnyčenko, in his "Otkrytoe pis'mo k russkim pisateljam" (*Ukrainskaja žizn'* 1913, 10). Even in the Ukrainian countryside opinions were split: there were among peasants both partisans and adversaries of Ukrainian education, and we have no means to establish their ratio. M. Hruševs'kyj wrote a series of articles designed to defend Ukrainian education that was published in the peasant newspaper *Selo* (1910, 1911), later collected in his *Pro ukrajins'ku movy i ukrajins'ku školu* (2d ed., Kiev, 1913). There he wrote: "Those who do not support education in Ukrainian usually reason like this: the Ukrainian language is a *muzhik* language, it does not open any doors. Children of the masters will be

---

[22] On the demonstration in Kiev, cf. the memoirs by S. Vasyl'čenko, 320.

taught in Russian, and the children of *muzhiks*, in Ukrainian. The masters' children will find all the doors open; the peasants', none any-where'' (Hruševs'kyj 30). Even in the Duma a favorite tactic of the extreme right was to make a Ukrainian peasant deputy speak against Ukrainian; it succeeded in that several times (e.g., the speech of M. Andrijčuk; *Stenogr.* 1910, 1279). The number of Ukrainian intelli-gentsia was growing rapidly and there were some signs of militancy (M. Jevšan, M. Sribljans'kyj, D. Doncov, et al., as well as some stu-dents; see Lotoc'kyj 2, 125, 141, 296), but the number was still extremely small. The nation continued to lack, with few exceptions, upper classes, large cities, and industrial regions; linguistically it remained, at least on the surface, Russian. To gain fully all national functions, as Czech had for the Czechs, Ukrainian had to achieve much more. The status of the Ukrainian language was clearly rising, but the movement had only just begun.

An unexpected ''help'' to the cause of the Ukrainian language came from the imperial prime minister, P. Stolypin, the most aggres-sive implementor of Russian conservative nationalism. While such languages as Georgian, Armenian, Tatar, and Lettish were granted some very limited rights, Ukrainian (and Belorussian) were denied any whatsoever, because whereas the former were the languages of ''other groups'' incorporated into Russia (*inorodcy*), Ukrainian and Belorussian were officially regarded as branches of the Russian language. The term *inorodcy* clearly bore derogatory connotations. Despite that, the Ukrainian intelligentsia sought to obtain at least some of the rights associated with that status. On 20 January 1910, Stolypin issued an order prohibiting all ''inorodčeskie'' societies, including, it said, Ukrainian and Jewish ones. A sort of *lapsus calami*, the wording of the order gave Ukrainians legal grounds for claiming such status, although Russian conservative groups continued to insist on the theory of the tripartite Russian nation (e.g., Count V. Bobrin-skij, in *Nacionalisty* 141).[23]

---

[23] See also *Stenogr.* 1913, p. 1074, and the support for the *inorodcy* policy towards Ukrainians by the left, p. 1333. Another disadvantage of not being classified as *inorodcy* pertained to the empire's customs policy. By agreement with Austria (1906), books imported from Austria to Russia in languages other than Russian were duty free; books in Russian were subject to rather high duty. As established by a

The nascent upward movement of the Ukrainian language was interrupted by the outbreak of war with Germany and Austro-Hungary. War was declared on 18 July 1914 (o.s.), and the Ukraine west of the Dnieper was placed under military government as the Kiev military district. Just two days later, on July 20, *Rada*, the only Ukrainian daily, was closed down by the authorities and already published issues of *Svitlo* and *Literaturno-naukovyj vistnyk* were confiscated, although none of the publications spoke against the government or the war. On 9 January 1915, all Ukrainian periodicals (as well as Jewish ones) were suspended (Petljura 2, 312), except for *Ridnyj kraj*, which switched to the Russian alphabet (Dorošenko 1, 11). Ukrainians and Jews were clearly considered inimical elements by the imperial military government. The ukase of 1876, never formally repealed, seemed to be in effect once again. The Ukrainian Scholarly Society in Kiev, though not formally suspended, became inactive (Dorošenko 1969, 36). For a short time, the new orders were not applicable in the Odessa military district, but soon they went into effect there, too. The monthly *Osnova*, a replacement for *Literaturno-naukovyj vistnyk*, founded in Odessa, was suspended with the publication of its third issue (Dorošenko 1969, 77). *Promin'*, a weekly which Vynnyčenko managed to begin publishing in Moscow in November 1916, was shut down a month later. A circular order by the minister of interior, A. Protopopov, issued 11 December 1916, summarized and reconfirmed all these measures.

The annihilation of everything Ukrainian, including the public use of the language, was a policy that the Russian army soon also imposed in Galicia and Bukovina. Soon after war broke out, on 22 August 1914, Lviv was occupied, and Bukovina and Galicia as far as Peremyšl' came under Russian military and civil rule. All Ukrainian institutions and periodicals, except the Moscophile ones were closed, and the leading Ukrainian intellectuals, including Metropolitan Andrej Šeptyc'kyj, were deported. The dream of the Russian rightists who sought the eradication of Ukrainian culture and literary language, with their strongholds in Lviv and Černivci—a sentiment expressed quite overtly as early as 1912–1913 by many speakers in the Duma (e.g., Gr. Laškarev—*Stenogr.* 1913, 1084 ff.) and promulgated by such

---

special letter of the Ministry of Finances of 9 July 1907, Ukrainian books printed in Galicia and Bukovina were to be treated as Russian (Lotoc'kyj 2, 244).

societies as the Galicko-Russkoe obščestvo, Russkoe sobranie, Klub obščestvennyx dejatelej, and Slavjanskoe blagotvoritel'noe obščestvo (Lotoc'kyj 2, 463ff.)—seemed about to be fulfilled. P. Struve welcomed the new situation, which promised the stifling of Ukrainian aspirations and the smothering of the Ukrainian language (Petljura 2, 297). A systematic Russification of the newly occupied territories began. Courses on the Russian language for Galician and Bukovinian teachers were established in nearly every city of the two regions, as well as in Kiev and in St. Petersburg (Dorošenko 1, 5). Symbolically, Nicholas II visited Lviv and granted an audience to one of Galicia's Moscophile leaders, V. Dudykevyč (Dorošenko 1, 6). No major acts of resistance to the regime east and west of the Zbruč occurred until late 1915, when an illegal periodical, *Borot'ba*, began to appear (Dorošenko 1, 14, 18). The occupation of Galicia and Bukovina was interrupted in May 1915, but in the early autumn of that year Russia again occupied the eastern part of Galicia and, in June 1916, all of Bukovina. The second Russian regime, headed by Governor F. Trepov and regulated by the "Provisional Rules" of General M. Alekseev, introduced a different policy. Ukrainian elementary schools, the Ukrainian *himnaziji* in Ternopil' and in Černivci, and the Ukrainian teacher's seminary in Ternopil' were spared. Textbooks in Ukrainian, including Šerstjuk's grammar, were brought from the Russian Ukraine—where they were not allowed (Dorošenko 1969, 67 f., 72).

The turnabouts in the war resulted in, among other things, a high number of prisoners held in Austria and Germany, among them many Ukrainians. At the intercession of the Vienna-based Union for Liberation of the Ukraine, in December 1914, Ukrainian prisoners began to be placed into special camps. Up to 80,000 Ukrainians passed through these camps, which became centers of Ukrainian education. There young Ukrainian men educated in Russian schools had an opportunity to read Ukrainian books and newspapers (some published especially for them, e.g., *Rozvaha* in Freistadt, *Rozsvit* in Rastatt, *Šljax* in Salzwedel), to listen to courses conducted in Ukrainian and, above all, to learn to read and write in Ukrainian. Galicians and Bukovinians led these educational and cultural activities; outstanding among them was V. Simovyč. It was for this audience that Simovyč published popular pamphlets like *Jak staty po-ukrajins'komu hramotnym* (Salzwedel, 1919), as well as the more sophisticated *Praktyčna hramatyka ukrajins'koji movy* (Rastatt, 1918), which became the nucleus of his later, more extensive *Hramatyka ukrajins'koji movy* (Leipzig, s.a. 1921). Simovyč's enlarged grammar became the most influential Ukrainian grammar of its time. It played a part in the standardization of the literary language. Though based on the traditions of S. Smal'-Stoc'kyj, Simovyč's grammar bore witness to his contacts with Ukrainians from Russia and struck a kind of compromise between the two traditions. It is exactly in this respect that its impact on the norms of the literary language was significant and mostly positive. Hence, the episode of the prisoner-of-war camps left a certain imprint on the internal development of the Ukrainian literary language.

It is more difficult to assess the impact of Galicia and Bukovina on the Ukrainians who were part of the Russian army occupying these regions. Čykalenko tells of an encounter with one soldier who switched from Russian to Ukrainian in everyday speech after his contact with the Galician population (II, 9b). We do not know how typical that case was. Čykalenko also mentions that after the occupation of Galicia and Bukovina the sale of Ukrainian books in the Russian Ukraine ''rose to unheard-of levels.''

Another circumstance of war that had a certain bearing on the Ukrainian language was the formation by Austria of the Regiment of Ukrainian riflemen, or Sičovi stril'ci, in August 1914. Linguistically, this resulted in the revival of Ukrainian military terminology and phraseology after a century and a half of dormancy.

The years of World War I brought no other gains to the Ukrainian language. On the other hand, the new persecutions of the Ukrainian language were too shortlived to effect the gains of the preceding decade. As already noted, the prewar gains consisted mainly of some—small as they were—successes in the use of the Ukrainian language in public life and of relatively widespread propaganda for the Ukrainian language among the Ukrainian and a certain segment of the Russian intelligentsia.

The events of the first sixteen years of the twentieth century should have had, and did have, an impact on the standardization of the Ukrainian literary language and on its very structure. The role of the intelligentsia as the consumer and shaper of the literary language was to be accepted; the orientation on the peasant language was realized to be too narrow and the ties of the literary language to its underlying dialect(s) was to be reassessed and relaxed. Finally, the interrelation of the Central Ukrainian variant of the standard language and its "Austrian-Ukrainian," that is, Galician-Bukovinian variant, as represented by the Lviv koine, was to be resolved especially after the "barbwired" boundary between the Russian and the Austrian Ukraine was if not smashed, then positively neutralized. This brought to the fore the problem of a common Ukrainian standard language in all Ukrainian territories. All these problems would be settled through discussion and, since there were no central authoritative institutions that could have settled them in an oral exchange, language discussion became the prerogative of the press and other publications.

After 1905 these problems had become practical and persistent ones. The nascent Ukrainian periodical press in the Russian Ukraine had to solve them not only theoretically, but in everyday usage. How does one say this and how does one write that?—such questions plagued every journalist every time he put pen to paper. His reader reacted to every innovation, accepting some and protesting against others. Hence language discussion concerned not merely the linguist, but every educated Ukrainian. It was due to practical applications that the degree to which Galician elements should be accepted became central to the discussion. Ukrainian journalistic experience and a Ukrainian journalistic language had, after all, existed only in the Austrian Ukraine, as Modest Levyc'kyj, for one, recognized: "When, starting in 1906, the possibility of publishing newspapers in the Russian Ukraine emerged, it became necessary to transfer from Galicia almost all the lexical material that had accumulated there during those thirty years [from the time of the ukase of 1876]" (Levyc'kyj 1918, 8). The recalcitrant Nečuj-Levyc'kyj seconded this opinion, in a different tone: "Publications of the *Zapysky* of the Kiev Scholarly Society, of *Selo*, of *Literaturno-naukovyj vistnyk*, of *Zasiv* are sometimes like Galician language schools established in the Russian Ukraine to teach Galician book language, style, and spelling" (1912, 35).

Galician elements in the journalistic language also constituted a political problem. They made the Ukrainian press difficult to understand for the reader unaccustomed to Galician publications. It is not by chance, then, that these problems were discussed even at the gatherings of political parties. For instance, in the fall of 1905 the convention of the Ukrainian Democratic Party devoted much attention to a discussion of Ukrainian spelling and made some compromise decisions (Čykalenko 412).

The acceptance of Galician elements was facilitated by a "new view" according to which the literary language was not to be adapted entirely to the peasants' language. In fact, its Galician components made the literary language more acceptable to the new intelligentsia because it was no longer ethnographically conditioned. This fact was also properly noted by contemporaries. Nečuj-Levyc'kyj wrote: "Our young writers lost contact with the people's language. Living in big cities, they became urban, armchair men" (1907, 45). The villainous young writers had to admit that this was indeed so, as M. Kocjubyns'kyj did: "The older writers, our teachers, had a better ear for the living language of the people (this cannot be denied), had a better eye for it than the young ones who have no contacts with the countryside or with the people: instead of the living language they take as their model the book language, often maimed and contaminated." Yet Kocjubyns'kyj continued: "I have hope that like new wine our literary language will after a certain time get rid of the froth and will become pure and strong. Such a transitional period is characteristic of many young literatures" (Kocjubyns'kyj 322).

The needs of current journalism and the new orientation of the literary language made absorption of new elements, including Galician ones, obligatory. Inveterate opponents of the innovations, such as Nečuj-Levyc'kyj, were becoming exceptional. In fact, some turncoats came out of that camp. For instance, B. Hrinčenko, who in 1891 had initiated a campaign against Galicianisms (see chap. 2, above) now, in the pamphlet *Tjažkym šljaxom* (1907), admitted that "a literary language arises from all its dialects," which for the Ukrainian literary language opened the gates to Galician elements: "The [Ukrainian] language will become the best and the most understandable when at its foundation there lies the people's language of the Central (*naddniprjans'koji*) Ukraine with expedient (*potribnymy*) supplements from the people's language of Bukovina and Galicia" (42, 88). In accordance with this turnaround in his views, Hrinčenko included in his dictionary many words from Galician sources. What remained unchanged was the rejection, now as before, of what Hrinčenko considered illegitimate borrowings from other languages—Polish, Russian, or German (49).

How deeply Galician elements penetrated the literary language is evident in their occurrence even in some official Ukrainian-language publications issued by the Russian administration, in the translation of the manifesto of 17 October 1905 initiated by the conservative *Oktjabrist* M. Rodzjanko (Čykalenko II, 153c), and in the pamphlet of the Ministry of Finance, *Zabezpečennja prybutkiv i kapitaliv deržavnymy oščadnyčymy kasamy* (Insurance of profits and stocks in the State Saving Banks; 1910)—which angered conservative Russian elements (Ščegolev 304).

Protests were heard not only from Russians. The new journalistic language was, at the beginning, truly difficult for the average reader. Čykalenko (467) saw this as one reason for the financial failure of the first daily in the Russian Ukraine, *Hromads'ka dumka* (1906): "The public, both educated and uneducated, is not accustomed to the Ukrainian newspaper language. . . . This is evident from letters sent to us [publishers] as well as from conversations with our readers. They are not accustomed to abstract notions unknown to other people. The language of our newspaper is alien to them, and even those who are sincerely in favor of developing our periodical press are indignant about that language."

Not surprisingly, the old opponent of linguistic innovations, Nečuj-Levyc'kyj, became the mouthpiece for such protest and disaffection. In 1907 he published "S'ohočasna časopysna mova na Ukrajini," and in 1912, *Kryve dzerkalo ukrajins'koji movy* (the latter is in many details a reiteration of the former). Irritated and irate, Nečuj-Levyc'kyj, then a septuagenerian (he was born in 1838) and out of touch with the times, could not understand what caused the changes that were affecting the language. He saw them as a conspiracy wrought either by the Galicians or by M. Hruševs'kyj, who edited *Literaturno-naukovyj vistnyk*, *Selo*, and other periodical publications. To Nečuj-Levyc'kyj the language of Lviv was anti-popular and outright bad. Nečuj-Levyc'kyj does not explain where, specifically, its failure lies, but from comments like the ones following it can be assumed that its main problem was an overabundance of foreign components: "Everywhere in Europe as the foundation and the basis (*grunt i osnova*) of literary languages central dialects (*movy*) were taken whose forms and vocabulary cover the widest area, and not subdialects (*pidmovy*) and strange jargons (*hovirky*), sometimes mixed along the borders with [those of] adjacent nations" (1912, 82).

Nečuj-Levyc'kyj was willing to accept eight words from Galician literature—*perevažno, zdijsnyty, vražinnja, perevažuvaty, zmist, vplyv, peresvidčytys', nemožlyvyj* (1912, 44)—and "perhaps a few more," but only a few more.[24]

Responses to Nečuj-Levyc'kyj's two attacks came from many fronts. Stešenko, for instance, found reasons for the influx of new words and constructions: "Time was passing, and Galicia exerted its influence upon the Ukraine. The younger [generation] had made Galician novelties in the language their own, for there were no others. . . . The older patriots, who like Nečuj now blame the language of our press, did not create a higher language for the Ukraine; yet the press and the institutions had to have something. . . . It is not Hruševs'kyj who takes us to that language, but he and others are prompted by the force of spirit, that primordial force in the face of which the lamentations of nearsighted people who want to hold our nation within the boundaries of domestic use, to the language of the peasant woman Palažka, do not matter" (Stešenko 315).[25]

M. Žučenko argued mainly from the vantage point of a little-educated speaker for whom Galician influences made Modern Ukrainian sometimes hard to understand, a rather obsolete view for 1912, rooted in an identification of the Ukrainian language with peasant speech. Yet Žučenko understood that the Galician layer in the Ukrainian standard language could not be eliminated. His final conclusion, somewhat contradicting the point of departure of his discussion, was that for the time being Galicianisms were to be accepted, but that they should slowly and gradually be replaced. (One can ask, why replace them once they have been accepted?)

Modest Levyc'kyj reacted to both of Nečuj-Levyc'kyj's pronouncements: to that of 1907 he replied in an article of 1909, and to the one of 1912, in a pamphlet of 1913. Levyc'kyj advised the educated to work for the organic unification of Central Ukrainian and Galician components, lest "God forbid, we fall into that sad situation that after

---

[24] The Galician source of some of these words is dubious.

[25] Palažka, a character in one of Nečuj-Levyc'kyj's works, is a rather primitive and narrow-minded villager who speaks in a colorful, traditional vernacular.

some time there will be two Ukrainian literary languages'' (1913, 11).[26]

A debate over language was to be expected because of the changes that standard Ukrainian was undergoing. Theoretically the discussion was not very engrossing, for the arguments of both Nečuj-Levyc'kyj and of his opponents often were too impressionistic or entirely subjective and lacking any understanding of language nature and history. The debate was important, however, because it showed that the innovations in the standard language, including the introduction of some Galicianisms, had no convincing adversaries. Inadvertently, the acceptance of the innovations was reaffirmed. In fact, the argumentation against them could have proceeded only from ignorance or from an overtly Russian orientation, or from both. Hrinčenko quoted a reader whose argument exemplified the situation: ''Put aside all things Galician. Although Galicia is our sister, who is closer [to us] of course than Muscovy, she lives pretty far from us and, to boot, she loafed among various Slavic nations and because of that introduced into her literature a lot of words which to our people seem at the beginning difficult to understand and more foreign than the 'Muscovite' ones because with the latter we had to get accustomed to willy-nilly'' (68). In the same vein was the complaint of a reader of *Hromads'ka dumka*, who asked for the meaning of the words *urjad* 'government' and *rux* 'movement' (among others) and after having received explanations advised that they be replaced by *pravytel'stvo* and *dvyženye*, respectively—that is, by the Russian equivalents (Čykalenko 467).

The discussions of 1907–1909 and 1912–1913 did not change the course of Ukrainian language development. Writers and journalists of the middle and younger generations generally accepted many innovations whose function was to urbanize the standard language and to broaden its dialectal base from Central Ukrainian to Central and West

[26] More detail is given in Shevelov 1966, 83–90. The following two items also belonged to that language discussion: ''Kil'ka jazykovyx uvah'' (editorial), *Dilo*, 27 August 1913 (unavailable to me); and Les' Martovyč, ''Pryčynky do statti i kil'ka jazykovyx uvah,'' *Dilo*, 2 September 1913. F. Korš discussed very much the same problems, albeit his polemics were directed against Russian rather than Ukrainian writers. A bibliography of the polemics on language appears in Tymošenko 2, 231ff., and, more completely, in Lotoc'kyj 2, 334ff.

Ukrainian. In a more general formulation these ideas were expressed, in 1911, by V. Hnatjuk: "Every peasant thoroughly knows his language (of course, practically), but only as his dialect. Every dialect can serve as the foundation for creating a literary language, but it cannot be one alone because it is too poor to supply all the notions necessary for a cultured nation. Those notions are taken from other dialects, from other languages living and dead, and especially they are created independently of other dialects and languages while using the general foundations of the language."[27] Similar ideas were expressed about culture in general (with language a component): "If a nation produces forces which can develop a higher national culture, it would be futile and even harmful for the development of the masses of people to direct these forces in the channel of 'popularization.' And the more conscious element of the masses of people understands perfectly well the enormous value of the higher national culture, for the achievements of which they already raise their requests and demands" (Petljura 2, 235 [1912]). A kind of linguistic commentary to these ideas was supplied by Nečuj-Levyc'kyj. He described his meeting with a journalist who happened to be Symon Petljura thus: "I often meet students and they speak the Ukrainian vernacular; only one student, S. Petljura, spoke with me so that I asked him if he was not from Galicia" (1912, 12).

Yet Petljura was not alone. Simovyč reminisces that Lesja Ukrajinka was very accepting of Galician influences in the language, and that she reproached only M. Hruševs'kyj's language because "he made his language exceedingly Galicianized" (1938, 50). The language of her works contains a great many Galician and "extradialectal" elements.[28] Similar was the stand of M. Kocjubyns'kyj. He grew up in Podolia, where the dialect was transitional from Central Ukrainian to some Galician usages. Kocjubyns'kyj did not, however, write in dialect. Except in his earliest, immature works, he worked on his language systematically, striving to write in a superdialectal

---

[27] Quoted from Tymošenko 2, 213. In a similar vein, F. Korš said about the discrepancies between Galician and other elements in the standard Ukrainian language: "Such a lack of harmony (*rasnogolosica*) is unavoidable at the beginning of the formation of any literary language" ("Nacionalističeskaja nauka," *Ukrainskaja žizn'*, 1913, no. 7/8, p. 321).

[28] Some of her Galicianisms are collected and analyzed in Shevelov, 1966, 93ff.

standard language that had absorbed various dialectal elements to become pliable, rich, and contemporary. While introducing a number of less familiar words into his work,[29] he did not lose sight of the criteria of understandability and an all-Ukrainian character for the resulting literary language. Hence his objections against works written in Galician dialects, such as those by S. Kovaliv, about which he wrote in November 1899: "The language of those short stories strikes one with its exceedingly local character, and even I, who considers the language of Galicia his own, occasionally cannot understand what Mr. Kovaliv is writing" (Kocjubyns'kyj 238); he also objected to superfluous regional terms. Thus in publishing the work of the Bukovinian writer Ol'ha Kobyljans'ka, Kocjubyns'kyj pleaded for her permission to replace some local words with those used in the standard language (25 October 1902; Kocjubyns'kyj 273). Particularly welcome to Kocjubyns'kyj were Galician words which conveyed notions of urban life. The Russian Ukraine had not developed a native urban vocabulary, so Kocjubyns'kyj enriched the language of his writings, and by the same token potentially the literary Ukrainian language, with a substantial number of interdialectal borrowings. They did not make his language Galician, but did render it consistently synthetic. As an exacting author and staunch Ukrainian citizen, Kocjubyns'kyj deemed it his duty to build a modern standard language on a polydialectal foundation.

To one degree or another this same characterization applies to the writings of many other authors of the time, such as M. Voronyj, H. Xotkevyč, and M. Černjavs'kyj. Due to the contemporary developments in literature and in journalism, it was Kiev rather than Lviv that became the main center for the expansion and incorporation of Galician elements. Those elements became an inalienable component of the standard language, modern in terms not only of time, but also of structure, in a systematic departure from the ethnographic tradition that had shaped the language in the nineteenth century, particularly during populism.

The "renovated" standard language that was typical of intelligentsia activists in 1900–1913 also came into vogue among some members of the bourgeoisie, which was beginning to take form in

[29] A selection with a commentary is given in Shevelov, 1966, 103ff.

those years. An accurate although very ironic portrait of one such man and his language was given by V. Vynnyčenko in his novel *Božky* (Idols):

> At that time a man came in, Skalozub. He was a slender, well-proportioned young man blamelessly dressed in the European manner, in a black tie, gloves, in patent-leather shoes with the uppers in yellow chamois. .... He behaved with an emphasized, refined official politeness. He spoke like a Galician although he had visited Galicia not more than twice and for a short time. He liked to use expressions little known in the [Russian] Ukraine and admired himself because of that somewhat. Skalozub dressed in the European way and spoke with an excess of Galicianisms not so much because he personally loved that manner, but mainly for the idea's sake, out of principle. Usually people deem Ukrainians a peasant, coarse nation. A Ukrainian, in other words that means a *muzhik*. For this reason Skalozub seemed to have taken it as an obligation to prove, by his own example, that Ukrainians were not *muzhiks* alone, that some of them dress in the European fashion, have good manners, and speak Ukrainian, but not the *muzhik* Ukrainian. Since he was a rich man, owner of many thousands of *desjatyna*s of land, of factories and mines, he bore the banner of his being Ukrainian in a confident hand. Previously he belonged to a certain current within the Ukrainian community whose task was to oppose Russification. .... The Ukraine for Ukrainians, down with Russians, Poles, and Jews! That was their program (*Tvory*, 244ff.).

As the result of all these combined processes, by 1914 the Ukrainian language could no longer claim that its *raison d'être* was understandability to the peasant. Whether contemporaries were aware of it or not, the Ukrainian language's main function became to preserve the national cultural tradition as deposited in works of literature, and to be a political banner for a nation in the making, or, one should say, in the process of reviving on new, modern foundations. As Franko put it in 1907: "the literary language becomes, in fact, the representative of national unity, a common link for all its own dialects, which combines them into an organic unity" (Franko 338).[30]

---

[30] The argument that the elevated Ukrainian language was incomprehensible to the uneducated passed, in fact, to the adversaries of a Ukrainian literary language (see, e.g., the speech of K. Rudič in the State Duma of 12 December 1914—*Stenogr.* 1914, 778). They forgot that the elevated Russian language was equally or even more incomprehensible to the Russian peasant of that time.

CHAPTER THREE

The Years of the Struggle for Independence (1917–1920)

The so-called February revolution that broke out in St. Petersburg (actually, on 12 March 1917) was an event essentially grounded in Russian social and political conflicts. Yet the deposing of the tsar and the virtual end of the monarchy could not but deeply affect the Russian Ukraine. The immediate effect was the revival of an active political life on an unprecedented scale, which opened new prospects for the public use of the Ukrainian language. This development was reflected in the rapid formation of a Ukrainian government and the revival or formation of diverse Ukrainian political parties. Very soon the activized use of the Ukrainian language encompassed a very high number of functions in other areas, among them military, juridical, financial, educational, and scientific, which until then were off limits for the Ukrainian language in the Russian Ukraine.

The government took the first step in Kiev in March 1917. The Society of Ukrainian Progressives (TUP, in existence since 1908), the only organized Ukrainian political group to keep functioning, illegally or semilegally, after the outbreak of war in 1914, founded the Ukrainian Central Rada (Council). The Central Rada was conceived as a single-party (i.e., TUP) institution, but from the outset it was reinforced by persons who appeared to represent all the Ukraine but actually represented only Kiev. The Central Rada was drastically enlarged and supplemented at the All-Ukrainian National Congress held 17–21 March 1917, the delegates to which represented the many Ukrainian organizations and institutions that had sprung into being by that time—political, professional, cooperative—as well as the various social classes of the Ukraine, except large landlords and industrialists. By that time the Presidium of the Central Rada alone counted ten members (*Visti z U.C.R.* 1, p. 1). The two All-Ukrainian Military Congresses (held 18 May and 18–23 June 1917) pledged their support to the Central Rada and sent their delegates to replenish it. Without being the government of the country in the strict sense, the Ukrainian Central Rada negotiated with the Russian Provisional Government on the problem of the autonomy of the Ukraine. Soon after the demand for autonomy was rejected, on June 18, the first nucleus of a Ukrainian government was established—the General Secretariat. It provided for "secretaries" (actually ministers) of the interior, of finances, of nationality affairs, of military affairs, of agrarian affairs, of justice, of education, and of food supplies, among others, but not of foreign affairs or of communications, because these were left to the Russian government. By July 20, after its recognition as the representative organ of the Ukraine, the Central Rada, together with its General Secretariat, until then exclusively Ukrainian, was replenished by representatives of the national minorities—Russians, Jews, and Poles. On 12 November 1917, the General Secretariat was extended to include secretaries of labor, of trade and industry, and of communications. On November 20, the Ukrainian National Republic, in federation with other republics arising from the ruins of the Russian Empire, was proclaimed. Popular support for this act was evidenced by the landslide victory of Ukrainian political parties in the elections to the All-Russian Constituent Assembly in November 1917. Then, on 22 January 1918, these federative links were broken, and the independent Ukrainian National Republic was proclaimed. With the proclamation the secretaries of the General Secretariat became ministers. On April 29, the Constitution of the Ukrainian National Republic was approved and Myxajlo Hruševs'kyj was elected president. The constitution was written in Ukrainian, but it said nothing about the rights of the Ukrainian language or any other language.

The political developments of the first year after the revolution, outlined very briefly here, did not have as strong an impact on the use, status, and internal development of the Ukrainian language as, theoretically, they might have had. One factor was the brevity of time that elapsed: crucial political and even social upheavals can occur within a year, but their impact on language is not reflected immediately. More important factors were the actual situation in the country and the character of the activity of the Central Rada. Of primary concern to the Rada were programmatic debate and the proclamation of overriding government principles. Much less was done about the execution of approved programs. In fact, the executive branch of the Rada and of its government was underdeveloped, if existent at all. For some time, the provincial commissars were appointed by the Russian Provisional Government and were beyond the control of the Rada. When Ukrainian provincial commissars were finally appointed, their ties with Kiev were loose (Dorošenko 1969, 180). All the big cities and even most towns were governed by municipal organs that were alien or hostile to the Rada. The free and truly democratic elections of municipal governments that took place in the summer of 1917 did not change the situation. The results of elections in twenty randomly selected localities show that Ukrainian parties received a majority in only five (Jelysavet, Romen, Loxvycja, Myrhorod, Konotop); only in five others did they garner more than one-third of the elected deputies (Kharkiv, Poltava, Černihiv, Čerkasy, Proskuriv). In Kiev Ukrainian parties received 20 percent of the vote, in Katerynoslav 10 percent, and in Odessa 4 percent (Dorošenko 1, 144).

The social base behind the Rada was the peasantry and the soldiers, that is, its support came primarily from the countryside. The cities were yet to be won, and time would run short for that. The conservative element in the cities was reinforced, especially after the Bolshevik coup of 7 November 1917, by the flight of many members of the upper classes from Russia; on the whole they favored the restoration of the integrity of the Russian Empire, and stood against Ukrainian autonomy or independence. On the other hand, the urban lower classes were organized into the soviets of workers and soldiers, which grew stronger as they succumbed more and more to Bolshevik agitation and propaganda. Although theoretically these soviets accepted the theme of national liberation, essentially they put all their emphasis on socioeconomic demands and tended to use the Russian language, thus contributing to its spread.

In Kiev itself, three political forces—the Ukrainian parties, the conservative Russians, and the basically Russian Bolsheviks—competed for power. On 11 November 1917, the conservative Russians staged an uprising. They were defeated and the Central Rada managed to survive, but only at the price of a temporary alliance with the Bolsheviks. In many other cities and towns the authority of the Ukrainian forces was even weaker. In addition, the Rada's contacts with the provinces were sporadic and uncertain. As a matter of fact, the very boundaries of the country were not stabilized. In the original negotiations and agreement with the Russian Provisional Government, five provinces were said to be under the jurisdiction of the Central Rada—those of Kiev, Poltava, Černihiv, Volhynia, and Podolia. It was in November 1917, that the Rada also claimed the provinces of Kherson, Kharkiv, Katerynoslav (to which most of the Donec' basin belonged), Tavria, without the Crimea, and optionally (by plebiscite) the Ukrainian-populated parts of Kursk, Voronež, and Xolm (the Third Universal, reprinted, e.g., in Dorošenko 1, 179ff.). Even within the original, narrower territories, the ties of the Rada were to a great extent illusory, based on ideology and moral authority rather than on the presence of any organized administrative machinery.

This political situation, coupled with the disorganization and turmoil prevailing throughout the country, explains why the large steps in Ukrainian political, cultural, and linguistic development taken under the Central Rada influenced Ukrainian society much less than might be expected.

The general situation in the Ukraine was faithfully reflected by conditions within the army. After the February Revolution there began in the Russian army a movement to isolate Ukrainians into special units; at first this was done against the general command of the Russian army and later with their consent. It is believed that such Ukrainian units grew to comprise sixteen divisions. The organization was done on a voluntary basis, and the units lacked stability. Some of these units were not let into the Ukraine, some underwent demoralization and dispersed, some later joined the Bolsheviks. The Ukrainianized units which were on Ukrainian territory were deliberately dispersed or demobilized. The socialist-minded Central Rada and the General Secretariat were lukewarm to the idea of a Ukrainian army, and introduced instead the so-called Free Cossacks, territorial units of men recruited from their native villages, with larger units from each district. They were to be administered, symbolically, not by the military, but by the Ministry of Interior. At their peak, the number of Free Cossacks reached 60,000, but they were demobilized, at the demand of the Germans, in the spring of 1918. A system resembling usual army units was initiated among them at the end of 1917 to early 1918, when war was already raging between the Ukrainian National Republic and Bolshevik Russia, and Kiev was under attack. The Bolshevik leader V. Antonov-Ovseenko estimated the number of defenders of Kiev as up to 20,000, but actually the number was much smaller (Dorošenko 1, 279). At any rate, on 16 January 1918 the Central Rada decided to abolish the regular army in favor of a "People's Militia," and only in April 1918 did systematic work to create a Ukrainian army of eight corps of infantry and four and one-half divisions of cavalry actually begin. According to Vs. Petrov (*EU* 1, 1178), the Ukrainian army at that time actually numbered about 15,000 soldiers. These were hardly favorable conditions for the elaboration of a standard Ukrainian military nomenclature and terminology. That process began only in the early 1918.

Under the Central Rada the Orthodox church remained as before, that is, it continued to be Russian. A council was founded in Kiev in 1917 to organize an autocephalous Ukrainian Orthodox church, but the dominant Russian high clergy blocked the consecration of bishops and the movement was hampered for several years, until late 1921.

The foundation for a Ukrainian monetary system came with the decision of the Central Rada, on 6 January 1918, to issue Ukrainian banknotes, which were to circulate alongside Russian money.

The coup d'état of 29 April 1918 abolished the Central Rada and proclaimed a monarchy with Pavlo Skoropads'kyj as hetman. The Ukrainian National Republic was replaced by an unspecified "Ukrainian State." The next regime dismissed "politicians" and instead sought out "experts." Very often these were Russians, especially members of the Kadet party, who opposed the independence or autonomy of the Ukraine. Such experts even demanded that Russian, alongside Ukrainian, be the official language of the country. If Ukrainian was not able to replace Russian as the vehicle of communication at the time of the Central Rada, it certainly had no chance to do so under the Hetmanate, although under the new regime Ukrainian culture would develop, as we will see below. The territory of the country was now precisely delimited and well guarded—by the German army of ca. 800,000 men. But the Ukraine was again subject to two competing authorities, one Ukrainian and the other German.

The Germans objected to the organization of a Ukrainian army. A new division of *serdjuky* was organized, but most units underwent disarmament and dissolution, so that in fact only a few units remained. In July 1918, new plans for the army were made, but they were not to be realized. In many of the existing military units the officers were Russians, which certainly did not enhance the prestige of the Ukrainian language. Hetman Skoropads'kyj's military and administrative policies may have been designed to create gradually, through education, new Ukrainian cadres while benefiting from the expertise of Russians. But this was a risky game, because the Russians, once in positions of authority, could easily take the upper hand, and the time was not suitable for slow developments. Thus, the Hetmanate period was in fact a setback for the use and development of the Ukrainian language.

On 14 December 1918, Hetman Skoropads'kyj's regime fell, and the Ukrainian National Republic, now headed by a five-member Directory, was reinstated (December 19). The Directory had little time for formulating domestic policy, however, because its attention was absorbed in struggling against threats to the existence of the country. Internal mutinies of an anarchic or communist character commanded large areas of the Katerynoslav, Kherson, Podolia, Kiev, and Černihiv provinces. Foreign challenges were the French-Greek landing at Odessa, the attack of Denikin's conservative Russian (White) army from the southeast, and, especially, the offensive of the Russian Bolsheviks which began on 17 November 1918, about a week after the revolution in Germany. Kharkiv was lost on 3 January 1919, and Kiev on 5 February 1919. The territory under the authority of the Directory shrank virtually to Western Volhynia and Podolia, with a provisional capital first in Rivne and then in Kamjanec'-Podil's'kyj. When, in the summer of 1919, the Bolsheviks were forced to retreat by Denikin's army and, on the other hand, the army of the Ukrainian National Republic grew to 85,000 men, territory was reconquered as far east as the outposts of Kiev (31 August 1919). Soon Denikin's army advanced westward to the Zbruč, only to flee under the attacks of the Bolsheviks and quit Ukrainian territory in December 1919. The Ukraine was reconquered, now by the Bolsheviks from the northeast and by the Poles from the west. The government of the Ukrainian National Republic had to abandon regular warfare and to switch to partisan tactics (4 December 1919). In 1920, an alliance with Poland and the Polish-Russian war brought Ukrainian armed units to Kiev (May 7), but they remained for only a month. On 11 November 1920, the last regular units of the army of the Ukrainian National Republic crossed the Zbruč and were interned in Poland, which recognized the Soviet government as the government of the Ukraine. Thus, during the time of the Directory, most of Ukrainian territory was in the hands of either Denikin's army, the Bolsheviks, or the Poles, or under the control of the Romanians (the Ukrainian parts of Bessarabia).

Denikin's policy was ruthlessly to suppress the Ukrainian language and culture, and to thwart any political aspirations. Under the Poles and the Bolsheviks (see chap. 5), circumstances were not favorable either. In the regions under the Directory, conditions were so unstable that no political undertakings, other than those diplomatic or military, were possible. The Ukrainian language, of course, enjoyed all rights under the Directory, but had little opportunity for their expression.

Thus, of the three periods in the struggle for Ukraine's independence—that of the Central Rada, of the Hetmanate, and of the Directory—the relatively most quiet was the middle period. Linguistically, however, the time of the Hetmanate was marred by strong Russian influences on all levels of government. Nevertheless, the advances in status made by the Ukrainian language in the critical years 1917–1920 were substantial, and in many respects crucial, in comparison with the preceding decades. After a lapse of nearly two centuries, the Ukrainian language again became the language of state legislation, of state administration, of public gatherings, and of the army. There was, however, a discrepancy in language use between various levels of administration. Whereas the countryside and the central administration used Ukrainian to conduct business, the cities very often stuck to Russian. Both city and town old-fashioned *dumy* and the newly formed municipal soviets were strongholds of Russian. The Ukrainian state's time was too short and its stability too uncertain to make the official use of Ukrainian self-understood and generally accepted. Very often the official use of Ukrainian was more of a challenge than a "natural" routine.

Along with the spread of Ukrainian for public and official use, another indisputable development was its functional diversification. There are no direct data about its expansion in urban life, but the indirect evidence, such as the conduct of education and the appearance of Ukrainian publications, speaks eloquently, although there can be no doubt that in large cities, especially those on the periphery of the Ukrainian state which were only briefly and intermittently within its boundaries (i.e., Kharkiv, Katerynoslav, Mykolajiv, and, especially, Odessa and the Donec' basin), Russian was unaffected as the vehicle of public communication. In terms of the language habits of various social classes, the situation hardly changed. But with the rise of Ukrainian political parties, Ukrainian became more an instrument of discussion and polemics on political matters than it had ever been before. If in early 1917 there was virtually only one Ukrainian political movement that used Ukrainian (i.e., TUP), now all shades of political thought, from the Ukrainian monarchists to liberals to socialists to anarchists and communists, resorted to Ukrainian as a means of communication. Characteristically, nearly every contemporary political party in the Ukraine was split into two parts: e.g., the Ukrainian Social-Democrats and the Russian Social-Democrats, the Ukrainian Socialist-Revolutionaries and the Russian Socialist-Revolutionaries. Among the mostly Russian anarchists and communists, there were small groups and some individuals who defended the rights of, at least, the Ukrainian language. Ukrainian probably also made some gains in terms of professional diversification, but precise data on that development are difficult to find.

More ample and more precise data are available about Ukrainian schools, books, cultural institutions, and the periodical press. In education, the problem of Ukrainian schooling was not an easy one to resolve. There were no precedents, no textbooks, and no experienced teachers of Ukrainian subjects; insufficient numbers of teachers were able to teach in Ukrainian at all. In cities a widespread phenomenon was the protests against education in Ukrainian raised by parents' committees (no data are available about whether this took place in villages as well). The Russian Provisional Government granted approval (in April 1917) for teaching in Ukrainian in elementary schools, with Russian to be taught as a subject from the second grade, as well as for courses on Ukrainian language, literature, history, and geography to be taught at teachers' seminaries, and chairs of Ukrainian language, literature, history, and law to be established at the universities (Dorošenko 1, 389). In July, two Ukrainian high schools (*himnaziji*) were founded (ibid., 396). The relatively radical Second all-Ukrainian Congress of Teachers (meeting August 10–13) demanded that teaching be conducted in Ukrainian in the lowest elementary grades from September 1, and that teachers of the higher grades and on the high-school level be required to attend summer courses to obtain the necessary qualifications for teaching in Ukrainian in the future (Dorošenko 1, 395). During 1917, 53 Ukrainian high schools were founded (Dorošenko 1, 388; according to *EU* 1, 933, the number was as high as 80), whereas the total number of *himnaziji* was about 800 (it was 828 by the end of 1918; Krylov, 35). In the existing Russian high schools, courses in Ukrainian language, literature, history, and geography were introduced, but otherwise these remained Russian (autumn of 1917). In the summer of 1917, up to 100 summer schools were conducted for teachers (Dorošenko 1, 396). In Kiev, the Ukrainian People's University (Ukrajins'kyj narodnij universytet) opened on October 9, followed a month later, on November 7, by the Pedagogical Academy (Dorošenko 1, 399ff.). The private Society for School Education, founded in March 1917, was very active in promoting and organizing education in Ukrainian. In adult education, a fairly wide network of Prosvita Society chapters was developed, with libraries, public lecture programs, etc.; their number, it is estimated, approached 5,000 (*EU* 2, 2370).

In sum, under the Central Rada the development of Ukrainian schooling proceeded slowly and in moderation, with the goal of gradual success over many years. Testimony to how cautious this policy was is a speech delivered by I. Stešenko, Secretary General of Education. On October 8, addressing in Ukrainian teachers of the Kiev school district, Stešenko told them that he was doing so because Ukrainian had become the official language of the country (Dorošenko 1, 397). One has to deduce that before October 8, the language actually used in Ukrainian school administration was Russian. The same conclusion, but this time about provincial administration, can be deduced from Dorošenko's mention (1969, 174) that when he was the provincial commissar of the Central Rada in Černihiv and Černihiv province, the only local commissar who sent him telegrams in Ukrainian was the one stationed in Nižen; apparently all other district commissars communicated in Russian. Such leading military commanders as Generals I. Omeljanovyč-Pavlenko and O. Hrekov were also known to be Russian speakers (ibid., 199).

No break in educational policy was evident with the change in government to the Hetmanate. In accordance with the hetman's declaration, his prime minister, F. Lyzohub, stated that in the spirit of 1918, Ukrainian remained the official language of the country, but Russian was permitted because many did not speak Ukrainian (state officials were to acquire command of Ukrainian; Xrystjuk 3, 35ff.).[1] The two main principles of the Hetmanate's educational policy were to promote the Ukrainianization of the elementary school, and to

---

[1] In practice, this requirement was rarely enforced (Xrystjuk 3, 75).

foster the establishment of new high schools and universities with Ukrainian as the language of instruction, while preserving the existing Russian institutions. About 150 Ukrainian *himnaziji* were founded by late 1918 (Dorošenko 2, 348), and, as already noted, summer schools in Ukrainian subjects were conducted. On the college and university level, the prerevolutionary Russian-language institutions were kept intact, except for the addition of chairs in Ukrainian subjects, but parallel new institutions were opened, where Ukrainian was the language of instruction: the (incomplete) Ukrainian university at Kamjanec'-Podil's'kyj, with ca. 1,000 students; the nucleus of a university, i.e., a historical-philological faculty, at Poltava, with ca. 200 students; and the People's University in Kiev, later reorganized as the Ukrainian State University, with ca. 3,000 students (Dorošenko 2, 349, 356, 360). National institutions enhancing the prestige of the Ukrainian language and culture were also founded: the Academy of Sciences, the National Library, and some others joined the Pedagogical Academy, the Academy of Arts, and the National Theater established earlier, under the Central Rada. A Ukrainian State Opera was preparing to open (Dorošenko 2, 367). The number of Prosvita branches at that time is given as 952 (Dorošenko 2, 344).

Under the Directory, military conditions and administrative instability precluded any major undertakings in education or culture. A few feverish attempts at outward Ukrainianization—such as the order to replace, within three days, all Russian shop signs with Ukrainian ones (Dorošenko 1969, 400)—were of little consequence.

The situation of the Ukrainian press during this time was determined, on the one hand, by the political awakening of readers (and journalists!), and on the other hand, by the unstable military, political, and economic conditions, which resulted in such purely technical obstacles as lack of paper, and sudden shortages of electricity. Statistically, Ukrainian publishing experienced an explosion. According to Žyvotko (147), the number of Ukrainian periodicals rose to 106 in 1917,[2] and to 212 in 1918. In Kiev alone, as early as the spring of 1917, six dailies had begun publication. Chronologically the first was *Nova rada*, successor to the prerevolutionary *Rada* (from 25 March 1917). Very soon it was joined by the Social-Democrats' *Robitnyča*

---

[2] According to Dorošenko 1, 403, the number was 63.

hazeta, by the Socialist-Revolutionaries' *Narodnja volja* and *Borot'ba* (begun as a weekly), and then somewhat later by *Hromads'ke slovo* and *Promin'*. An important, distinctive feature was the territorial distribution of the press: periodicals appeared in all provincial centers and in many smaller towns, including the Kuban' area and the Ukrainian parts of the Voronež and Kursk provinces. It is estimated that by the end of 1917 about 30 Ukrainian or Ukrainian-Russian dailies were published in towns, with a total of about 100,000 readers (Večernyc'kyj 78). That number grew spectacularly in 1918. The new periodicals were marked by political differentiation, representing all the parties of the time, as well as by professional differentiation, addressing teachers, students, women, children, historians, physicians, military men, agriculturalists, nurses, and postal workers. There were also periodicals in literature, bibliography, theater, art, cooperation, religion. Three magazines of satire and humor appeared. A novelty of the time were official bulletins initiated by the *Kyjivs'ki hubernijal'ni visti* (bilingual, in Ukrainian and Russian) and *Visti z Ukrajins'koji central'noji rady* and followed by publications of the General Secretariat, headquarters of the army, and various ministries. The publishers were political parties, cooperatives, government offices, *prosvity*, *zemstva* (called now *narodni upravy*), professional organizations, and, of course, private individuals. Even in the most difficult circumstances, when the government was pushed as far west as Kamjanec'-Podil's'kyj, the extent and richness of the new Ukrainian press remained striking.

Yet behind this impressive flourishing there were dark shadows. Most publications were unstable or ephemeral; many were poorly edited and in an uncertain language; the majority were geared to the little-educated reader (among the exceptions were *Nova rada* edited by A. Nikovs'kyj, *Robitnyča hazeta* headed by V. Vynnyčenko, and *Naše mynule* edited by P. Zajcev); little or nothing is known about the circulation of most periodicals. What is certain is that they did not match the long-standing Russian publications, such as *Kievskaja mysl'* and *Južnyj kraj*; during the time of the Hetmanate these Russian publications were joined by such organs of the Russian monarchist emigration as *Russkij golos* in Kiev and *Golos juga* in Odessa.

The effect of the Ukrainian press on the prestige of the Ukrainian language and on its expansion in everyday use was, presumably, twofold. On the one hand, the Ukrainian periodicals spread knowledge about and use of the language. On the other hand, those that were poorly edited could not but compromise the language. Occasionally, the latter provided material for "Ukrainian jokes" directed against the Ukrainian language.

The publication of Ukrainian books was numbered at 747 titles in 1917, 1,084 in 1918, and 665 in 1919, striking figures when compared with the 242 titles published in 1911 (see chap. 3), although the items published in 1917–1919 included many small pamphlets. The number of publishers and publishing companies was estimated at 78 in 1917, and 104 in 1918 (*EU* 1, 975ff.), Among published books, school textbooks held a position of special importance. In 1918, circulation of elementary school textbooks, for example, reached 950,000 copies (Dorošenko 2, 369). For other types of publications, some data on circulation can be found in *Knyhar'* (1917, 3, 160): e.g., *Jakoji my xočemo avtonomiji*, by M. Hruševs'kyj, sold 80,000 copies within about four months; his *Iljustrovana istorija Ukrajiny*, sold 19,000 copies in about a month; *Pro narodne samovrjaduvannja*, by V. Koroliv, sold 50,000 copies.

By no means all the books published were satisfactory technically or linguistically. Yet books were in such demand that their publication became a profitable business. An editorial published in *Knyhar'* (1917, 2) described the situation as follows: "Even in small towns publishing enterprises arise, which are unacquainted with our good traditions of 1905 and less so with the earlier ones, and which are unaware of literary customs and publishing ethics. They publish books of dull poetry priced a *karbovanec'* for 24 pages of bungled print. . ., in their endeavor to get into their greedy hands a fresh, even if paperprinted, penny" (p. 50).

Quite extraordinary was the number of books devoted to the Ukrainian language. A tally made from the bibliography by Červins'ka and Dykyj shows that 59 titles published in 1917–1919 were designed as manuals for self-instruction in the Ukrainian language, as compared with 11 such items published during the entire preceding century. Some of the manuals appeared in Russian, including *Kratkoe rukovodstvo k izučeniju ukrainskogo jazyka dlja znajuščix russkij jazyk*, by I. Blažkevyč, 39 pp. (1918), and *Dlja russkix na Ukraine: Naibolee legkij i skoryj sposob praktičeskogo izučenija ukrainskogo jazyka* by I. Krok (Kiev, 1918). The average size of these publications was 50 to 60 pages; only 13 items exceeded 100 pages, and only the publications of I. Ohijenko (matched by the works of Simovyč published abroad) had more than 200 pages. The majority appeared in Kiev, Kharkiv, and Odessa, but some were published in such places as Čerkasy, Kozjatyn, Braclav, Romen, and Kherson. The authors varied: some are renowned scholars, and others, unknown persons. Among the former was the history of the Ukrainian language written in Russian by an outstanding Russian scholar: S. Kul'bakin's *Ukrainskij jazyk* (Kharkiv, 1919). Previously, patriotic considerations had prompted the preparation of manuals on the Ukrainian language; now, profit undoubtedly joined such motives. High demand opened a broad market for such books. This, in turn, bore indirect witness to the spread of Ukrainian, if not for active, everyday use, then at least as a potential medium of communication, and probably also to the growth of its prestige.

Preparation of a dictionary requires more time than preparation of a grammar. Nevertheless, the years 1917 to 1919 saw an impressive upsurge in the publication of dictionaries. According to Červins'ka and Dykyj (434, 435, 440),[3] three Ukrainian-Russian dictionaries were published and, characteristically, fifteen Russian-Ukrainian ones (443, 444, 446, 448, 449, 452, 453, 454, 456, 459, 460, 466, 468, 469, 503), testimony that Russian speakers were switching, at least passively, to Ukrainian. A plethora of terminological dictionaries also appeared: 4 medical (473, 511, 578, 587); 4 in physics and chemistry (491, 527, 582, 599); 2 linguistic (502, 591); 3 in natural history and geography (511, 547, 593); 1 military (515); 4 technological (594–97); 1 mathematical (602); and no less than 8 dealing with legal and administrative terminology, a reflection of the rise, for the first time in two centuries, of a bureaucracy working in Ukrainian. It is highly typical of the period that the publication of Russian-Ukrainian dictionaries, followed by Ukrainian-Russian ones, was predominant, whereas no dictionaries of other languages, nor of Ukrainian alone, were published. The beginning of a switch from Russian to Ukrainian was clearly taking place. This was true not only for speakers of Russian in the countryside, but also for those who spoke Ukrainian daily but had become used to turning to Russian to express ideas beyond everyday conversation. The quality of the dictionaries published varied, but the

---

[3] In this paragraph, numbers in parentheses refer to corresponding items in Červins'ka and Dykyj.

general level was rather low. As a rule, they were quick responses to an urgent need, and their compilers often had no preparation in lexicography.

The lack of trained lexicographers was not the only reason for the shortcomings of most dictionaries published in 1917 to 1920, nor was it the haste with which the dictionaries were compiled. Another and no less important reason was the very situation in which the events of 1917 and the following years found the Ukrainian language. For many decades, and even centuries, left outside so many avenues of life, Ukrainian had very little time to make up for all its ensuing deficiencies. It was in need of both standardization and of (to some extent artificial) supplementation, a situation typical for all languages in transition from having only colloquial and literary use to fulfilling all the needs of a modern, national society. Vocabulary, phraseology, and terminology had to be regulated, and, often, newly introduced, be it from colloquial sources, from dialects, from historical sources, from other languages, or by invention.

There was little language planning in the years of the struggle for independence and, under the conditions of permanent turmoil, even fewer means of enforcing what had been planned. Nonetheless, some such steps were undertaken, for the first time in the history of Ukrainian under Russia. A commission on the regulation of orthography (*pravopysna komisija*) was appointed by the Ministry of Education. It consisted of three linguists—I. Ohijenko, A. Kryms'kyj, and Je. Tymčenko; on 24 May 1918, the Ministry approved their submitted *Najholovniši pravyla ukrajins'koho pravopysu*. These regulations were published in 1919 in Kiev (after an initial publication in *Vil'na ukrajins'ka škola*, 1918–19, no. 10). Although they covered only a few of the most disputed issues and comprised but eight pages, the rules were nevertheless a first step toward centralized language planning.[4] Also some terminological dictionaries appeared, as recom-

---

[4] More precisely, the terminology should be Ukrainian-centered. In 1907, the Russian Academy of Sciences in St. Petersburg made an attempt to regulate Ukrainian orthography. The immediate pretext was the forthcoming publication of B. Hrinčenko's dictionary. Chaired by F. Fortunatov, an outstanding Russian linguist, the Academy's so-called Little-Russian Commission, at its session of 6 January 1907, discussed a project by P. Stebnyc'kyj (a minor Ukrainian writer) and approved its proposals for Ukrainian orthography, subject, however, to further discussion. The commission basically accepted the then predominant spelling (including the letter г

mended by other ministries, e.g., the Ministry of Transportation published a *Terminolohičnyj zbirnyk* (Kiev 1918). The degree to which such publications were binding is difficult to ascertain; my guess would be that it was rather low. The questions of how the terminology was elaborated and regularized and what sources were used to fill gaps was never systematically studied. Here, only a few observations and tentative generalizations, based on limited data, can be made.

The prevailing trend seems to have been romantic, which had two major manifestations: as historical romanticism, and as ethnographic romanticism. Historical romanticism leaned on the resuscitation of the terminology of the seventeenth-century Cossack state, and became prominent in such areas as state structure and military organization. In this tradition, the solemn announcements of the Central Rada were called *universaly*, the parliament was to be called *sojm*, the state chancellor *heneral'nyj pysar*, the term for ''province,'' *gubernija*, was to be replaced by *zemlja*. Monetary units were *karbovanec'*, *hryvnja*, and *šah*. In the army, the officer ranks were *rojovyj*, *čotovyj*, *bunčužnyj*, *pivsotennyj*, *sotnyk*, *kurinnyj*, *polkovnyk*, *otaman* (of *brygada*, *korpus*, etc.). After the fall of the First Ukrainian National Republic, the very title *hetman* was based on these traditions. Some concessions were then made to more modern terminology: a *rada ministriv* was appointed, *zemli* became again *huberniji*, the *heneral'nyj sud* was replaced by the *deržavnyj senat*. But the guard of the Hetman was called *serdjuky*, and the military ranks were *hurtkovyj*, *rojovyj*, *čotovyj*, *bunčužnyj*, *xorunžyj*, *značkovyj*, *sotnyk*, *bulavnyj staršyna*, *osavul*, *polkovnyk*, *heneral'nyj xorunžyj*, *heneral'nyj bunčužnyj*, and *heneral'nyj oboznyj* (Hnatevyč 391, 428). The Second Ukrainian National Republic continued to use many of the terms of its

---

for the sound *g*), but with some alterations of a clearly Russianizing character, such as the abolition of the apostrophe and its replacement by the ''soft sign,'' and the abolition of the spellings *jo* and *'o* and their replacement by the letter *ë*. Hrinčenko objected, referring to the impossible changes in alphabetical order that would ensue for his dictionary, which was ready to be printed. Many other Ukrainians joined in the protest and so did the press (*Rada* 33, dated 9 February 1907). Thus the recommendations of the Russian Academy were never, in practice, implemented. Stebnyc'kyj's paper and the decisions of the commission were published in *Izvestija Imperatorskoj akademii nauk*, ser. 6, 1907, no. 9, pp. 225–41. Dzendzelivs'kyj (70–79) published the reactions of Hrinčenko and P. Žytec'kyj (with censored omissions).

republican predecessor, but the terms *dyrektorija, trudovyj kongres,* and *rada narodnyx ministriv* were impossible in the seventeenth-century Cossack state (whereas *holovnyj otaman,* the title of S. Petljura, had its roots there).

Relying on the Cossack state for administrative, legal, and military terminology also had a more recent tradition. It began, in fact, with the Galician paramilitary organization, *Ukrajins'ki sičovi stril'ci,* of 1913–1914, and its predecessors, the *Sič* societies existing from 1900. In these organizations the very name *Sič, sičovi* refers to sixteenth- and seventeenth-century traditions and had no reference to actual Galician life in the twentieth century. The tradition was brought to the former Russian Ukraine in late 1917 by Je. Konovalec' and his brigade of *Sičovi stril'ci.* The underlying tendency in all these Cossack-based terminological innovations and resuscitations was toward nationalization of the entire nomenclature. The Turkic origin of a great many of the terms was irrelevant.

The historical-romantic principle could be applied only very limitedly or not at all to other branches of terminology. There ethnographic romanticism had a free field. Its leading idea was that the bulk of new terminology should be based on dialectal data. For notions unknown to villagers the collected data might have to be semantically reinterpreted or new words might have to be created from morphemes used in rural speech. This was more or less the position of O. Janata when, in 1917, he suggested that a comprehensive collection of terms known to the "people" (i.e., the peasantry) should be undertaken and, on the basis of these data, all terminological issues should be resolved.

Janata's view was opposed by M. Hruševs'kyj in the same newspaper, *Promin',* where the idea had originally been expressed. He pointed to the urgency of creating Ukrainian terminology for child and adult schooling. In Hruševs'kyj's opinion, there was no time for Janata's terminological plan. Whatever terminology already existed had to be used. Practically, this meant a combination of popular terminology (as represented in various dictionaries, especially that of Hrinčenko), of Galician terminology, and of elements borrowed from the West European languages and Russian. Characteristically, Hruševs'kyj did not reject Janata's proposal on theoretical grounds. He would perhaps have adhered to it, too, were it not for the practical considerations of time.

On 11 April 1918, a Terminological Commission was appointed at the Kiev Scholarly Society. As if following Hruševs'kyj's advice, the commission listed among its most important sources "materials of the Lviv Scientific Society, Galician school textbooks, works by I. Verxrats'kyj and other Galician scholars" (Xolodnyj). The resulting terminology was eclectic, but no one denied that an ethnographic foundation was the most desirable and should be used whenever practically feasible.[5]

The application of the principles of historical and ethnographic romanticism was not, of course, uniquely Ukrainian. It emerged in nearly all standard languages at the time of their renascence and during the broadening of their functions and their inventory. This was true of Czech, Slovak, Serbian, Croatian, Lithuanian, Lettish, and many others. What varied was usually simply the proportions of their historical to ethnographic orientations.

The principles of ethnographic romanticism were broadly applied in language planning later, at the time of Ukrainianization; specific examples are given in the corresponding section below (see chap. 6).

The part played by Galicia in the years 1917–1920 was, in terms of the development of the literary language, insignificant or none, except for a more active dissemination of some older Galician features of the language, due to more lively contacts between Galicians and the population of the UNR/Hetmanate (such as through the so-called *Ukrajins'ka halyc'ka armija,* that is, the Ukrainian Galician Army). But in Galicia itself the development of the Ukrainian language was for the most part hampered, due above all to the conditions of war prevailing there. The independence of the West Ukrainian lands was proclaimed on 18 October 1918 and realized by armed coup d'état on 1 November 1918. But virtually immediately, a military conflict with the Poles ensued. Lviv was lost in three weeks. The Ukrainian-Polish war continued, absorbing all the energy of the populace and of the government, until mid-July 1919, when the government of the West Ukrainian National Republic had to leave the country, first for

---

[5] The populist approach to language proved extremely tenacious in the Ukraine. As late as 1917, V. Samijlenko, a popular poet, advised that the best criterion for the evaluation of the language of a literary work would be "to listen to how a Central Ukrainian peasant (*prostoljudyn*) speaks," even though he would admit words alien to an "illiterate peasant" (Samijlenko 367, 373).

Kamjanec'-Podil's'kyj and later (November 1919) for Western Europe. During the eight months of its existence the West Ukrainian National Republic proclaimed and used Ukrainian as the official language, although it entitled the minorities to use their own languages in contacts with the administration. This new status of the Ukrainian language was deprived of major consequences, however, because of its short-lived nature, as well as limited territory of application and the continuous battle environment; also, in Galicia the Ukrainian language had already been prepared to serve such functions.

In Bukovina the independent Ukrainian administration (in union with Galicia) existed for but five days, from 6 to 11 November 1918, when the country was occupied by the Romanian army. In Bessarabia (Xotyn area), a strong anti-Romanian uprising rallied under Ukrainian national slogans flared in January 1919, but it was soon crushed (Dorošenko 1969, 420). In Transcarpathia several "people's councils," and their congress at Xust (21 January 1919), voted for union with the rest of the Western Ukraine, but that same month the land came under the occupation of Czecho-Slovakia, Romania, and Hungary. Of these occupants, the Central Ruthenian Council in Užhorod opted for Czecho-Slovakia (5 May 1919), a choice confirmed by the peace treaty of Saint-Germain (10 September 1919).

The irrelevance of the events of 1918–1919 in Galician Bukovina, and Transcarpathia for the development of the Ukrainian literary language is indirectly reflected in the fact that no grammars or dictionaries were published there during that time.[6]

Thus, in the years of the struggle for independence, it was the development of the Ukrainian language in the former Russian Ukraine that proved to be crucial for not only that part of the country, but for the entire Ukraine. There actual independence lasted the longest, the status of the Ukrainian language changed most radically, and the dynamics of its expansion were the most striking.[7] None of the

---

[6] The books by the Galician V. Simovyč are not an exception: they were published in Germany, and they were originally intended for prisoners of war from the Russian Ukraine, not for the Galician population.

[7] On 14 June 1917, *Robitnyča hazeta* published, as follows, a speech by S. Petljura at the Second All-Ukrainian Congress of soldiers: "Soldier-citizens, members of organizations, must always be on guard as to the achievements of the revolution and make themselves into (*vyxovaty z sebe*) real sons of their nation and speak exclusively Ukrainian as well as write letters to their homes exclusively in their mother tongue"

language changes was completed at the time the independent Ukraine fell. All were brought to a standstill by the Sovietization of the country accomplished primarily through the invasion of the Russian Red Army. Nevertheless, they could not be immediately extinguished, and to a great extent they determined the zig-zags in the ensuing Soviet language policy within the Ukrainian S.S.R., as well as the vicissitudes of the Ukrainian language in the parts of the Ukraine occupied by Poland, Romania, and Czecho-Slovakia.

(Petljura 2, 372). It is immaterial whether the naive combination of guarding the attainments of the revolution with speaking Ukrainian comes from Petljura or from the newspaper reporter. What is important is that the call was typical of the early months of the revolution.

To what extent was the attitude out-of-date by the end of the struggle for independence? Of interest in this context is that the Constitution of the Ukrainian National Republic adopted by the Central Rada on 29 April 1918, a day before Hetman Skoropads'kyj's coup (i.e., it was never enforced), did not claim that Ukrainian was the state language, nor did it treat the language problem at all (reprinted in Xrystjuk 2, 175). The same was true of all four *universaly* of the Central Rada (reprinted in full in Dorošenko 1, 89, 115, 179, 264). The spreading use—or at least knowledge—of Ukrainian at the time of the Ukrainian National Republic and of the Hetmanate is an indisputable fact. What the quality of that language was is another question. Very often it was a peculiar mixture of Ukrainian and Russian, with many hybrids unique to that particular time; some of those that cropped up in oral speech and in correspondence are quoted in Solovej 112f. Newspapers of the time have not been studied from that point of view; they would certainly supply a rich harvest of linguistic misnomers.

A characteristic example in print is the pamphlet of S. Mazlax and V. Šaxraj entitled *Do xvyli* (Saratov, 1918). Ardent defenders of Ukrainian rights and talented journalists, the authors wrote in a language full of Russianisms and of pseudo-Ukrainian words which are actually distorted Russian ones (e.g., *naslidok* 'consequence' with the meaning 'patrimony' as influenced by Russian *nasledstvo*; *osobystyj* 'personal' with the meaning 'particular' under the influence of Russian *osobennyj*, etc.—Mazlax 7).

It is obvious that while the spread of Ukrainian to all avenues of life enhanced its prestige, the actual inadequacies of the language and its distortion by unprepared and unqualified users undermined that prestige. The latter was reflected in the appearance of some hostile and derisive "Ukrainian jokes." Some of these are recorded in Solovej 112.

CHAPTER FOUR

The Soviet Ukraine
Before Ukrainianization

Three stages in the Soviet-Russian occupation of the Ukraine are dealt with here; the first occupation, lasting from January to March/April 1918; the second occupation, lasting from January to August 1919; and the third occupation, which began in December 1919 (in some parts of southern Ukraine, from February 1920), and lasted until the initiation of the policy of Ukrainianization, which was formally introduced by the Council of People's Commissars on 23 July 1923 (in practice from April 1925). Thus, this chapter deals with the years 1918–1924, excepting the brief periods when the Soviets were forced out of the Ukraine. The three Soviet Russian occupations of the Ukraine can be examined together because during all three the policy toward the Ukrainian language and its status were basically identical.

The prevailing Russian character of the occupational forces is clearly evident in Lenin's telegram to Stalin sent 22 February 1920, if it needs any corroboration: "It is imperative without any delay to engage interpreters in all headquarters and military organs of the military forces in the Ukraine, and to oblige unconditionally all their officers to accept applications and other documents in the Ukrainian language. This is unreservedly necessary—all concessions should be made in what concerns the language and in the maximum equality of languages" (Lenin 51, 141f.). Ukrainian forces, of course, would not have needed interpreters. Two other principles of Communist policy, which would apply in the years to come, are implicitly formulated here: (1) concessions should be made regarding language, but not other matters; (2) not the domination of the Ukrainian language, but rather its admittance alongside Russian should be fostered (in other words, Russian was one of the two accepted languages of the Ukraine).

All three Russian occupations were accompanied by severe mass terror, often preventive, led by the military and by the All-Russian Extraordinary Commission (Če-Ka, 12 December 1917–6 February 1922). Numerous Ukrainian activists were killed in those years (including H. Čuprynka, a popular poet), often even those who were not engaged in any action against the Soviet regime (see, e.g., Majstrenko 41; Mazepa 1, 42; Vynnyčenko 2, 271 and 3, 311). However, specifically anti-Ukrainian actions as such more often than not resulted from the personal, hostile attitude of one or another commissar towards things Ukrainian rather than from actions by the Če-Ka. Acts of terror were directed against anyone suspected of opposing the Soviet regime and against everyone who belonged to the previously privileged classes. True, everywhere in the Ukraine power was not in the hands of local soviets (contrary to the name of the system), which did not exist in towns or villages and which were powerless in big cities, but in the hands of appointed ad hoc revolutionary committees and plenipotentiary commissars who could act arbitrarily. Zatons'kyj wrote in 1918: "Every [party] organization, almost every party member, resolved his own questions concerning tactics vis-à-vis the Ukrainian national movement, which grew incessantly and was becoming a more and more important factor of political strength in the Ukraine" (quoted from Levyns'kyj 13). M. Skrypnyk, in 1920, mentioned that the number of individual injunctions against the use of Ukrainian known to him had reached two hundred (Skrypnyk 17).

No one punished such individuals for their irresponsibility, which violated the general principles formulated (as late as 1919!) by Lenin. As Zatons'kyj admitted in 1926, the Soviet Ukraine was built "in spite of the suspicious attitude of the significant majority (one must state the truth) of the working class and, at the beginning, even of part of the peasantry" (*Budivnyctvo* 11). In addition, virtually all Ukrainian institutions were dissolved and dispersed, including the numerous Prosvita chapters (1922), private publishing houses, and cooperative organizations. However, *Nova rada* continued to be published during the first Soviet occupation of Kiev (the right-wing Russian *Kievljanin* and *Kievskaja mysl'* were closed; Dorošenko 1969, 230). One interesting detail mentioned by D. Dorošenko is that the letterheads of various soviets were printed in Ukrainian and in Russian, and the parties concerned in any case were given a choice between the two (1929, 228). The Ukrainian Academy of Sciences was spared dissolution, but it was reduced to a starvation budget (990 rubles in 1921, at the beginning of the third Soviet occupation; *Zvidomlennja* 1921, 63) and its access to printing facilities was restricted. Such a situation could not but create an atmosphere of fear, including fear to use Ukrainian in public.

The legislation of the Soviet regime, beginning with the second occupation (there was no time for legislation during the brief first occupation) had a different spirit. It contained no prohibition aimed at the Ukrainian language. The Constitution "of the Ukrainian Socialist Soviet Republic," adopted by the All-Ukrainian Congress of Soviets on 3 March 1919 and sanctioned by the Central Executive Committee on 19 March 1919, said nothing about Ukrainian or any other language. It only stated the inadmissibility of any national privileges or of national suppression, while, on the other hand, proclaiming the desire to dissolve the Ukraine itself "in one international Socialist Soviet Republic as soon as conditions have developed for its rise" (*Politika* 116, 113). This implied toleration of the Ukrainian language, but nothing more. (The coat-of-arms adopted for the state, for instance, had text in Russian and Ukrainian.)

At the end of the same year (December 21) the following general appeal, signed by H. Petrovs'kyj, V. Zatons'kyj, and D. Manujil's'kyj, was published: "In the labor school of the Ukrainian Soviet Socialist Republic, the Ukrainian language will become a powerful and active means for liberation of the Ukrainian working people from [intellectual] darkness and ignorance" (*Politika* 118). It implied recognition of (elementary?) education in Ukrainian, but, of course, like every popular appeal, this one had no binding force.

Beginning in the spring of 1919, several decrees favoring the use of the Ukrainian language were issued. The most important of these stipulated the following: the Ukrainian language, as well as the history and geography of the Ukraine, must be taught in schools (9 March 1919, Third Congress of Soviets); Ukrainian must be admitted alongside Russian in all government institutions and offices (21 February 1920, All-Ukrainian Central Executive Committee, and 2 May 1920, Fourth Congress of Soviets); Ukrainian subjects must be taught at teachers' seminaries and courses (4 May 1920, People's Commissariat of Education: "not in the old, predominantly philological direction, but so as to become the source of a living understanding of the cultural and socioeconomic [*kul'turno-pobutovoho*] situation of the present-day Ukraine'': *Zbirnyk*, 2–12 May 1920, no. 9, p. 220); the Ukrainian language as a subject must be introduced in schools and should be used in government institutions and offices (21 September 1920, Council of People's Commissars [CPC]); teaching in Ukrainian is recommended for schools, as is the use of Ukrainian in filmmaking; courses in the Ukrainian language should be organized for government officials (19 February 1921, CPC). On 3 March 1921 the Fifth Congress of Soviets approved the work of the People's Commissariat of Education (PCE) ''aimed at the elimination of national animosity and at the development of the Ukrainian language as the language of the majority of the toiling masses of the Ukraine.'' In 1922, the preceding measures were codified in a single *Kodeks zakoniv pro narodnju osvitu v URSR*, which stated (§ 25): ''The Ukrainian language as the language of the majority of the population of the Ukraine, especially in villages, and Russian, as the language of the majority in cities and as the All-Union language, have in the Ukrainian S.S.R. national (*obščegosudarstvennoe*) significance and must be taught in all educational (*učebno-vospitatel'nyx*) institutions of the Ukrainian Soviet Socialist Republic'' (Durdenevskij 155). The Criminal Procedures Code of 13 September 1922 spoke, in paragraph 22, of legal proceedings ''in one of the two state languages, Ukrainian or Russian'' (Durdenevskij 78). On 27 July 1923, the CPC issued a new decree, ''On measures for the Ukrainianization of schools and educational and cultural institutions''; on 1 August 1923, the AUCEC and CPC issued a joint resolution, ''On measures of safeguarding the equality of languages and on assistance to the development of the Ukrainian language'' (*Sobranie uzakonenij* 1919, 3, p. 347ff.; 1920, 4, p. 5; 1920, 24, p. 713; *Zbirnyk uzakonen'* 1920, 9, p. 220; 1923, 29, p. 896ff.; 1923, 29, p. 913ff.).

Party decisions about these matters were also not lacking, in either Kharkiv or Moscow. They included the following: the resolution of the Central Committee of the Russian Communist Party (RCP) and of its Eighth Conference, ''On Soviet power in the Ukraine,'' dated 3 December 1919; the resolution of the Tenth Congress of the RCP, ''On current tasks of the party in national policy,'' dated 15 March 1921; the resolution of the First All-Ukrainian Conference of the Communist Party of the Ukraine (CPU) on the national problem, of 2–4 May 1921; the resolutions of the plenary session of the Central Committee of the CPU dated 6 February 1922 and 17 October 1922;

of the Seventh All-Ukrainian Conference of the CPU, dated 9 April 1923; of the Twelfth Congress of the RCP, dated 25 April 1923, preceded by L. Trockij's programmatic *Zadači 12 s"ezda RKP (b)* (Moscow, 1923), which emphasized the explosive power of nationalism while admitting the failure of the Communist Party to unite nations by stimulating the development of their cultures (quoted extensively in Sadovs'kyj 45); the resolution of the plenary session of the Central Committee of the CPU, dated 22 June 1923, on the Ukrainianization of the internal party education and propaganda (*Kul'turne budivnyctvo* 229ff.). At that plenary session (as well as before it) the Ukrainian party minority (headed by Šums'kyj?) strived to secure implementation of the policy of Ukrainianization in everyday life; in particular, they proposed that Ukrainian, alongside Russian, be proclaimed the official language of the Soviet Ukraine. The proposal won a majority at the preliminary session, over the protest of H. Petrovs'kyj and M. Frunze, but it was defeated at the full plenary session. The term "official language" was replaced by "two generally used languages" (Babij 283).

The very number of such decrees and resolutions, calling for nearly identical measures, shows that the situation did not undergo any essential changes and that the published laws and ordinances were not consistently enforced. The resistance against or hostility toward Ukrainian resulted from the recent wars with the Ukrainian governments, the attitude of Russians and Russianized groups in the population, and, most important—in fact, decisive—the situation in the CPU itself, which controlled the machinery of dictatorship. In its political orientation, cultural ties, and even individual makeup, the CPU was essentially a Russian party based in the Ukraine. According to official statistics, even later, by 1923, only 23.3 percent of its party members were Ukrainian (Borys 89); in 1918 the percentage was just 3.2 (*Vsesojuznaja kommunističeskaja partija [bol'ševikov]. Social'nyj i nacional'nyj sostav VKP [b]. Itogi vsesojuznoj partijnoj perepisi 1927 g.* [Moscow, 1928], p. 158). As one of the party's leaders, V. Zatons'kyj, had bluntly stated a few years earlier, "here [in the Ukraine] the Bolshevik Party, as well as the majority of the industrial proletariat, consists chiefly of Russians (Great Russians), if not by nationality, then by culture" (*Kommunist* 1918, 3–4; quoted from Levyns'kyj 14). No wonder, then, that neither the leaders nor most party members wanted Ukrainianization. Many went even farther. As

Je. Boš' put it: "The worker and the peasant of the Ukraine demand and strive for the indivisible (*edinaja*) Soviet Russia" (her *Nacional'noe pravitel'stvo i sovetskaja vlast' na Ukraine* [Moscow, 1918]; quoted from Levyns'kyj).[1]

The most outstanding personality in the Ukrainian and pro-Ukrainian faction (or factions) in the party was Mykola Skrypnyk. Consistently an advocate of Ukrainianization, he found himself in an absolute minority, in fact, often in opposition to the majority. Characteristically, he was not elected to the Central Committee of the CPU at the First, the Second or the Third Party Congress, nor to the Politbureau at the Fourth, the Fifth, or the Sixth congresses. Skrypnyk became a full-fledged member of the Politbureau only at the Ninth Congress, in December 1925, in spite of the fact that he was a leading founder of the party. Another Ukrainian member of the CPU, Ju. Lapčyns'kyj, actually formed an oppositional group (federalists), whereas V. Šaxraj was on the road to that step in 1919–1920. V. Zatons'kyj, on the contrary, was quite docile on the national question (which did not preclude his execution later, in 1937).

The situation began to undergo slight change when the CPU absorbed the left elements of the Ukrainian Social-Democrats (Je. Neronovyč's group, ca. 40 persons) in 1918, the Ukrainian Socialist-Revolutionaries, or so-called *Borot'bisty* (Borot'bists), in 1920 (possibly up to 4,000 persons, of whom by 1923 only 119 are said to have remained: Majstrenko 45, 67, 72ff.), and some members of the Ukrainian Communist Party in 1925. Some legislative initiatives by the Soviet Ukrainian government in 1920–1921 might have been brought about by the former Borot'bists. From 1920 H. Hryn'ko, a former Borot'bist, led the People's Commissariat of Education; he was removed, in 1923, for what was labeled "excessive [though actually very moderate] Ukrainianization." Hryn'ko was replaced by Zatons'kyj, but in 1925, when vigorous Ukrainianization began, this

---

[1] The general situation is reflected in language selected for official government publications. Begun entirely in Russian as *Sobranie uzakonenij. . .*, this series became bilingual, with parallel Ukrainian and Russian texts, with no. 4 (21–25 March 1920), entitled *Zbirnyk uzakonen'. . .*; but it relapsed into Russian with no. 22 (1–10 August 1920), later to become bilingual again, and then, still later, exclusively Ukrainian. For some peculiarities in the laws of 1919–1924, see chap. 7 (in part 2), where these decrees are compared with those of 1925.

position was again entrusted to a former Borot'bist, O. Šums'kyj.

The zigzags in the language policy of the Soviet Ukrainian government, as well as the discrepancies between legislation and practice in those years, were partially due to the hidden but abiding conflict between the active Ukrainian minority and the pro-Russian majority in the central organs of the party and the government. The official historian of the CP(b)U, M. Popov (265), characterizes the years 1921 – 1923 as a time of slowdown in the Ukrainianization that had been pursued more vigorously in 1920. The slowdown may have been connected with the appointment of Hryn'ko in 1920 and the subsequent hampering of his activity by Russophile elements. In November of 1920, at the Fifth Conference of the CPU, the emissary of the Central Committee of the RCP(b), G. Zinov'ev, downgraded the policy of Ukrainianization as follows: "What is the essence of the national policy in the Ukraine?... We must act so that no one can say that we want to be in the way of Ukrainian muzhiks who want to speak Ukrainian. .... In some years [to come] that language will win that has more roots, that is more vital, more cultured. Thus, our policy consists in showing, in deeds, not in words, sincerely and honestly, that the Soviet power does not stand in his [the Ukrainian muzhik's] way of speaking and of teaching his children in the language he prefers" (quoted from Popov 236). Here Zinov'ev reduced the Ukrainian language to the idiom of villagers, and the party's policy toward it to not hindering the language in that capacity. A poignant fact is that no one attending the conference objected to the statement (Popov 277).

X. Rakovs'kyj, chairman of the CPC of the Soviet Ukraine in 1919 – 1923 (he himself was Bulgarian) passed over the problem of the Ukrainian language in silence in his declaration on the policy of the Soviet government made in Kharkiv and in Kiev (January and February 1919). Asked a question on the envisaged status of the Ukrainian language, he responded: "In answering the demand to declare [Ukrainian] the official language of the Ukraine, I do declare in full responsibility... on behalf of the workers' and peasants' temporary government of the Ukraine: this would be dangerous to the Ukrainian revolution" (quoted after Popov 182).[2] Rakovs'kyj referred to the great number of Russians in the Ukraine; the Russian-speaking

---

[2] A group of former Social-Democrats [independents] did demand that Ukrainian be declared the official language (Borys 260).

population in Kiev, Odessa, and the centers of the working class, as well as to the alleged mutual understandability of Russian and Ukrainian.

Rakovs'kyj defended his stand on the Ukrainian language also in the article "A hopeless affair" (*Izvestija*, 3 January 1919), the title of which, however, referred not to the promotion of the Ukrainian language, but to the military campaign of the Directory. In the article Rakovs'kyj wrote: "Of course we do not intend to deny either the Ukrainian language or a certain [degree of] national consciousness [on the part of Ukrainian peasants], but this is so far a potential force whose development the Soviet form of power will not only not impede but, on the contrary, will create conditions for a complete flourishing" (excerpts from both the speech and the article can be found in Xrystjuk 4, 173, and in Mazlax 196ff., but the selection is somewhat biased). Hence, the principle underlying Rakovs'kyj's language policy was the legal equality of the Ukrainian and Russian languages.

In the years to come Rakovs'kyj, without betraying his earlier views, even made a kind of defense of the Ukrainian language. In a speech at the Twelfth Congress of the RCP(b), in April 1923, he said: "Sometimes I have heard comrades call the Ukrainian language an invention of Galicians. Has not, after all, the great-power attitude of a Russian man crept into this, [the attitude of a man] who has never experienced national oppression but, quite the reverse, has oppressed other nations throughout [several] centuries?" (*Dvenadcatyj s"ezd* 579). There is no real contradiction between Rakovs'kyj's utterances of 1919 and 1923. As in 1919 he did not deny the existence of the Ukrainian language—writing in "A hopeless affair" that "Danger of Russification under Soviet power is entirely unthinkable. Insofar as the Ukrainian peasants and the Ukrainian workers need schooling and the administration to be in Ukrainian, this will be secured by Soviet power much better than it would be by Ukrainian intellectuals from among the newly-made officials...who see in Ukrainian independence...conditions for their own bureaucratic supremacy"—so in 1923 Rakovs'kyj did not opt for proclaiming it the official language or for fostering it at the expense of Russian. Yet he clearly learned from his experience with Ukrainian-Russian relationships in the CPU and CPC.

The Russian-Ukrainian friction within and without the CPU bearing on the status of the Ukrainian language was reflected in the uncertainties of the legal status of the Soviet Ukraine. At the time of the Second Soviet occupation, it was legally an independent state (Borys 297). So the Ukraine was called by Lenin ("The RCP[b] holds the view of recognition of the independence of the Ukraine"—Lenin 39, 334). His view was adopted in the resolution of the Central Committee, and it was restated in Lenin's "Letter to Workers and Peasants of the Ukraine on the Occasion of the Victory over Denikin": "The independence of the Ukraine has been recognized by both the All-Russian Central Executive Committee of the RSFSR and the RCP" (Lenin 40, 42). The same view is reflected in the leaflet Trockij addressed to Ukrainians at the time of the Soviet invasion (Vynnyčenko 3, 494; Mazepa 2, 168). On 12 December 1920, the legally independent Soviet Ukrainian state entered a union with Soviet Russia whereby it relinquished its sovereignty in the spheres of the military, finances, labor, communication, and the economy, but preserved separate citizenship and foreign diplomatic contacts (Borys 301ff.). At the same time (from December 1917), however, it was accepted that all decrees issued by the CPC of Soviet Russia were also valid in the Ukraine. On 2 May 1918 the Commissar of Nationality Affairs ordered in Moscow that an office for Ukrainian affairs be established and headed by a certain Je. Petrenko (*Politika* 109). In mid-1919 the All-Russian Executive Committee published a decree "on the amalgamation (*ob"edinenie*) of the Soviet Republics—Russia, Ukraine, Latvia, Lithuania, and Belorussia—for the struggle with world imperialism" (*Politika* 11), leaving it unclear whether a political union or a military alliance was meant. When the Russian army occupied the Ukraine, as early as 16 December 1917, the commander-in-chief of the Russian Soviet army, N. Krylenko, ordered that the Ukrainianization of military units be stopped (*Politika* 108). The ruling party was part of the Russian party, and the Russian government dispatched many commissars who held all power in their hands, according to some estimates up to 1,000 (Borys 255), and according to others up to 3,000 (Majstrenko 61). The same applied to the First Secretaries of the Central Committee of the CPU after G. Pjatakov, who were, in sequence, F. Sergeev (party name Artem), E. Kviring, S. Kosior, V. Molotov, and D. Manujil's'kyj, the sole Ukrainian among them.

The decrees issued and actions taken had created a complete legal mess, as expressed by Zatons'kyj in March 1921: "I personally do not know in what relation we are at present with the RSFSR, we who live in the Ukraine. I personally cannot make it out. So what can be said of the broad masses!" (*Desjatyj s"ezd* 205). In May 1921, the resolution of the First All-Ukrainian debate (*narada*) of the Central Committee of the CPU came up with the statement: "In the history of Soviet Ukrainian statehood there were moments [*sic*!] of complete independence (*nezaležnosty j samostijnosty*) of the UkrSSR..., moments of federative connection..., of political independence on the basis of military and economic amalgamation with the RSFSR.... State relations between the two sister republics are still in the process of being shaped and have not acquired certain stable forms" (*Rezolju-ciji* 125). It should be added that at the time of federation, no formalities about rights guaranteed to the participants were set down (as correctly observed by Vynnyčenko 3, 306). The confusion was legally disentangled only in the period December 1922 to June 1923, when the Union of Soviet Socialist Republics was founded and its constitution approved. The Ukraine became an integral part of the union, losing the right to separate citizenship, the right to diplomatic relations with other countries, and many other rights. Even then, as late as April 1923, Rakovs'kyj stated: "There is no step a national republic can take about which one can say from the outset that it was entitled to take it" (*Dvenadcatyj s"ezd* 582). Under such legal conditions it was, theoretically, equally possible to foster the Ukrainian language and to suppress it.

The actual state of the Ukrainian language during the years 1918–1924, under Soviet domination, shows some ups and downs and an interplay of give and take. On the one hand, Ukrainian was never outlawed by the central government; on the other hand, the same government, and especially the party, found many of its manifestations undesirable. It is impossible to evaluate statistically the use of the language, orally and in writing, in the Soviet administration. One must rely on the impressions and evaluations of contemporaries. These are nearly unanimous, regardless of whether expressed by adversaries or functionaries of the system. The three utterances selected for inclusion here are representative. Vynnyčenko said (3, 309): "In actual fact, all clerical work is done in Russian, all the officials (*urjad*) speak in Russian, whereas the Ukrainian language is made fun of and is called the 'dog's language'" (Vynnyčenko is referring to the situation in 1919). Hryn'ko said in 1923: "The state machinery from top to bottom works in the Russian language, with quite small exceptions in the staff of the People's Commissariat of Education in the provinces and some others. Our cooperative organization functions in Russian in at least 60 to 70 percent [of cases]" (Popov 270). No less a person than E. Kviring, First Secretary of the Central Committee and for many years a staunch opponent of the Ukrainianization, summed up the situation thus: "We must say that our government (*vlada*) is still excessively (*nadto*) non-national, still strikingly non-Ukrainian, and that in this we certainly have not gone too far" (Popov 272).

Newspapers published in the Ukrainian SSR were as follows, according to *Knyžkova palata* :

Year	In Ukrainian	In Russian
1918	60	227
1919	127	228
1920	87	266[3]
1921	45	95
1922	30	102[4]
1923	28	86
1924	36	95

Circulation (*tyraž*) in thousands of copies was as follows:

Year	In Ukrainian	In Russian
1918	not given	not given
1919	not given	not given
1920	35	147
1921	99	199
1922	83	353
1923	80	492
1924	176	752

(*Presa* 174).

[3] Completely different data are given in EU 1, 591: 73 and 151.

[4] Completely different data are given in Žyvotko 158, with reference to Ihnatijenko, 173 and 222.

The ratio of Ukrainian to Russian newspapers was highest in 1919 (when newspapers published under non-Soviet regimes were probably also included, although this is not stated explicitly). It is the only year for which Ukrainian titles number more than one-half of the Russian ones; in other years, they number roughly one-third, and in some cases, especially in circulation, fall as low as one-fifth.[5] If one considers that Russian newspapers were regularly imported from Russia, for which no statistical data are available, the low number of Ukrainian newspapers becomes even more striking. It must also be mentioned that some Ukrainian newspapers were published by the Borot'bists and the UCP, who put out papers in Kharkiv, Katerynoslav, and Kamjanec'-Podil's'kyj, as well as in Kiev. (All "bourgeois" newspapers were closed at the very beginning of the Soviet regime.) The organ of the Communist government, the Russian-language *Izvestija*, became the Ukrainian-language *Visti* from 1921, but the organ of the Central Committee, *Kommunist*, remained Russian throughout the period (it occasionally included articles in Ukrainian). Chronologically, the first periodical publication of the Communist party in the Ukraine was the organ of the Kiev Provincial Party Committee, *Bil'šovyk*, published from March 1919. Several Ukrainian newspapers for peasants started to appear in 1921, but most of them did not survive into 1923 (Popov 267).

The number of Ukrainian newspapers being published was low, but if one recalls (following Majstrenko 36) that, in 1917, the CPU published nothing in Ukrainian (the *Vistnyk Ukrajins'koji narodnoji respubliky*, published in Kharkiv from 19 December 1917, had a Ukrainian title, but nearly all the contents were in Russian: Žyvotko 159), clearly progress was being made. Communist periodicals in Ukrainian and in Russian numbered as follows, according to Ihnatijenko (1926, 73):

[5] For all periodicals, including newspapers, Ihnatijenko 1926, 70, gives the following table:

Year	Total Ukrainian	In the Russian Ukraine	In the Austrian Ukraine	Russian periodicals in the Ukraine
1917	172	106	21	751
1918	252	218	15	321
1919	243	173	49	222
1920	139	79	36	151
1921	181	77	55	188
1922	168	43	68	287

Year	In Ukrainian	In Russian
1917	—	4
1918	1	6
1919	21	30
1920	63	120
1921	75 (?)	169 (?)
1922	43 (?)	146 (?)

According to data from *Litopys ukrajins'koho druku* (1924, 2), these numbers would be 62 and 160, respectively, for 1923. The publication of Ukrainian newspapers in the Soviet Ukraine (although some data are uncertain, as marked with question marks above) fairly adequately reflects the official Soviet attitude toward the Ukrainian language: limited toleration, but no promotion.

A similar situation obtained for journals. In the early years of the Soviet regime, non-periodical almanacs prevailed: *Červonyj vinok*, 1919; *Grono* and *Zšytky borot'by*, 1920; *Štabel'* and *Vyr revoljuciji*, 1921; *Žovten'*, 1922; *Šturm*, 1923; *Kvartaly*, *Pluh* and *Žovtnevyj zbirnyk*, 1924 (compiled after Lejtes 1, xiii f.). Periodicals begun in 1919 – 1922 rarely survived into the following year, although not necessarily due to political reasons; the exceptions, according to Lejtes (1, xiv ff.) were only four: the literary *Šljaxy mystectva*, the pedagogical *Šljax osvity*, the youth-oriented *Student revoljuciji*, and the professional journal *Sil's'kohospodars'kyj proletar*. In 1923 some more solid periodicals appeared: the literary-political monthly *Červonyj šljax*, the illustrated biweeklies *Hlobus* and *Nova hromada*, and the popular scientific biweekly *Znannja*. So, the number and the circulation of journals published were extremely low, but no complete halt in publication occurred, and, from 1921, some growth, albeit slow, is evident.

The status of the Ukrainian language in the Soviet Ukraine in those years is reflected in that compilers of almanacs and editors of journals seemed to be embarrassed to be publishing in Ukrainian. They tried to justify themselves or to publish a combination of writings in several languages: most consistently, M. Semenko in *Semafor u majbutnje* published materials in Ukrainian, Russian, English, French, and German (reprinted in Lejtes 2, 107ff.); also, Semenko, together with M. Xvyl'ovyj and others, took part in joint Ukrainian-Russian enterprises (Lejtes 2, 67). The almanac *Žovten'* was introduced in 1921 by a declaration which, among other things, stated: ''We here in the

Ukraine feel ourselves to be but a part of the universe-wide workers' soul surpassing the frontiers of states and nations. We take the Ukrainian language to be a certain rich material left to us as a patrimony by generations [who lived] thousands of years, our forefathers, the Ukrainian peasantry'' (signed by Xvyl'ovyj, V. Sosjura, M. Johansen; reprinted in Lejtes 2, 66). The literary organization Hart proclaimed: ''The Union [of writers] wants to unite proletarian writers of the Ukraine who aspire to create the universal international communist culture while using the Ukrainian language as the vehicle of their work,'' and continued: ''This is to emphasize the urgency (*udarnist'*) of work in that language which is spoken by tens of thousands of peasants who should be subordinated ideologically to the influence of the proletariat'' (signed by V. Blakytnyj; reprinted in Lejtes 2, 95). Finally, *Červonyj šljax* was introduced by the statement: ''The Ukrainian language itself is a major factor in the process of the creation of a new life, and it requires continual perfection and broadening to meet the requirements posed by the cultural rise of the toiling masses. *Červonyj šljax* must carefully approach this task and mobilize literary and scholarly forces for the work of molding the Ukrainian language into a powerful tool for the cultural development of the toiling masses'' (reprinted in Lejtes 2, 98). In such declarations, a guilt for writing in Ukrainian seems to combine whimsically with a peculiar stubbornness and pride in the undertaking.

For book publication, at least for belles lettres, a table showing the number of titles in Ukrainian vs. Russian literature can be used. In 1918 to 1924, the publication of translations of literary works from Ukrainian into Russian and (to a lesser extent) from Russian into Ukrainian was atypical, so that the numbers below should correspond, roughly, with titles published in each language (a correction should be made for works translated from other languages):

Year	Ukrainian Literature	Russian Literature
1918	304	52
1919	149	98
1920	106	61
1921	62	72
1922	71	128
1923	48	73
1924	153	82

(*Presa* 94ff.).

The low number of books in Russian literature published in 1918–1919 is probably explained by the inclusion of non-Soviet publications. The general decline of 1921 to 1923 was caused by economic ruin and by the liquidation of private publishing houses (which would be reversed in part with the introduction of the "New Economic Policy," in 1921). The most striking feature is the overtaking of first place by Russian book publications in 1921–1923, which undoubtedly reflects the status of the Ukrainian language and culture at the time and the insufficiency of government efforts to protect it. Also, Soviet-Ukrainian publications, especially in 1920–1922, included a large number of small pamphlets aimed against things Ukrainian, such as the 1920 *Pravda pro petljurivs'ki brexni, Pro Petljuru, pans'ku škuru*, etc. (Siropolko 181).

The same conclusion can be drawn from the table below, which gauges book production as a whole:

Year	In Ukrainian	In Russian	Percent in Ukrainian
1918	1,084	386	64.4
1919	665	726	47.0
1920	457	369	53.1
1921	214	448	32.0
1922	385	927	29.3
1923/4	855	1,848	31.0
1924/5	1,813	2,535	40.2

(Siropolko, 184, who compiled his data from *Knyhar* 1923, 2; *Radjans'kyj knyhar* 1932, 31; and Ju. Meženko's *Ukrajins'ka knyžka časiv velykoji revoljuciji* [Kiev, 1928]).

In education, instruction in Ukrainian survived best in elementary schools through the time when official policy maintained the equality of the Ukrainian and Russian languages. (Statistical data for every year are not available to me.) According to Popov (266), in 1920 "many rural elementary schools switched to instruction in Ukrainian" (in fact, the schools were allowed to continue teaching in Ukrainian, as they had before the Sovietization). Siropolko (201) quotes from the report of the People's Commission of Education to the Sixth Congress of Soviets (December 1921; not available to me) that in 1921, 63 percent of schools were conducted in Ukrainian in the Ukraine as a whole, 80 percent in the Podolia, Kiev, and Poltava regions, and ca.

20 percent in the Kharkiv and Donec' regions; in the large cities, however, the percentage was much lower—in Kiev, 25 percent, Katerynoslav, 20 percent. By 1923, according to Zatons'kyj, 95 percent of rural elementary schools in the Kiev and Poltava regions were Ukrainian (quoted after Popov 268); but Popov also states (168) that in the Donec' region there were no Ukrainian schools at all (were they liquidated in 1922?). Rakovs'kyj, in 1923, stated that the number of Ukrainian elementary schools corresponded to the percentage of Ukrainians in the population, except for the Donec' and Kharkiv provinces (Popov 270).

Urban schools at that time, however, were almost entirely Russian. As late as June 1923, Skrypnyk reported that the Ukrainian language was not taught even as a subject in those schools. He also stated that "in the majority of higher schools instruction is conducted in Russian; the percentage of elementary and high schools where instruction is given in Russian is much higher than the percentage of Russians in the population" (Skrypnyk 37, 50). It may be assumed that factory vocational schools (*fabzavuč*) were entirely Russian. This also was the situation in the army and in military training, despite the demands of Skrypnyk (1924, 39ff.); a striking exception was the founding of two Ukrainian schools for army officers, one in Kharkiv (as early as 1920; Majstrenko 224), and the other, much later, in Kiev (1927?; Popov 267).[6]

The language situation in education made the contrast between the countryside and urban centers sharper than ever and further diminished the prestige of the Ukrainian language, suggesting that it was the language of a lower, backward culture and that studying it had few prospects. That attitude found expression in such pronouncements as that by Dm. Lebed', Second Secretary of the Central Committee of the CPU from 1921 to 1923: "We know theoretically that the conflict of the two cultures [Ukrainian and Russian] is inevitable. In our case, in the Ukraine, due to historical circumstances the urban culture is Russian, the culture of the countryside is Ukrainian"; from this he drew the conclusion that the Russian and not the Ukrainian language and culture should be supported (*Kommunist*, 4 April 1923; quoted from Popov 269). Lebed's views met with criticism from members of the

---

[6] Cf. the list of military schools as of 1926 in *Kievskij krasnoznamennyj: Istorija krasnoznamennogo kievskogo voennogo okruga 1919–1972* (Moscow, 1974), p. 79.

central organs of the party, yet they accurately reflected the split between the cities and the countryside that had resulted from actual policy.

The real situation of the Ukrainian language, and the real attitude toward it, are best reflected in the data on the publication of Ukrainian grammar textbooks. In 1920–1921 none was published; in 1922, 1; in 1923, 7; in 1924, 5; altogether 13 in five years, as compared with 59 published during the three years of the struggle for independence, 1917–1919 (figures are derived from the data of Červins'ka and Dykyj). Another telling fact is that of the 13 items, 8 were designed for elementary schools and only 5 for higher schools or self-education.

Identical conclusions follow from an analysis of the publication of dictionaries (again tallied from the bibliographical lists of Červins'ka and Dykyj). No dictionaries were published in 1920; 2 in 1921; 1 in 1922; 5 in 1923; and 7 in 1924; totaling 15 in five years, as compared to 45 in 1917–1919. Of the fifteen dictionaries published, 2 were general Ukrainian-Russian (439, 442),[7] 3 were general Russian-Ukrainian (461, 462), and the remaining 10 were terminological: 2 medical (474, 578), 3 legal and administrative (478, 501, 561; in 1917–1919, 8 such dictionaries appeared); 1 chemical (532); 1 mathematical (577); 1 technological (584; on the sugarbeet industry; it was perhaps designed for rural readers); 1 anatomical (603); and 1 geological (601).

Not much was done about the regulation of orthography. The brief "rules" prepared at the time of the Hetmanate (1919) were revised slightly by the Academy of Sciences[8] and sanctioned by Hryn'ko as Commissar of Education. Numbering sixteen small pages, the booklet was printed twice in 1921. An interesting detail is that the Academy accepted the rules set forth in the 1921 edition at three sessions, on 17 May and 12 July 1919, and on 29 February 1920. Apparently there was some discussion and probably some changes were suggested, but nothing is known about them; we do know that the chairman of the

---

[7] Numbers in parentheses refer to positions in Červins'ka and Dykyj.

[8] The Academy's "Section on Orthography" by 1920 had as its manager V. Durdukovs'kyj, a specialist in pedagogy, and V. Tutkovs'kyj, the son of academician Pavlo Tutkovs'kyj, a specialist in the natural sciences. The section was part of the Commission on Spelling and Terminology headed by A. Kryms'kyj and (in 1918) by A. Nikovs'kyj (*Zvidomlennja za 1920*, 82).

commission was H. Holoskevyč. The rules were published in 40,000 copies, which sold out that same year (*Zvidomlennja za 1921*, 19; Ohijenko, 13; Bahmet 130). Incidentally, the initial printing of the 16-page booklet took one year.

The orthographic rules of the Academy were not its only work bearing on the standard of the Ukrainian language. Several of the dictionaries summarily characterized above were prepared by the Academy. In 1921 an Institute of the Ukrainian Scientific Language was founded at the Academy; until 1925 it functioned under the general guidance of A. Kryms'kyj. The Institute's task was to prepare terminological dictionaries, primarily Russian-Ukrainian ones. During 1923, two were published: P. Tutkovs'kyj's dictionary of geological terminology, and O. Kurylo's dictionary of chemical terminology (Gregorovich, pos. 3, 4; these will be discussed in the next chapter).

A commission on the compilation of the contemporary (*žyva*) Ukrainian language began to function, also under A. Kryms'kyj. Its first achievement was the publication of the first volume of a *Rosijs'ko-ukrajins'kyj slovnyk* (A–Ž) (Kiev, 1924); prepared by V. Hancov, H. Holoskevyč, and M. Hrinčenko under the general guidance of Kryms'kyj (A. Nikovs'kyj and O. Synjavs'kyj had participated earlier, in 1919). The commission in charge of the compilation of the dictionary also employed a staff of 6 full-time and 75 casual workers. In 1921, these numbers were 10 and 19, respectively; in 1922 they dwindled to 4 and 5 respectively; and in 1923 they were 4 and 16 (*Zvidomlennja za 1922*, 8; . . . *za 1923*, 50). In the preface the editors state that their aim was to compile a dictionary of the Ukrainian literary language as it had developed over the last decades (i.e., since 1905), and especially during the last five years. Their list of sources, however, does not include a single writer of the Soviet period or any Soviet periodical (the only newspaper listed is *Nova rada*). In fact, the only Soviet source referred to is N. Buxarin's *Azbuka kommunizma*, in translation from the Russian; translations of the Holy Scriptures are also cited broadly. It was only in 1924 that some contemporary writers were included as sources of excerpts, among them M. Xvyl'ovyj, H. Kosynka, M. Ryl's'kyj, and P. Tyčyna (*Zvidomlennja za 1924*, 36).

What strikes the user of the dictionary is that in addition to literary works (beginning with Kotljarevs'kyj), a large number of ethnographic records from the Eastern and the Central Ukraine is included.

Their appearance clearly continues the tradition of populist lexicography, above all, of B. Hrinčenko's dictionary of 1909. The Academy dictionary was thus a compromise between the populist approach, oriented on the peasantry, and the more modern attitude, reflecting the language of the intelligentsia and shaping it. The two trends may also reflect the interests of the two editors-in-chief: the populist proclivities of Kryms'kyj are obvious in all his writings, and a different trend might have been promoted by S. Jefremov (who did not participate formally in the preparation of volume 1; to accelerate publication, Kryms'kyj was in charge of volumes 1 and 2, whereas in April 1924 Jefremov became chief editor for volumes 3 and 4).

The first volume of the dictionary relied on a copious collection of lexical and phraseological cards (ca. 400,000). It included numerous synonyms and phrases and marked some words as characteristic of certain styles, though rather infrequently. It was a new phenomenon in Ukrainian lexicography, but its vacillations between standard and dialectal, urban and rural (often folkloric), made it somewhat eclectic, and the effort to represent the standard language often collided with a desire to introduce the richest material available. As the editors themselves put it, it was "sometimes not quite polished" and seemed more like "materials for a dictionary" (p. ix). For instance, under the Russian *videt'* one finds: *bačyty, vbačaty, vydity, zrity. Vydity* bears the remark "western," but nothing is said about whether the word is dialectal or regional. Under the entry for Russian *vnutrennosti*, one finds alongside other words such expressions as *skyndéji, bándury, bél'baxy*, without any note that they are slang terms. Among the phrases given for the word *voda*, one finds the Russian *voda žurčaščaja* translated as *dzjurkoton'ka* and the Russian *bol'šoe skoplenie vody* as *dunaj*; these are examples of stylistically neutral Russian expressions being translated into strikingly folkloric Ukrainian ones, in fact limited to folksongs, occasionally ad hoc formations conditioned contextually (this is probably true of *dzjurkoton'ka*, which in Hrinčenko's dictionary is cited from a poem by P. Kuliš and in the Academy dictionary appears without reference or stylistic qualification). Such a general romantic-populist attitude, as well as a sheer insufficiency of lexicographic training on the part of some compilers, undoubtedly undermined the practical value and impact of the dictionary. But the very appearance of an Academy dictionary must have enhanced the prestige of the Ukrainian language, as did its other publications.

The Academy produced 12 pre-Soviet publications in 1918–1919, followed, under the Soviets, by none in 1920, 3 in 1921, 2 in 1922, 22 in 1923, and then 19 in just the first months of 1924 (*Zvidomlennja za 1923*, 162ff.)—this despite the fact that the state subsidy to the Academy was woefully inadequate (in 1924, 1,000 rubles per month for all operational expenses: *Zvidomlennja za 1924*, 7); it was even less in the preceding years, so that the paid staff of the Academy dwindled from the originally planned 600 to 147 at the beginning of 1922 to 117 by the end of 1923: *Zvidomlennja za 1924*, 7). Financial difficulties were the main cause of the delay in compiling and publishing the second and third volumes of the Academy dictionary, which did not appear until 1927.

In its publications the Academy appeared as an entirely Ukrainian institution, although that was not actually the case. *Zvidomlennja za 1920* stated that the historical and philological branch of the Academy was filled with Ukrainian collaborators, whereas "in the branch of mathematical sciences and natural history...representation of the Ukrainian element was very limited, even too limited, and the absolute majority of collaborators were purest Russians. In accordance with this makeup...all conferences of the historical and philological branch were conducted in Ukrainian, as were most [but not all—G.S] conferences in the division of economic and social sciences, but in the division of mathematics and natural history the conferences were held exclusively in Russian" (p. 2). *Zvidomlennja* continues: "But, following the statute of the Academy of Sciences, all studies without exception are published in Ukrainian...so that the outcome of all research of the Academy in all its divisions is in Ukrainian" (ibid.). One example (cited in *Zvidomlennja za 1922*, p. 46ff.) is the list of 52 papers read by members of the Association of Zoologists at the Academy. Of the 52, only seven were delivered in Ukrainian, and the remainder in Russian. In 1924, the leading economist at the Academy, K. Voblyj, published 18 items, many in periodicals with Ukrainian titles, yet all but one in Russian; his single Ukrainian article appeared in an Academy publication (*Zvidomlennja za 1924*, 53). Beginning with *Zvidomlennja za 1925*, all titles of papers read are given in Ukrainian, so that it cannot be known how many were actually delivered in Ukrainian.

The rise of literary associations had some bearing on the state and status of the Ukrainian language. Most leading writers of the pre-Soviet period emigrated (Vynnyčenko, Oles', Samijlenko, Čerkasenko, Voronyj among them) or fell silent. But gradually new voices that accepted the Soviet system let themselves be heard. Aside from the several ephemeral Futurist groups and regroupings, two stabler literary organizations emerged. First chronologically was Pluh (The plow; 1922). In harmony with the actual policy of the Communist party at the time, which accepted Ukrainian as the language of the peasantry but made no serious attempts to propagate it in the urban and industrial milieu, Pluh proclaimed that it would be an association of "peasant writers," that the toiling part of the peasantry is "the future proletariat," and that it aimed to recruit writers from among "the revolutionary, conscious peasantry" (Lejtes 2, 74).

Very soon, in 1923, a reaction came. Those who resented the restriction of the Ukrainian literature and language to the countryside and wanted to see Ukrainian conquer the city and the class that was officially the most advanced, the bearer of the future and the subject of dictatorship in the present—i.e., the workers—proclaimed themselves the mouthpiece of the proletariat. Led by the former Borot'bist V. Blakytnyj, they founded the association of "proletarian writers" called Hart (Hardening [of steel]). In contrast to Pluh, which, essentially, continued to espouse traditional populist topics, style, and language, at least some members of Hart took up urban topics and problems having a universal character, and afforded themselves fairly bold experimentation (M. Xvyl'ovyj, P. Tyčyna, a.o.). Without overtly breaking the party line, they broadened the use of the Ukrainian language much more than officially advised, and, by the same token, introduced substantial corrections into the party line, while propagating communist ideology in general policy and in their world view.

By the end of the Soviet pre-Ukrainianization period, in the press, in periodicals, in publications, in scholarship, and in literature, a new, Soviet-minded intelligentsia had begun to press against the locks which were intended to confine the Ukrainian language to the countryside. In a sense this was a resumption of the efforts made by M. Kocjubyns'kyj and his colleagues at the turn of the century, following the setback of the Soviet-Russian occupation. It augured the need for at least some changes in party policy or, perhaps, politics. That would happen in 1925. The attempt to suppress the Ukrainian language, during the first and, in part, the second occupations, and then to confine it, had failed. The vitality of the Ukrainian language had proved itself in the probations of the years 1918 to 1924.

Looked at from another angle, in those years both the social and internal deficiencies of the Ukrainian language had become clearly apparent. Because it was deprived of state protection, these were open to view. Socially, Ukrainian remained the language of the peasantry and the intelligentsia, in most cases humanistic—that is, of teachers, writers, artists. The language split within the Academy of Sciences (humanities vs. sciences) mirrored the situation in the entire society. The novelty was that new promoters of the Ukrainian language merged within the upper strata of the governing party, both the old Ukrainian Communists and the new recruits from among the Borot'bists and the like. The promoters were in the minority, however, and the party remained an essentially Russian organization. Among the industrial workers Russian continued to be the main means of communication, and peasants joining the industrial cadres (not many during that time) probably succumbed to Russification rather than Ukrainianized the older strata of workers.

Internally, the language absorbed a great number of Sovietisms in the areas of administration and ideology, which more often than not were loan translations from Russian, although many were not slavish translations (e.g., Russian *kombed* = *komitet sel'skoj bednoty* 'committee of poor peasants'—Ukrainian *komnezam* = *komitet nezamožnyx seljan*; Russian *dom krest'janina* 'peasant house'—Ukrainian *seljans'kyj budynok ~ sel'bud,* etc.). The main avenue for the introduction of such words were newspapers, followed by oral propaganda, and stylistic editors were often their creators. Interestingly enough, in areas where newspapers were not influential—i.e., outside administration and political agitation and propaganda—borrowings from Russian were not typical of the standard language (they abounded in the substandard language).

There was little regulation of the language by linguists, but what there was relied on native resources rather than resorted to borrowings. That policy characterized the linguists connected with the Academy of Sciences and its Institute of the Ukrainian Scientific Language. Dormant for several years, due to a lack of funds and, hence, of collaborators (e.g., in 1922 it had one paid worker:

Zvidomlennja za 1922, 9) the Institute was reactivated in 1924, when H. Xolodnyj became the de facto director. In scientific and technological terminology, in the broad sense, the main method was to collect dialectal data and to promote ''felicitous'' words and expressions to literary status, either as they were or by modifying their meanings to fit the notion being rendered (e.g., *prohonyč,* originally 'shutterbolt'—i.e., an object of rural use—obtained the ''industrial'' meaning of 'bolt [in general, of any kind]', as an equivalent of the Russian *bolt*; see Shevelov 1977, 255). If no material for such semantic shifts was available, and no term for a given notion was present in the language, the coining of a new word from existing, native components was preferred to the adoption of a Russianism. It is no surprise that in 1918 to 1924, most such words remained in the cardfiles of the Institute.

The language gap between the countryside and the cities, which neither time nor circumstances had allowed to be eliminated in the preceding period, became deeper and more blatant during the first five years of the Soviet regime. The situation cried out for change.

CHAPTER FIVE

The Years of Ukrainianization
(1925 – 1932)

As a body of official documents, decrees, and resolutions, the policy of Ukrainianization can be traced from the year 1923, or even from 1920. But as a series of practical measures implemented consistently and persistently, it hardly began earlier than 1925. As Popov rightly reported: "The broad work of the party in the field of Ukrainianization unfolded. . . some time around the summer of 1925" (282). In June of 1926, L. Kaganovič justly spoke of the first anniversary of Ukrainianization (*Budivnyctvo* 48). By that time, two prerequisites for the policy had emerged in the Ukraine: a new, urban-based intelligentsia who had broken with the countryside, not yet very numerous but large enough to be taken into account; and a marked, though still very limited, Ukrainian element within the party. Other factors favoring the introduction of the new policy were the reconstruction, by 1925, of industry ruined during the years of civil war, and the proclamation of industrialization made at the Fourteenth Congress of the Communist Party of the Soviet Union (CPSU) in December 1925; these would precipitate an influx of peasants to the industrial centers. Whether the peasants would become Russianized or whether, on the contrary, they would Ukrainianize the cities was now a development indisputably on the horizon—and one fraught with consequences for decades to come.

The impending development was important not only for the Ukraine, but also for all other non-Russian parts of the USSR. There were other—in fact, crucial—considerations of an all-Union character at play that made the Central Committee of the CPSU cast the dice for Ukrainianization and press for its speedy materialization. They brought about the downfall, in December of 1925, of E. Kviring as the First Secretary of the Central Committee of the Communist Party of the Ukraine (CPU), a Latvian who since 1918 had been actively against Ukrainianization and who in 1925 was at best lukewarm to it. L. Kaganovič was appointed in his place and received the special task of actively promoting the new policy while making sure that it did not exceed the limits acceptable to the party—i.e., that it did not overflow into separatism in politics nor, in fact, in culture. Kaganovič had been tried and tested on numerous occasions and in various places— Saratov, Homel', Nižnij Novgorod, Voronež, Turkestan; from 1922 he had worked in Moscow. Probably the only First Secretary of the Central Committee of the CPU who to that time had mastered Ukrainian and occasionally used it in public, he was a ruthless party man and an ace troubleshooter. Kaganovič was appointed on 6–7 April 1925 (*Visti*, 8 April 1925, no. 79). Just two months later, on July 13, V. Čubar, a Ukrainian, became chairman of the Council of People's Commissars (CPC), and Rakovs'kyj was sent to London as the Soviet ambassador, even though by that time he seems not to have opposed Ukrainianization. Rakovs'kyj's signature had appeared on a decree of 8 August 1923 that strongly favored an actual Ukrainianization (*Zbirnyk uzakonen'* 1923, 29, p. 919; other signatories were Petrovs'kyj and Bucenko).

The reasons for the new direction of the Central Committee of the CPSU were the collapse of expectations for a proletarian revolution in the industrialized countries and the stabilization of Europe. The party turned to the new policy of supporting colonial revolutions in the hope that they would weaken the West and hasten its downfall. Although he did not mention the first consideration, Stalin fairly frankly expounded on the second at the Twelfth Congress of the CPSU, in April 1923:

> One of two things: either we put in motion, revolutionize the deep rear of imperialism, the oriental colonial and semicolonial countries, and thus accelerate the downfall of imperialism, or we miss [doing so] and herewith strengthen imperialism and by the same token weaken the power of our movement. . . . The entire Orient looks at our Union as at an experimental field. If in the framework of that Union we solve correctly the national problem in its practical application, [if] we here, in the framework of that Union establish really fraternal relations among the nations, an actual cooperation. . . the entire Orient will see that in our federation it has the banner of liberation, has the advance guard, in the wake of which it must go, and this will be the beginning of the collapse of world imperialism. (*Dvenadcatyj s"ezd* 480)

As an additional consideration he pointed out that "formerly oppressed nations occupy the areas most needed for economic development and the places most important from the point of view of military strategy" (481).

The national republics were to become showcases of these developments. Stalin did not conceal that even the small Asiatic Soviet republics carried more weight than the Ukraine in this regard: "If we commit a minor mistake in the Ukraine, this would not be so sensitive a matter for the Orient. But a minor mistake in a small country, an Adjaristan (population 120,000), would create a reaction in Turkey and in the entire East" (659). Nonetheless, the Ukraine was to follow the same path. There the general policy of *korenizacija* (going to national roots) was to become Ukrainianization, even if in Stalin's thinking the process was superfluous.

Stalin's utterances should be supplemented (and in part corrected) by the materials of the Fifth Congress of the Communist International. The congress held three special sessions devoted to the national question, on 30 June and 1 July 1924, at which D. Manuil'skij was the main speaker. The outcome was the adoption of a resolution that focused not on the Orient, but on Central Europe and the Balkans. After stating that "the national question after the World War has acquired a new importance and, at this time, is one of the most essential political questions of Central Europe and the Balkans" (*Cinquième congrès* 427), the resolution devoted a separate section to the Ukrainian question in Poland, Czecho-Slovakia, and Romania, which began: "The Ukrainian question is one of the most important national questions in Central Europe" (430). One overall solution should be sought for the Ukrainian lands occupied by the three states: just as colonial movements in Asia and Africa were regarded as crucial for the coveted collapse of the great Western states, so the Ukrainian question would be the key to the dissolution of Poland, Czecho-Slovakia, and Romania. The ultimate goal of the policy adopted by the congress was the unification of all the West Ukrainian lands with the Ukrainian SSR. Kaganovič, already in charge of the Ukraine, expressed the new principle thus: "If for Oriental nations the Uzbek, Turkmen and Kazakh republics can and must be the model, for the Western nationalities the Ukraine must serve as an example and a model of solving the problems of national liberation of oppressed masses by the proletariat'' (*Budivnyctvo* 41; also pp. 42, 50).

In 1925 these problems became more acute. On the one hand, in the bitter struggle within the CPSU Stalin needed support from every quarter, including the not very numerous national communists (he did receive the support of Skrypnyk; e.g., Skrypnyk 114); it was not by chance that Zinov'ev, his main opponent at the Fourteenth Party Congress in December 1925, made overtures to these same ''comrades'' (*Dvenadcatyj s"ezd* 604). On the other hand, the international situation, with the formation of S. Baldwin's conservative, anti-Soviet government in England (1923) and the conclusion of the Treaty of Locarno (1 December 1925), was perceived in the Soviet Union as the beginning of an encirclement by enemies. Finally, events in Poland, which in 1926 led to the coup of J. Piłsudski, could have had some importance specifically for the Ukraine.

It was in the wake of these internal and, especially, external events that the Ukrainian minority in the CPU found itself tolerated and even encouraged in its long-dreamed-of policy of Ukrainianization. The fact that this policy was most strongly motivated by circumstances outside the Ukraine, that even internally motivation came more from within the CPSU than from within the CPU, and that, in any case, it did not arise as any popular movement, explains its strengths and weaknesses as well as the relative ease with which it would later be discontinued. The policy did not reflect a movement of Ukrainians against Moscow, but, to a great extent, represented just another turn in the policy of the Kremlin. As Petljura prophetically wrote in a letter to M. Šumyc'kyj (3 November 1923): ''In general the affair of Ukrainianization makes the impression of a certain tactical move on the part of Bolsheviks; if it does not yield the desired outcomes, it will soon be abandoned'' (2, 542).

In anticipation of the decisions of the Twelfth Congress of the CPSU, the Seventh Conference of the CPU (4–10 April 1923) spoke of ''the complete independence of the Soviet republics in their national-cultural development and sufficient independent action in economics'' (*Rezoljuciji* 221). In April 1925, at its plenary session, the Central Committee of the CPU gave a broad survey of the state of Ukrainianization, and in June 1926, at the next plenary session, it issued ''Theses on the results of Ukrainianization,'' which would serve as political guidelines for the next five years. Afterwards there was hardly any major meeting of the CPU in which these problems did not figure prominently. One indirect testimony to the importance they had is the speech of S. Kosior, First Secretary of the Central Committee, at the November 1928 plenary session of the Central Committee of the CPSU. That was the year collectivization of the peasantry had been undertaken. Kosior devoted 13 pages of text to the collectivization, and 34 pages to Ukrainianization (Kosior 21ff.).

No less attention was given to Ukrainianization by the government. Of basic import were the decree of the All-Ukrainian Central Executive Committee and the CPC on 30 April 1925, "On measures for the speedy completion of Ukrainianization in the Soviet State machinery," and the decree of the CPC on 16 July 1925, "On practical measures for the Ukrainianization of the Soviet State machinery" (*Zbirnyk uzakonen'*, 6 June 1925, no. 26, pp. 202f.; 10 August 1925, no. 56, pp. 653ff.). They were supplemented by several others concerning specific matters: e.g., "On the form for texts (signboards) on buildings of Soviet institutions," of 10 October 1925; "On the order for installing, on the territory of the Ukrainian SSR, signboards, inscriptions, letterheads, seals, and labels in Ukrainian," of 31 December 1925 (*Zbirnyk uzakonen'* 78, 1925, pp. 653, 983—viddil I; 27, pp. 486, 483f.—viddil II); "On the Ukrainianization of clerical work at the commodity exchanges," of 15 June 1926 (Durdenevskij 158). In 1926 the People's Commissariat of Education published a whole book of decrees and directions, entitled *Ukrajinizacija radjans'kyx ustanov* (*Dekrety, instrukciji i materijaly*, no. 2, Kharkiv). All the decrees and laws were summarized and reconfirmed in the extensive "Regulations on securing the equality of languages and on assistance to the development of Ukrainian culture," dated 6 July 1927 (Durdenevskij 145–54).

If one compares party resolutions and government decrees of 1925 to 1927 with those of preceding years, some important differences in phrasing and content become obvious. In 1919, "all local languages are declared equal in their rights" (*Sobranie uzakonenij* 1919, 23, p. 347); in 1920, it is stated that "the Ukrainian language should be used alongside the Great Russian one" (*Sobranie uzakonenij* 1920, 1, p. 5); in 1923 this is explicitly rejected: "The formal equality of the two languages most widespread in the Ukraine, Ukrainian and Russian, as applied so far is insufficient" (*Zbirnyk uzakonen'* 1923, 19, 914). Now the exclusive use of Ukrainian is required of all civil servants, to begin not later than 1 January 1926; those who cannot or do not want to comply must be fired (*Zbirnyk uzakonen'* 1925, 26, 381); no one who does not have a command of Ukrainian is to be employed in any government office; everyone who applies as a student at a university, institute, or college should pass an examination in the Ukrainian language (Durdenevskij 149).

The very motivation for Ukrainianization had changed. Previously the impetus was the necessity of accommodating the peasantry (as shown in part 1, chap. 5). Even in June 1923, the association of the Ukrainian language with the countryside was preeminent. The resolution passed by the June 22 plenary session of the Central Committee of the CPU contained such stipulations as "In organs of the provincial [party] committees, materials concerning work in the countryside, both official and by local authors, must be published in Ukrainian"; also, "The work of conferences of delegates, [and] of circles and discussions (*spivbesidy*) in villages, should be conducted in the Ukrainian language" (*Kul'turne budivnyctvo* 231f.). The clear implication was that party life beyond the countryside was to proceed in Russian, as before.

Now such use of Russian was being rejected outright, as implying the inferiority of Ukrainian culture and language and its imminent withering away in confrontation with the superior Russian culture and language; the latter was assumed in the "theory of the conflict of two cultures" allegedly launched by D. Lebed' (see part 1, chap. 5), who was removed from the Ukraine at the same time as Kviring, in 1925.[1]

---

[1] The "theory" incriminated to Lebed' was stated in his article "Nekotorye voprosy partijnogo s"ezda," published in *Kommunist*, 17 March 1923, no. 59. Its main thesis was: "The active Ukrainianization of the Party and consequently of the working class (the Party cannot undertake it without also transferring it onto the working class) would now be a reactionary measure in relation to the interests of cultural advancement, because artificial introduction of the Ukrainian language in the Party and in the working class with the present political, economic, and cultural interrelation between the city and the countryside would mean taking the position of the lower culture of the countryside in comparison to the superior culture of the city."

Lebed' recommended that the Ukrainian language be admitted where the Ukrainian peasant wanted it, but no further. He envisaged the future engulfment of the Ukrainian language and culture by the Russian ones.

The first strong reaction to these views came from O. Šums'kyj, in his article "Po povodu odnoj formuly," to which Lebed' answered in the article "Pomen'še pospešnosti"; both appeared in *Kommunist*, 4 April 1923, no. 78.

In 1926, the identification of the Ukrainian culture and language with the village was flatly rejected (e.g., by Zatons'kyj—*Budivnyctvo* 12), as was any assertion of the superior character of the Russian culture and language. Zatons'kyj declared that such contentions were based on a false identification of the Russian culture with the proletariat and the Ukrainian one with the peasantry (*Budivnyctvo* 16). When Skrypnyk was reproached for the suppression of the Russian language in the Ukraine—which must have been a reference to the situation in the cities—he responded that there was no such suppression, because "in *rajony*, in the countryside" party and state machinery operated in Russian if the *rajon* or the village were Russian (Skrypnyk 55). This followed the resolution of the Central Committee of the CPU (of 19 July 1927) suggesting that *rajony* with such a national minority must have enough "agricultural literature in Russian, which takes into account peculiarities in the agricultural work of Russian peasants in the Ukraine" (*Budivnyctvo* 204). Both Skrypnyk and the Central Committee were silent about the policy of Ukrainianization aimed at the retreat of the Russian language from the cities, and the summary regulations of 6 July 1927 bluntly state that cities and towns could not be made into separate "national-territorial administrative units" (§ 8, Durdenevskij 146). Some unpublished circulars on the matter must also have been sent out; for instance, in the Artemivs'k district (Donec'k region) there was a requirement that 75 percent of books purchased by libraries be in Ukrainian (Xvylja 1930, 40).

Theoretical foundations for the policy of Ukrainianization are few in the programmatic party documents of the time. This is hardly surprising, for it is indeed difficult to reconcile the policy with the Communist program as a whole, in which all national problems are only of tactical interest. Thus L. Kaganovič, the factual supervisor if not the major proponent of the policy, in his programmatic report at the Tenth Congress of the CPU (November 1927), could only refer to the international situation and to "our answer to the imperialists and their henchmen, the petty-bourgeois democrats" (*Budivnyctvo* 150). Implicitly, this constituted recognition of the tactical nature of Ukrainianization.

The practical measures that made up Ukrainianization concerned the use of the Ukrainian language in the state machinery, on the one hand, and in culture, in the broad sense, on the other. Of course, in both areas, this entailed the de-Russification of the cities and industrial centers and affected only the urban centers of the country. The countryside did not need any Ukrainianization. The entire policy was centralized and conducted from the Central Commission for Ukrainianization of state institutions, headed by V. Čubar, chairman of the CPC. The Commission was founded on 16 July 1925, and branches were established in the administrative centers of the country (*Zbirnyk uzakonen'* 1925, 26, 384).

Ukrainianization was compulsory for all state officials. Every official was required to pass an examination in the Ukrainian language and culture. For those who did not know Ukrainian or knew it insufficiently, special courses were organized. At the beginning such courses were free, but instruction was scheduled for two hours after the regular work day; from 1927 those lagging behind in Ukrainianization had to pay for their instruction (Regulations of 6 July 1927, § 65, Durdenevskij 153). Those who evaded or, after completing the course, still failed an examination were to be fired without any unemployment compensation (ibid., § 72). Those who passed were required to use Ukrainian in all written correspondence and in all oral communications with Ukrainian visitors and parties (*Ukrajinizacija* 12, 23, passim). All courses of instruction in Ukrainian were under the supervision of so-called Central Courses of Ukrainian Subjects (*Central'ni kursy ukrajinoznavstva*) organized in Kharkiv, which established programs of instruction and sent inspectors to check on how the Ukrainianization measures were being implemented in various offices and institutions.

The language of the army remained basically Russian. Yet besides the Ukraine's two schools for Red Army officers, one in Kharkiv and the other in Kiev, a Cavalry Corps of Red Cossacks was organized in Hajsyn, Podolia. Skrypnyk demanded that the army be reorganized into territorial units bound to the area from which the recruits came (Majstrenko 115f.), but little was done in this regard.

In education, the success of Ukrainianization in the elementary schools (grades one through four) was stunning. While in 1922 the number of Ukrainian schools was 6,105 and those Ukrainian in part (i.e., Russian-Ukrainian) was 1,966, in 1925 the numbers were 10,774 and 1,128, respectively (the totals were 12,109 in 1922 and 15,209 in 1925; *Ukrajinizacija* 62). By 1930 the number of Ukrainian elementary schools had again jumped, to 14,430 vs. 1,504 Russian schools; for seven-grade schools, the numbers were 1,732 vs. 267 (Skrypnyk

210f.). In all non-Ukrainian schools, the Ukrainian language was taught as a subject. According to Siropolko (25), by the end of 1927, 77 percent of elementary school students were Ukrainian, a figure almost equaling the percentage of Ukrainians in the population (80.1 percent).

The change was less dynamic in other types of schools, but it was definitely noticeable. Among professional schools, the number of Ukrainian schools equaled 65.8 percent, supplemented by 16 percent Ukrainian-Russian and 5.3 percent Russian-Ukrainian schools (as of 1 November 1929; Siropolko 61). For workshop schools (*fabzavuč*) even the most rigid laws on Ukrainianization, the regulations of 6 July 1927 that had demanded the use of Ukrainian in all schools, were more lenient, insisting only on the "native language" of students (Durdenevskij 149). Nonetheless, even the vocational schools numbered 42 Ukrainian, 48 Russian, and 100 bilingual (Siropolko 72). The so-called workers' faculties (three- or four-year courses designed to prepare little-educated workers to enter schools of higher education) were, at the same time, 48 Ukrainian, 7 Russian, and 18 bilingual (Siropolko 77). Institutes of higher education numbered 14 Ukrainian, 2 Russian, and 23 bilingual (Siropolko 92). By speciality, the numbers were as follows: agricultural—3 Ukrainian, 6 bilingual; pedagogical—6 Ukrainian, 4 bilingual; technological and medical—2 Ukrainian, 2 Russian, and 7 bilingual (Siropolko 204). According to Skrypnyk (184), by 1929 the institutes were up to 30 percent Ukrainianized. But one must keep in mind that in most bilingual schools of higher and industrial education the most important subjects were more often than not taught in Russian, whereas Ukrainian was used to teach such marginal subjects as political education and the like.

The Ukrainianization of the press reached 68.8 percent in 1930, and 87.5 percent in 1932 (Siropolko 191). Landmark events were the Ukrainianization of the central organ of the Central Committee of the CPU, *Komunist*, on 16 June 1926; the founding of the Ukrainian newspaper for industrial workers, *Proletar*, in 1926; and the Ukrainianization of the *oblast'* newspaper in Odessa, *Čornomors'ka komuna*, previously entitled *Izvestija* (31 August 1929; Skrypnyk 134f., 142, 148). According to Majstrenko (112), in 1930 only three major newspapers in the Ukraine were still published in Russian: in Odessa (the important *Večernie izvestija*), in Stalino, and in Marijupol' (now Ždanov). In 1930 the circulation of *Komunist* was 122,000; of

Proletar, 79,000; of *Visti*, 90,000; yet that of *Radjans'ke selo*, geared
to the peasantry, reached 600,000 (Skrypnyk 24). Factory newspapers
were 63.4 percent Ukrainian-language in 1930. In some instances the
Ukrainianization drive brought about cut-backs in circulation, and in
others, its growth (e.g., in Kryvyj Rih; Kosior 27).

The number of journals grew quickly, and so did their differentiation by types. The traditional literary and political "thick" journals
represented by *Červonyj šljax* alone from 1923 now included regional
publications (*Žyttja j revoljucija* in Kiev, *Zorja* in Dnipropetrovs'k,
Metalevi dni in Odessa, *Literaturnyj Donbas* in Artemivs'k-Stalino),
and those representing specific literary organizations (*VAPLite,
Literaturnyj jarmarok, Prolitfront*—the group led by M. Xvyl'ovyj,
Nova generacija—the futurist group of M. Semenko, *Zaxidnja Ukrajina, Molodnjak, Hart*—the All-Ukrainian Union of Proletarian Writers, etc.). Various other types of journals proliferated, among them
political, technological, theatrical, scholarly, illustrated, popular, and
journals of music, as well as those of literary criticism, of the cinema,
of satire and humor. The total number of Ukrainian journal titles
reached 326 in 1929 (Siropolko 191).

In book production, publications in Ukrainian constituted 45.8 percent in 1925/26, 53.9 percent in 1927/28, and 76.9 percent in 1931,
according to Siropolko (184). According to Skrypnyk (212), in 1931
Ukrainian titles comprised 65.3 percent of publications, while in circulation they were 77 percent. The difference, clearly, was due to
mass publications in Ukrainian. Among scholarly books, up to 50
percent were published in Ukrainian; among textbooks for higher education, up to 79.4 percent were in Ukrainian.

Russian theater, including opera, was practically expelled from the
Ukraine. Major theatrical buildings in downtown urban areas were
assigned to Ukrainian companies that had previously performed in
peripheral and often poor locales. Sometimes these measures encoun-
tered resistance, e.g., by the Odessa opera, with its long-standing
Italian and Russian tradition. In 1931 there were in the country 66
Ukrainian theater companies, 12 Jewish, and 9 Russian (*EU* 2, 3328).
The production of Ukrainian cinema grew markedly (36 films in
1928), and Ukrainian radio began to broadcast (in 1924/25).

After many lean years, the budget of the Ukrainian Academy of
Arts and Sciences in Kiev soared. Although technical publishing
facilities were still inadequate, the Academy published 46 books in

1925 (*Zvidomlennja za 1926*, 5, 11), 75 in 1926 (ibid., 125ff.), 93 in 1927 (*Zvidomlennja za 1927*), 90 in 1928, and 136 in 1929 (*EU 2*, 3336). The staff of the Academy increased at a roughly equivalent rate.

Ukrainianization crossed the frontiers of the Ukrainian SSR to touch the millions of Ukrainians who lived in other Soviet republics, especially Russia. The movement was particularly successful in the Kuban' region, but in some other places, too, Ukrainian schools, Ukrainian newspapers, and Ukrainian clubs were founded.

The main goal, however, was clearly the de-Russification of the cities and industrial centers of the Ukraine. Unrelentingly, and often blindly, the heavy machinery of the totalitarian state struck against these strongholds of Russian language and culture in the Ukraine. At the beginning of the Ukrainianization drive, individual voices spoke out, demanding that the workers be Ukrainianized (e.g., V. Zatons'kyj, 1926—*Budivnyctvo* 13f.; Xvyl'ovyj 1926—Shevelov 1978, 40). The demand was risky as a slogan, because it implied that Ukrainianization was not desired by the proletariat, but imposed on it. Yet such slogans did appear in the provincial press, e.g., the Stalino-district newspaper *Diktatura truda* (published in Russian!) carried phrases like "acceleration of the Ukrainianization of the masses" and urged the government "to push forward the actual Ukrainianization of the proletariat of the Donbas" (quoted from Xvylja 1930, 49f.).

It was Skrypnyk who rescued the situation, with his theory that Russian-language workers in the Ukraine formed two groups: those who were Ukrainian by origin but were partly Russianized and spoke a mixture of the two languages; and those who were completely Russian. For the first group, more numerous, Ukrainianization was but a help in their precarious situation of being neither one thing nor the other. The Russian nationality of the second group was to be respected: its members should be attracted to the Ukrainian culture and language by its intrinsic value, without coercion (*Budivnyctvo* 31, 61ff.; Skrypnyk 151). This highly vulnerable thesis was incorporated into the programmatic party documents of the plenary session of the Central Committee of the CPU in June 1926, under the title "On the results of Ukrainianization."[2]

---

[2] Skrypnyk's theory of Ukrainian workers who have forgotten their native tongue is strikingly similar to the "theory" of Romanians who have lost their mother tongue

Coercion was, theoretically, admissible only in relation to state officials and only when they were on duty. In reality, however, Ukrainianization was implemented (and probably conceived) as a frontal offensive against the language and cultural pursuits of the cities. In undertaking to Ukrainianize this or that newspaper, and in all other measures, it was impossible to distinguish between the two groups of workers, not to speak of the overall infeasibility of assigning individuals to only one of the two groups (for instance, even workers of Russian descent spoke Russian with some Ukrainian admixture). And, of course, no one asked the members of the nominally Ukrainian group whether they wanted to return to their original, allegedly pure Ukrainian environment. Some sense of the workers' attitude is contained in reports of a poll organized among workers of Artemivs'k, in the Donec'k region (Kosior 1929, 25). Eighty-four persons were questioned about their attitude toward Ukrainianization. Their responses to the initial questions showed that 49 understood Ukrainian well and 14, poorly—from which it follows (though this was not stated explicitly) that 21 (or 25 percent) did not understand Ukrainian at all; 35 could read Ukrainian, 19 could write Ukrainian, 18 could speak the language fluently, and 2 could speak it poorly. Eighteen subscribed to Ukrainian newspapers, and 24 read Ukrainian books and journals. In response to the prime question, 59 said—probably reflecting some preliminary indoctrination by the press and radio— that it was desirable to organize discussion groups on Ukrainian subjects for workers, and 14 wanted Ukrainian books to be less expensive.

Xvylja (1930, 54) quotes an active member of the Komsomol as saying: "I need that Ukrainianization as you [need] the Jewish Talmud!"; he also cites workers who were said to have been in favor of Ukrainianization, among whom some could well have been sincere. The opponents were undoubtedly sincere, but there is no way to determine who and how many the supporters were. After all, Ukrainianization was the official line, a campaign to bring it about was in full swing, and in the communist system, it was easy to solicit the desired response, however insincere.

---

applied in Romanian legislation to justify the Romanization of Bukovyna Ukrainians. See below, chap. 7, section 2.

In world history, during industrialization some cities are known to have changed their language under the impact of the surrounding countryside; for instance, Prague lost its German character, as did Riga and Tallin. But the process usually took at least one generation. The Ukrainian promoters of Ukrainianization must have felt pressured to move more quickly, given the industrialization drive launched in November 1926, at the Fifteenth Conference of the All-Union Communist Party, and its supplementation a year later, in December 1927, by the drive to collectivize the peasantry announced at the Fifteenth Congress of the CPSU. They knew that the industrial centers of the Ukraine had to become Ukrainian before the mass migration of peasants into the cities if the newcomers were to avoid becoming subsumed in the urban Russian-speaking environment. In their zeal, party members, bolstered by the Bolsheviks' traditional conviction that the masses are pliable and that coercion and fear are the foundation of politics, applied coercion bordering on violence. Occasionally they showed surprising naïveté. One example of the latter is the request of Kosior (23) addressed to party members: "At meetings, conferences, encounters with your comrades—do speak Ukrainian." Ironically, it recalls a similar appeal attributed to S. Petljura (2, 372) ten years earlier (see part 1, chap. 3).

The impact of the policy of Ukrainianization on the status and prestige of the Ukrainian language was complex and often contradictory. Xvyl'ovyj's declaration that "Ukrainianization . . . is the result of the invincible will of a nation of thirty million" (Shevelov 1978, 17) was at best wishful thinking. Launched from Moscow, taken up and directed by the Communist party with its specific methods, Ukrainianization met with sympathy and support from some groups of the Ukrainian population and a cautious neutrality from some others. In the party itself, the policy was promoted by a minority. According to the official data, Ukrainians formed 37 percent of the party in 1925 and 47 percent in 1926 ("Tezy CK KP(b)U," June 1926. *Budivnyctvo* 61). The increase should be viewed with caution: in those years Ukrainians were often being advanced faster than non-Ukrainians, and many a careerist could profitably declare himself to be a Ukrainian without being one. How many of these old and new Ukrainians genuinely supported Ukrainianization? There are many statements to the effect that resistance to Ukrainianization was strong within the party (e.g., Čubar, *Budivnyctvo* 37), in the trade unions (see, e.g.,

Kosior 1929, 26), and in the state institutions; moreover, there is evidence that even during the years of Ukrainianization, Ukrainians in the party experienced harassment (e.g., Šums'kyj, 1927—*Budivnyctvo* 134). There were charges that Ukrainianization was merely an artificial camouflage which too often was in the hands of non-Ukrainians (e.g., Šums'kyj 1927, Čubar 1926—*Budivnyctvo* 135, 37). Finally, the Ukraine's Russian minority, which in the large cities and industrial centers was often the majority, tried (with a few exceptions) to ignore or circumvent the policy whenever possible.

As a result, the effects of Ukrainianization were far from straightforward. On the one hand, more people than ever mastered Ukrainian and became to some extent familiar with Ukrainian literature and culture; some of them even switched to speaking in Ukrainian. The Ukrainian language was heard more frequently in the streets of the major cities, although in none did Ukrainian replace Russian as the vehicle for everyday communication. On the other hand, the aura of coercion and artificiality accompanying the policy aroused hostility. The number of derisive jokes about the Ukrainian language (which, unfortunately, have never been collected or published) ran high.

The social basis for the policy of Ukrainianization was thin; in fact, it comprised only the Ukrainian intelligentsia that belonged to or sympathized with the Communist party. The proletariat and the middle class were at best indifferent. There was also no overt enthusiasm on the part of the peasantry, but this fact should not be misinterpreted. In those social and cultural spheres that were not yet in party hands, e.g., in the church, Ukrainianization progressed vehemently and rapidly. Founded in October 1921, after several years of groundwork, the Ukrainian Autocephalous Orthodox Church (UAOC) became influential and grew very fast, in both rural and non-rural settings. In 1927 it had about 1,050 parishes (Vlasovs'kyj 151) vs. 8,324 traditional Russian ones (Curtiss 223, with reference to *Antireligioznik* 1929, 4, 115). Most of the Ukrainian parishes were very active and found support among the population.

The Ukrainian church was strong in the Podolia, Kiev, Poltava, and Černihiv regions. On the other hand, Kharkiv had only 12 parishes, Dnipropetrovs'k–Zaporižžja had 29, Odessa–Mykolajiv–Kherson had 6 (Vlasovs'kyj 152). The number of parishes belonging to the UAOC was only 11 percent of all parishes (ibid., 154). But one has to take into account that the Ukrainian church had grown rapidly, that its beginning was non-canonical, that it had married bishops, and that it was constantly being chicaned and persecuted by the regime (ibid., 155ff.). In addition, the number of Ukrainian parishes increases if one considers that in addition to the UAOC there were two other Ukrainian church organizations: the Ukrainian Autocephalous Church headed by Feofil Buldovs'kyj (ibid., 194), and the so-called Active Christ Church, which the Soviet authorities supported in its activity against the Ukrainian Orthodox Autocephalous Church (ibid., 164).

Another channel into which peasants' energy was directed was the cooperative movement. In 1928 there were 41,734 cooperatives, which carried on 74 percent of the retail trade (*EU* 2, 1126). Some unions of cooperatives, such as *Vukopspilka* and *Sil's'kyj hospodar*, were large and influential.

Neither the UAOC nor the rural cooperatives needed any Ukrainianization. They were Ukrainian in their very essence, as was the mass of Ukrainian peasantry. In fact, while supporting or promoting their church and cooperatives, the peasants appeared indifferent to official Ukrainianization. Whether a *Narkomfin* wrote a letter to a *Narkomjust* in Ukrainian or in Russian was a matter of little concern to the peasants, and most of them cared little about the language used in Communist propaganda.

A potential source of support of Ukrainianization was the Ukrainian intelligentsia not aligned to the party, especially scholars, teachers, and writers. The return of the emigrants M. Hruševs'kyj, M. Voronyj, V. Samijlenko, and many others in 1924 – 1926 exemplified the will of these groups to cooperate with the new policy. But the Soviet regime was paranoically suspicious of any initiatives in the policy of Ukrainianization coming from outside the party. Studying the chronology of events in the Ukraine gives one the impression that every escalation of Ukrainianization brought about the destruction of a Ukrainian force or of a potential Ukrainian force.

The first blows fell on party members who genuinely supported the policy. The attacks on the "nationalist deviations" of M. Ravič-Čerkasskij (a Jewish historian of the Ukrainian Communist party, as opposed to the official Communist Party of the Ukraine) in 1923 – 1924 (Majstrenko 101), the repression of M. Xvyl'ovyj in 1925, initiated by Stalin himself, the purge of the virtually all-Communist editorial board of *Červonyj šljax* in 1926 (*Budivnyctvo* 101), the banishment of Šums'kyj and Hryn'ko to Russia in

1926–1927, the liquidation of the historian M. Javors'kyj and his school in 1930 (Polons'ka 1, 66) were among the many such measures undertaken. In 1930, Skrypnyk announced the unmasking of nine (specifically nine!) "counterrevolutionary organizations" (Skrypnyk 222).

From 1927–1928 on, intellectuals who were not party members became targets of the attacks. The fate of the Ukrainian intellectuals connected with the Ukrainian Academy of Sciences in Kiev is well documented. Until 1926–1927 scholars affiliated with the Academy and their researchers were paid by the state and were relatively free to pursue their work. A new approach was introduced by Skrypnyk himself. During a visit to the Academy in 1927, he ordered the dismissal of two academicians, K. Xarlampovyč and F. Myščenko (Polons'ka 1, 53). About the same time (March 1927), P. Ljubčenko demanded that the Academy be completely Sovietized (*Budivnyctvo* 131ff.), and a little later L. Kaganovič called that it be "freed from bourgeois influences" (*Budivnyctvo* 152). The party assigned young Communists to study under Academy members without even asking the latter's consent (Polons'ka 1, 51). In 1928, seven party men were imposed on the assembly of the Academy (ibid., 54). The newly reelected secretary of the Academy, A. Kryms'kyj, who was also one of its founders, was removed from that post (ibid., 55). In 1929, the CPC declared that henceforth candidates to the Academy would be nominated by the public and not by the Academy members themselves. As a result, on 28 June 1929, at a session open to the public, under intense pressure and in a voice vote, seven party candidates of high rank, including Skrypnyk, were elected to the Academy (ibid., 61). As early as July 1928, the Academy declared its readiness to work within the Five-year Plan (ibid., 56), and in 1929 it entered into "socialist competition" with the Belorussian Academy (ibid., 63).

With the addition of "new blood," the time had come to purge the Academy of the old "bourgeois-nationalist" influence. In the summer of 1929, all voluntary scientific societies affiliated with the Academy were disbanded (Polons'ka 2, 119). At the same time, scores of the Academy's associates were arrested, including the chairman of its Ruling Board and its actual *spiritus movens*, S. Jefremov. There followed the arrests of, it is estimated, several thousand people who were indirectly connected with the Academy or who had engaged in the national liberation movement of 1917–1920. Thus, the background was set for the highly publicized court trial of "traitors," "bourgeois agents," and "nationalistic wreckers" allegedly united in a counterrevolutionary *Sojuz vyzvolennja Ukrajiny* (SVU), or "Union for the Liberation of the Ukraine" (9 March – 19 April 1930). Of the 45 individuals put on trial (others were sentenced without a trial), 29 were affiliated with the Academy (Polons'ka 1, 74). In effect, these actions crushed the Academy and the intelligentsia of the Ukraine who had participated in the fight for the country's liberation some ten years before. In early 1931, the reprisals continued, bringing banishment of the other pillar of the Academy, M. Hruševs'kyj, to Russia (where he died in unclear circumstances) and the final dismissal and arrest of A. Kryms'kyj. The publications of the Academy were suspended. All work in the humanities was charged with being "bourgeois national-ist," while the sciences were directed to undertake the technical tasks posed by industrialization.

In literature the apolitical "neoclassicists" were forcibly silenced. The writers' organizations VAPLite in Kharkiv and MARS in Kiev were forced into "self-dissolution" (1927, 1929) and "self-criticism," and many of their members were persecuted. To counter-balance the influence of these organizations, new "proletarian" organizations were founded under the protectorate of the party. Two such organizations were ostentatiously greeted by L. Kaganovič at the Tenth Congress of the CPU in November 1927 (*Budivnyctvo* 152): "Molodnjak" (1926) and VUSPP (All-Ukrainian Union of Proletarian Writers, January 1927). Devoting their work entirely to party pro-paganda, the members of these organizations produced a large quan-tity of writings, none of which had any literary value. Analogous developments took place in theater, music, and the arts. Čubar stated in June 1926 (*Budivnyctvo* 39) that Ukrainian culture and its indispensable vehicle, the Ukrainian language, would attract the popu-lation, especially city-dwellers, by its high achievements. Yet every-thing possible was done to preclude such achievements, so that Ukrainian writings were identified as low-level pieces of propaganda. Similar developments took place in Russian culture, but there not all artistic or cultural achievements were eliminated. Whether this differ-ence was due to a deliberate policy or to the lower cultural level of the Communist rulers in the Ukraine is a moot question.

Simultaneously with the "proletarization" of Ukrainian culture, all manifestations of "spontaneous" Ukrainianization met with severe reprisals. In ecclesiastical matters, the year 1928 brought the arrest of Metropolitan Vasyl' Lypkivs'kyj, all the bishops, and many priests of the UAOC. By 1931, that church, as a separate entity, was completely destroyed and, by the same token, the Ukrainian language eliminated from church use. In the cooperative movement, restrictions began in 1927. Soon direct interference by the government in the form of high taxation and similar measures crushed what had been the relatively independent Ukrainian cooperatives (*EU* 1, 1127). This meant further limitations on the use of the Ukrainian language in the economic realm.

Thus, Ukrainianization was actually a two-sided process. Measures aimed at spreading the Ukrainian language were paralleled by measures aimed at degrading the Ukrainian culture and language. The latter measures spread fear among the population. Speaking Ukrainian publicly, though officially encouraged, was in general considered to be risky, unless an occasion was explicitly designed to be conducted in Ukrainian. The stigma attached to the use of Ukrainian in the large cities did not dissipate;[3] instead, it acquired new dimensions. Well-educated people were to speak Ukrainian in public when prescribed, but not spontaneously. Those who wanted to succeed were expected to pass examinations in Ukrainian, but not to use it any more than required.

Occasionally Russian chauvinism was exposed and counteracted, and its perpetrators were persecuted. Among such cases were those of M. Romanovskij, theater reviewer for Russian newspapers in Kharkiv, who was charged with hinting at the alleged inferiority of Ukrainian culture (Skrypnyk 62ff.); A. Malickij, a professor of law who ridiculed Ukrainianization (Majstrenko 138); the Odessa Philharmonic Society (Skrypnyk 89ff., 144), which disdained Ukrainian music. But no exponent of anti-Ukrainian, pro-Russian views was legally persecuted. In the worst scenario, they were publicly criticized

---

[3] Note the resolution of the CPC of 1 December 1925: "Some functionaries know the Ukrainian language but are ashamed of using it" (*Ukrajinizacija* 62); Zatons'kyj, in 1926, noted the same in relation to industrial workers (*Budivnyctvo* 14). There is no way to establish where the shame ended and the fear began.

and dismissed, whereupon they left for Russia and obtained good positions there.

The most publicized case was that of D. Lebed', who was transferred from the Ukraine to Russia in 1925. Although thereafter often criticized in the Ukrainian press, Lebed' used a new post in Russia to fuel the anti-Ukrainian side of Ukrainianization. In 1928 he published in the organ of the Central Committee of the CPSU an article on "the theory of the conflict of two cultures," a theory he was credited with devising. There he contended that any surviving Russifying tendency constituted no immediate danger in the Ukraine, whereas that "which knocks on the door, the elemental force (*stixija*) of Ukrainian *kulak* chauvinism, today requires special attention" (Lebed' 1928, 87).

Torn from its only real potential social basis, imposed by a non-Ukrainian party and state machine, deprived of sincerity and spontaneity, consistently counterbalanced by anti-Ukrainian measures, Ukrainianization appeared to the average Russian or pro-Russian city dweller as a kind of comedy, occasionally having some dramatic overtones but still above all a comedy. He learned in what circumstances and to what degree he had to reckon with this official façade, he learned that these were relatively limited and small, and he learned that it was wise not to transgress the boundaries. He knew that, by law, those officials who did not have a command of Ukrainian were to be fired; he also knew that whereas a messenger, a typist, or a secretary was occasionally dismissed on these grounds, the high functionaries, or *specy*, were in practice excused from Ukrainianization. He knew that whereas signboards were scheduled to be redone in Ukrainian (by the resolution of the CPC of 3 October 1925— *Ukrajinizacija* 14), behind the façade the old Russian bureaucratic machine continued to exist (cf. Kosior 29).

The city dwellers who actually discovered for themselves the Ukrainian language and culture and wholeheartedly embraced them were most clearly a minority. For the majority, Ukrainianization was but a mimicry, a pretense, a ruse. One small example epitomizes their attitude and the situation. An issue of the *mnogotiražka* (internal circular) *Za radjans'ku akademiju* (1931, no. 9 [11]) printed for the Ukrainian Academy of Sciences in Kiev, supposedly the foremost exponent of Ukrainian culture and the stronghold of the Ukrainian language, carried a front-page appeal by five academicians to join in the spirit of socialist competition. The text was accompanied by portraits of the signatories and facsimiles of their signatures. The appeal was in Ukrainian and the names typeset under the portraits were in Ukrainian transcription: *Symins'kyj, Je. Paton, Fomin, Plotnikov.* The signatures, however, read *Siminskij* and *E. Paton*—both Russian forms—and *Fomin* and *Plotnikov*—written with *i vos'meričnoe* (Russian *и*). It was obvious that the appeal had been put together in Russian, and that for publication it had donned a Ukrainian guise, or else that the academicians, for whatever reason, deliberately chose to sign it in Russian.

In some industrial centers even the guise of Ukrainianization was ferociously resisted. As late as 1930, in Artemivs'k (the Donec'k region), out of 8,323 clerks, 3,681 (44.2 percent) did not comply with the orders to Ukrainianize, and 796 succeeded in being excused. In the industrial centers of the Stalino (now Donec'k) district, out of 92 elementary schools, only 2 were Ukrainian; none of the higher schools were Ukrainian (Xvylja 1930, 40, 47). As one of the workers said: "We talk a lot about the Ukrainian language; it is high time to try to talk *in* Ukrainian. I advise our union to conduct the first general meeting of workers in Ukrainian" (ibid., 51). The implication, of course, is that until that time (mid-1930) no such meetings were conducted in Ukrainian.

These situations show that all too often, in the large cities and industrial centers the use of the Ukrainian language was no more than a pretense. When it came to important events, Russian was used consistently. In such circumstances, a derisive attitude toward the Ukrainian language became widespread. One of the most frequent anti-Ukrainian jokes was to ask: "Do you speak seriously or in Ukrainian?"

A coercive administrative campaign could hardly succeed in transforming Russian and pro-Russian city speakers into Ukrainians. This was even less possible in the milieu of a two-faced, contradictory policy which, on the one hand, encouraged and required the use of Ukrainian and, on the other hand, viewed any sincere personal move in that direction as suspect and dangerous. Šums'kyj was perspicacious enough to declare, as early as in November 1926, that "forced Ukrainianization of the state machinery is nonsense" (*Budivnyctvo* 107). Xvyl'ovyj had one of the characters in his novel *Val'dšnepy* (published in 1927) call Ukrainianization "idiotic" and "a drag on social processes'' (Shevelov 1978, 44).

The successes of Ukrainianization, if any, lay elsewhere. Passive mastery of Ukrainian, though still not universal, now encompassed much broader circles. No statistics are available, but it is beyond any doubt that the number of people interested in Ukrainian culture grew substantially. Probably some intellectuals who under different circumstances would have worked within Russian culture opted, instead, for the Ukrainian one. One such individual was Ivan Kaljannikov, who became the Ukrainian poet Kaljannyk (and was later liquidated as an "Ukrainian nationalist"). No doubt more such cases can be uncovered and documented. Finally, the policy of Ukrainianization left an indelible imprint on the normalization of the standard Ukrainian language.

A rapid upsurge in the publication of manuals and textbooks of the Ukrainian language characterizes the years of Ukrainianization. Their circulation was unprecedentedly high. In fact, the compilation and publication of such materials became highly lucrative. According to an incomplete listing given in Červins'ka and Dykyj, in 1925 – 1928, 60 textbooks and manuals of Ukrainian were published in the Ukrainian SSR (each edition was counted as one item). These included textbooks for various school grades as well as self-instruction manuals. Many of these appeared in several editions. Presumably, the number of published textbooks climbed even higher in 1929 – 1931, after rules for Ukrainian orthography were published. Some of these books were written or compiled by outstanding linguists, such as O. Kurylo, O. Synjavs'kyj, and M. Sulyma.

The years 1925 – 1928 also saw the publication of two new Ukrainian-Russian dictionaries and four Russian-Ukrainian ones, some of which appeared in several editions. Of the Ukrainian-Russian dictionaries, the most important and interesting was the new edition of B. Hrinčenko's *Slovar ukrajins'koji movy*, edited and supplemented by S. Jefremov and A. Nikovs'kyj. Three volumes appeared, for the letters A – N, in Kiev in 1927 – 1928. Leaving the entire text of the original Hrinčenko dictionary intact, the editors added twentieth-century materials, including many loan words about which Hrinčenko had been very cautious. Thus the new dictionary was planned to be a synthesis of old and new. Unfortunately, it was never completed because the editors became embroiled in the trial of the SVU.

The *Rosijs'ko-ukrajins'kyi slovnyk* the Academy began to publish in 1924 added five more volumes, covering words through the letter P (1927–1933). Editorial techniques had improved considerably in comparison to the first volume. Excessive populism was in part overcome, and the dictionary grew into a representative, reliable, and fairly complete collection of Ukrainian words and idioms. Its novelties were, in the words of the editors, "improvements in differentiation between meanings of Russian and Ukrainian words, more precision in commentary, clearer delimitation of stylistic nuances in the meanings of Ukrainian words and phrases" (II, 1054).

Great emphasis was placed on the compilation of terminological dictionaries. This work was concentrated in the Academy of Sciences, where in 1921 an Institute of the Ukrainian Scientific Language had been founded. The institute comprised five departments (agriculture, technology, society and economy, natural history, arts) and thirty-three sections (Polons'ka 1, 80). In 1926 it occupied 11 editors, 2 philologists, 3 technology experts, 21 paid (irregularly) collaborators and 250 unpaid collaborators, who were responsible to the institute's head, H. Xolodnyj (*Zvidomlennja za 1926*, 14). After the SVU trial (1930), where Xolodnyj was accused of "terminological sabotage" and was condemned, the institute was formally liquidated, but in practice it became (from 1931) part of the Institute of Linguistics. During 1925 to 1932, the Institute of the Ukrainian Scientific Language and its continuator published more than 27 terminological dictionaries (Gregorovich 10ff. lists 27, but the list is incomplete: e.g., *Rosijs'ko-ukrajins'kyj slovnyk vijs'kovoji terminolohiji* by S. and O. Jakubs'kyj [1928], *Slovnyk antropolohičnoji terminolohiji* by A. Nosiv [1931], *Rosijs'ko-ukrajins'kyj slovnyk pravnyčoji movy* edited by A. Kryms'kyj [1926] are not included; according to *Slavjanskoe jazykoznanie* 1, 252ff., the total number of terminological dictionaries then published in the Ukraine was 49). The institute also had contracts to publish 34 more such dictionaries.

Virtually all dictionaries published in 1925–1932 were Russian-Ukrainian or Ukrainian-Russian. There were almost no dictionaries based on languages other than Russian, the single apparent exception being I. Šarovol's'kyj's German-Ukrainian dictionary (1929).

The compilation of terminological dictionaries on private initiative for the most part died, and the work was essentially centralized. This reflected what was probably the most important novelty of the period:

the effort to achieve normalization of the language. In the Academy dictionary this effort manifested itself moderately, mostly in editorial remarks on style accompanying debatable words. Terminological dictionaries were as a rule prescriptive, even though in most cases they were subtitled "Project." Their data were incorporated into school books and "adopted" by general publications. Following their prescriptions was the responsibility of style editors and proofreaders, as decreed by the CPC (*Zbirnyk uzakonen'*, viddil II, 31 December 1927, p. 483). However, the penetration of new terminology into the spoken language, if any, was very limited, due to the general character of Ukrainianization.

Work on normalization of Ukrainian spelling had the most far-reaching and most durable effect. The Academy's "main rules" (*najholovniši pravyla*) were clearly both insufficient and debatable. Some supplements were provided in the *Ukrajins'kyj pravopys* by M. Hruns'kyj and H. Sabaldyr (1925), but it was generally agreed that a thorough revision was needed. Revision of these rules started with the appointment, on 23 July 1925, by the CPC, of a special commission. The commission originally consisted of 36 persons, including ten Academy affiliates and ten prominent Communist party members. Formally, its first chairman was Šums'kyj, Commissar of Education, later succeeded by M. Skrypnyk; in fact, direction was in the hands of O. Synjavs'kyj, an outstanding linguist. The commission undertook to revise and expand the Academy of Sciences' previously published *Najholovniši pravyla ukrajins'koho pravopysu*, approved by the Commissariat of Education in 1921. It was then to present a draft for general discussion and approval by a specially convoked conference and, finally, by the government. It was decided that the commission would establish not only the rules of orthography, but also of morphology (in its written form), of punctuation, and of some elements of orthoepy and accentuation (Synjavs'kyj 94). The guiding principle for the normalization was "the tradition and the nature of the Ukrainian language," with attention to its history (ibid., 95f.). The written rules set down by the commission were edited by A. Kryms'kyj, V. Hancov, and Synjavs'kyj (the orthographic dictionary, by H. Holoskevyč), and then were passed along for final additional editing to Synjavs'kyj.

In August 1926, a draft was printed and made subject to public discussion. About sixty letters proposing changes were received (Synjavs'kyj 98); subsequently a Conference on Spelling (*Pravopysna konferencija*) was convened in Kharkiv, participation in which was by invitation only. It was in session from 25 May through 6 June 1927. The participants were four high functionaries of the Commissariat of Education, five members of the Ukrainian Academy of Sciences, twenty-eight university professors of linguistics and philology, eight teachers, seven journalists, and eight writers (Synjavs'kyj 109). Three participants represented the Western (Polish) Ukraine: K. Studyns'kyj, I. Svjencic'kyj, and V. Simovyč.

The conference was obliged to confront the difficult problem of two orthographic traditions, the Central-East vs. the West Ukrainian. On the question of the rendition of *l* and *g* in loan words (*l* or *l'*, *g* or *h*), the conference did not reach agreement. Resolution of this issue, as well as the final form of the written rules, was entrusted to the presidium of the orthographic commission: Skrypnyk, A. Pryxod'ko (Deputy Commissar of Education), Kryms'kyj, Synjavs'kyj, and S. Pylypenko, a writer. After ten meetings and long discussions, the presidium approved the final text (prepared by Synjavs'kyj). On the controversial question of rendering foreign *l* and *g*, a compromise was introduced: to use *l* and *h* in loan words of Greek origin or mediation, and to use *l'* and *g* (for foreign *g*) in loan words of Latin and modern European origin or mediation. These rules were signed into law by Skrypnyk on 6 September 1928; published in 1929, they became compulsory in all schools and publications of the Ukrainian SSR. The text of these rules comprised 103 pages, as compared with the no more than 20 of the Academy's previous rules on spelling. Never before was the spelling and the morphology of the Ukrainian language codified in such detail and precision.

The work of the orthographic commission was by no means simple or easy: it had lasted more than three long years. Behind each discussion of this or that orthographic rule stood two different cultural traditions and two disparate schools of linguistics. The new code was a compromise that did not satisfy either party. What was worse, the compromises did not correspond to any one tradition or school, but introduced rules of spelling and pronunciation that were totally new. It is impossible (and unnecessary) to note all the controversial spelling problems here. To illustrate the contradictions it suffices to focus on two rules, concerning the rendition of foreign *l* and *g*. Typically, as already stated, usage in the Western (Polish) Ukraine had foreign words with *l'* and *g*, and that in the Central-Eastern (Russian) Ukraine, with *l* and *h*; in both cases there were some exceptions. Synjavs'kyj presents this discrepancy as being chiefly a West European tradition vs. a Byzantine one. For the most part, this presentation is invalid. Politically dependent (colonial) nations usually acquire the bulk of their loan words through the mediation of the governing nation. This was the Poles in the Western Ukraine, and the Russians in the Central-East. Many words borrowed in the late sixteenth or seventeenth century from West European languages throughout the Ukraine were adopted, because of the Polish mediation, with *l'* and *g*; later, however, under Russia, they were readopted with *l* and *h*. Vice versa, some words introduced into Old Ukrainian (up to the fifteenth century) with *l* and *h* (from the late twelfth and early thirteenth century, all instances of *g* changed to *h* in Ukrainian, both in native and borrowed words) in the Western Ukraine were readapted to Polish, receiving *l'* and *g*. Thus, with a few exceptions, all loan words in the Ukrainian language of the Central-Eastern Ukraine have *l* or *l'*, as does Russian, with *h* used consistently as a substitute for Standard Russian *g*; in the Western Ukraine the same words all have *l'* and *g* (for Western *g*). Seeking other sources for this development may bolster Ukrainians' self-respect, but historically no other explanation is valid.

In the two parts of the Ukraine then separated by a political frontier, the choice of *l* or *l'*, of *h* or *g* was dictated by Russian or Polish mediation. In each part of the country, the system of the other part was unknown in everyday communication. Prescribing the unknown pronunciation, and then only to a portion of loan words, constituted a radical linguistic experiment. It is questionable whether such an experiment could succeed in an independent state; certainly, it had little chance to succeed in the conditions of a bilingual intelligentsia and of a low level of education among other social groups just beginning to accept Ukrainianization. In other words, none of the social and political prerequisites for the experiment's success existed. Although elaborated very carefully by the best linguists, the orthographic rules of 1928/29 were utopian and doomed to failure. From the very beginning, they were highly unpopular. The planned reconciliation of two cultural traditions remained unachieved. The preservation of two different traditions could not be brought about by a peculiar, artificially imposed compromise.[4]

Innovations in vocabulary caused a different reaction, because at issue was not a change in known language components, but the addition of lexical items to the vocabulary already in use. The use of Galicianisms in the standard language, so important before 1925, now gained a new topicality. A. Nikovs'kyj gave a fit characterization of the new situation: "The question. . .of the influence of the 'language of Galicia' ('*halyčanščyny*'), once so live and acute in our press, is now subsiding in the Central-Eastern Ukraine. Previously the situation was such that because of Galician phrases, the reader of Ukrainian books could find himself annoyingly distressed by drastic words and become antagonistic to reading in Ukrainian. Now, when there are Ukrainian schools, Ukrainian institutions, more of the press, and plenty of dictionaries, the achievements of the Galician literary language should not be rejected. On the contrary, they should be welcomed and applied for general use, as material well worked out (*vyroblenyj*), very often to the point, and conveying West European influences" (Nikovs'kyj xv). Similar pronouncements were made by other lexicographers of the time, e.g., Z. Vysoc'kyj (1926), P. Horec'kyj (1928), O. Kurylo (1928, see Wexler 153), and H. Xolodnyj (1928). Xolodnyj, as director of the Institute of the Ukrainian Scientific Language, wrote: "The works of Verxrats'kyj have pointed out the main road to be trod in future" (*Visnyk IUNM* 1).[5] The Academy dictionary also included many Galician words and phrases, some of which were labeled as regional and some of which were not, indicating that they were considered regular components of the standard language. For instance, the primary equivalent of the Russian word *zavod* (s.v.) is given as *vyrobnja*, without any comment, whereas in the discussion of this choice reference is made to four previous

[4] A parallel development with a similar outcome occurred in Belorussia. A Conference on Spelling (with guests from the West) took place on 14–21 November 1926; its proceedings were published in 1927; the draft of its resolutions was published in 1930. The rules were abolished by the decree of the CPC of Belorussia in 1933 (Mayo 26ff.).

[5] In this context, it is interesting to note how a Galician student of Verxrats'kyj's assessed his language: to him, Verxrats'kyj wrote "in such a heavy language" that his subject became the most difficult of all (Šax 36).

dictionaries (by O. Partyc'kyj, F. Piskunov, Je. Želexivs'kyj, and V. Kmicykevyč), three of which are Galician (Shevelov 1966, 119); in the entry *zavidovat'* (s.v.), on the other hand, the word *pozavydity* is marked as Galician.

This new attitude toward things Galician was reflected in attempts to establish contacts with West Ukrainian linguists. Their invitation to the Conference on Spelling of 1927 was one such measure. The election of four Galician scholars to membership in the Academy in 1929 was another. (At the demand of the government, they were expelled from the Academy in 1934: Polons'ka 1, 62; 2, 22.) During the first years of its work, the Institute of the Ukrainian Scientific Language sent drafts of its terminological dictionaries to Lviv for suggestions and revisions (Shevelov 1966, 119). During Ukrainianization, a number of Ukrainian language instructors were Galicians who had immigrated in the revolutionary years 1917 – 1920 or even later (Shevelov 1966, 117).

The willingness to include some Galicianisms in the standard language was another manifestation of the general attitude. Those who worked at normalizing the standard language by filling its gaps generally gave priority to the internal resources of the language. It was expedient, therefore, to open the standard language to various dialects, to treat it as "a common interdialectal and superdialectal (*mižhovirkovu j nadhovirkovu*) Ukrainian literary language" (Synjavs'kyj 100). This general attitude underlay the "spelling compromise" between the West and the Central-East discussed above. Lexical Galicianisms were, however, different from the material of other dialects. They did not come directly from local dialects. Rather, they were components of the Lviv koine, that is, they were sublimated by having risen to an urban and—to some extent, even if low—literary standard. Other dialects were typically rural and virginally primitive; at best, some of them had been expanded and generalized through use in folklore.

Such considerations did not stop the language legislators from seeking out Galician dialectisms and, at least in theory, elevating them to the standard language. Time and again, they referred to dialectal expeditions, to recording dialectal vocabulary, and to using it in general and terminological dictionaries. M. Hladkyj wrote (1928): "We turn the attention of our collaborators. . .to the need of studying. . .Ukrainian folklore and the materials of dialectological and ethnographic collections'' (translated and quoted in Wexler 115). O. Kurylo added (1925): ''The Ukrainian folk mentality, as expressed in the language, has in it much material for rendering abstractions, and this should be used in the scientific language instead of coining new and artifical expressions'' (Kurylo 1942, 9; Wexler 115). Accordingly, expeditions were sent to various localities, with directions that typically read as follows: ''[The material must be gathered] for the most part from people who, by living in villages, have preserved a sufficiently pure language, people who are tied in their work to the conditions and needs of the village: peasants, potters, smiths, locksmiths, carpenters, weavers, fishermen, hunters, mechanics, etc.'' (Wexler 116). Data collected on dialectological expeditions, records of dialectal materials made by paid and unpaid collaborators, and excerpts from earlier dialectal records constituted the foundation of the very rich card files of the Institute of the Ukrainian Scientific Language.

In the use of these data, words were often semantically recycled, that is, words semantically rooted in village life, including agriculture and handicrafts, were assigned a new ''industrial'' meaning, as in the case of *vyrobnja*, originally 'workshop', then 'factory, mill,' or *prohonyč* (mentioned above), originally 'shutterbolt', then 'bolt' in general (Shevelov 1977, 255). Such a recycling is a natural, spontaneous process in the languages of societies that industrialize. In the Ukrainian case, however, the recycling was part of a planned, organized reshaping of the language.

Alongside the use of colloquial and dialectal materials, new words were coined on the basis of existing morphemes, most frequently by affixation (e.g., *dvyh-un* and *ruš-ij* 'motor', *vy-myk-ač* 'electrical switch', etc.). Some of these, such as *dvyhun* and *vymykač*, have been accepted into the language (Shevelov 1977, 255f.), but the majority exist only on the pages of terminological dictionaries. Words were also created by compounding, though less frequently, e.g., *sklo-riz* 'glazier's diamond', *vodo-zbir* 'cistern', etc.

The restoration of archaic elements, a device widely used in developing languages at the time of national rebirth (e.g., in Czech), was generally not typical of the normalization of Ukrainian at the time of Ukrainianization. In scientific terminology, such restoration was exceptional; it was used only a little more frequently in legal (court) terminology. Restoration was rare in military terminology, where the

Cossack terminological tradition of the seventeenth and eighteenth centuries, resuscitated by the national army of 1918 – 1921, was rejected, with but a few exceptions (e.g., *sotnja* 'company', *šanci* 'entrenchment' – Jakubs'ki s.vv.). The reasons for this restrained attitude were probably twofold: on the one hand, there was the strong populist tradition established as early as the nineteenth century; on the other hand, there was the desire to stay away from the usages of the military in the Ukrainian National Republic and the Hetmanate. Nonetheless, in the preface to the *Rosijs'ko-ukrajins'kyj slovnyk pravnyčoji movy* (Kiev, 1926), its "editors" (i.e., A. Kryms'kyj) declared: "We have deliberately introduced into the dictionary many words from the old Ukrainian legal language in order to disclose the tie of the contemporary language with the old one, to buttress the present-day legal language with a historical foundation, and to show how many words the contemporary language of the Ukraine retains from the old legal language and how gravely err those who accuse the present-day Ukrainian language of being artificial, forged, Galicianized. It proves that the Ukrainian language some two or three hundred years ago used those same words that at times, it seems, so grate on our Russianized ear" (Kryms'kyj 1926, viii). This dictionary was severely criticized by Skrypnyk in 1931. In fact, however, it contained only ca. 2,000 archaic words (the total number of words was over 67,000), which were singled out by the editorial comment *star.* (ancient) and had no prescriptive intent (Krymskyj 1926, v).

Behind all these practices, no doubt, was an effort to purge Ukrainian of excessive patterning on Russian. This was the same process which occurred in Czech, during its national rebirth purged of Germanisms, in Bulgarian in relation to Turcicisms, in Romanian in relation to Slavicisms. The crucial difference in those cases, however, was that Bulgaria and Romania were fully independent states and that the Czechs were benefitting from cultural autonomy in a constitutional state. Neither situation was true of the Ukraine at the time.

The decision to rely upon internal lexical resources, primarily those of the "unspoiled" popular language, was one on which all Ukrainian language legislators seemed to agree, but not all of them wanted to implement the decision equally. One can distinguish their division into two main groups.

One group aimed at filling gaps in the language that up to then had typically been filled by inserting Russian words. Linguists in the second group proposed, in addition to filling the gaps, to replace elements considered non-native with native ones. One can call the trend of the second group ethnographic, that of the first, synthetic (i.e., striving for a synthesis of native rural components with urban, European ones; cf. Shevelov 1962, 314ff.); the first group was extremely puristic, whereas the second was moderately puristic. The main representatives of the ethnographic, extremely puristic school were Kryms'kyj, Je. Tymčenko, O. Kurylo in her early writings, M. Hladkyj, S. Smerečyns'kyj, and, outside the Soviet Ukraine, V. Simovyč in his early writings and I. Ohijenko. The synthetic, moderately puristic trend was represented by O. Synjavs'kyj, M. Sulyma, M. Nakonečnyj, O. Kurylo in her later writings; close by them stood V. Hancov and A. Nikovs'kyj.[6] The extreme puristic trend was stronger in Kiev, the moderate one in Kharkiv. The volume *Normy ukrajins'koji literaturnoji movy*, by O. Synjavs'kyj, although published in Kiev (1931), was written in Kharkiv, as were two detailed surveys of the modern standard Ukrainian language, collectively written and edited by L. Bulaxovs'kyj: *Zahal'nyj kurs ukrajins'koji movy dlja včytelivzaočnykiv* (1929) and *Pidvyščenyj kurs ukrajins'koji movy* (1931). These three were major achievements in the description of the standard Ukrainian language of the time. Conventionally, the two groups, and the trends they represented, are also labeled the Kiev versus the Kharkiv school.

The Kiev, extremely puristic, school was strongly represented in many terminological dictionaries. For instance, on its recommendation *ekvator* was to be replaced by *rivnyk, paralel'nyj* by *rivnobižnyj, konus* by *stižok, sektor* by *vytynok, štepsel'* by *prytyčka, kursyv* by *pys'mivka*, etc. Linguists of this school were also active in studying syntax. Here, too, the tenor of their activity was to bring the literary language close to the spoken language while freeing it from blind patterning on Russian syntax. Forms and constructions untypical of

---

[6] Cf. Nikovs'kyj's statement: "Now that the state, the state machinery, business correspondence, professional and technical groups, science and school are placing demands on the Ukrainian language, our language can undergo, along with a quantitative growth, a severe drain of blood, jetting up [from the ground] to, after all, empty heights of routine and illusory technical perfection" (vi).

colloquial speech, whether based on Russian or on the traditions of Greek or Latin, were rejected by the extremely puristic school: active participles, passive constructions, and substantives denoting processes were considered non-Ukrainian. Kryms'kyj went so far as to have the word *zmist* 'contents' replaced by the phrase *De ščo je*, literally 'what is where', in publications of the Academy of Sciences. The simplistic approach became nearly humoristic in *Zrazky prostoho slova* (Kiev, 1929) by Oleksander Synjavs'kyj (not to be confused with Oleksa Synjavs'kyj). In general, verbal constructions were recommended at the expense of nominal ones.

The Kharkiv, moderately puristic, school was not so categorical in its prescriptions. It fully admitted constructions based on European tradition and practice, while also supporting the expanded use of "native" constructions. Linguists of this school clearly distinguished between various styles and genres, whereas the extremists virtually disregarded such differences. As in lexicography, in syntax the moderates defended the synthesis of popular "colloquial" elements with assimilated European components. (In lexicography, this approach is well represented in *Praktyčnyj rosijs'ko-ukrajins'kyj slovnyk*, by M. Johansen, M. Nakonečnyj, K. Nimčynov, and B. Tkačenko—1926.)

Interestingly enough, the ethnographic school found hardly any followers in belles-lettres. A few works recorded colloquial rural speech—e.g., by A. Holovko and K. Hordijenko—but these were stylizations offered through the mediation of a narrator. The general trend clearly favored the urban language. Within this trend one can speak of writers who cultivated a refined "Europeanized" language (e.g., M. Zerov, M. Ryl's'kyj) as opposed to those who adopted the colloquial urban language, with its choices that easily included some Russianisms (e.g., M. Xvyl'ovyj, M. Semenko). A chasm separated prescriptive linguistics from the writers. It is telling that M. Hladkyj wrote a full volume of criticism, occasionally strident, of the language of contemporary writers (*Mova sučasnoho ukrajins'koho pys'menstva*, Kiev, 1930; first published in *Žyttja j revoljucija* 1928, 11–12, and 1929, 1–6). Couched in softer language but essentially in the same vein was a study by M. Sulyma on the language of Xvyl'ovyj ("Frazeolohija Mykoly Xvyl'ovoho," *Červonyj šljax* 1925, 1–2, pp. 263–86), in which Sulyma systematically contrasted the "most original, most cardinal peculiarities of popular Ukrainian mass phraseology," to "the Russianized language of the big cities, of Donec'k factories, of barrack colonies, of sanatorial zones, of responsible specialists" (263f.), to "the contemporary intelligentsia's chat (*balačku*) about writers, about scholars, about newspapers, the language of city-dwellers" (283).

This discrepancy between writers and linguists (at least those representing the ethnographic trend) was symptomatic. It showed that the "perfect" Ukrainian standard language devised by linguists was an abstract ideal which might, at best, prevail in the long run, but was for the time being utopian (as was "spelling" which required relearning all foreign words). In an interplay of what existed with what should have existed, a compromise would gradually have been found. It probably would have occurred if Ukrainianization lasted. But Ukrainianization did not last. It began to weaken and wither in 1931. With the year 1933 it would be officially discontinued.

The work of the Ukrainian linguists of the Ukrainianization period was not entirely in vain, however. For the first time in the history of Ukrainian, the language was normalized, and the normalization was conducted, basically, on a scholarly basis. Much of the language legislation would be rendered null and void; yet much remained through the traumatic events of the 1930s, when virtually all the linguists of the period of Ukrainianization were silenced or destroyed.

For all its artificiality, groundlessness, internal contradictions, tragi-comic excesses and zigzags, Ukrainianization reasserted the existence of Ukrainian as a standard language, rather than just a sum of rural dialects. It extended the mastery of that standard language through various strata of the population, and contributed to its survival during the coming years of constraint and persecution.

CHAPTER SIX

Between 1933 and 1941: The Ukraine Under Postyšev and Xruščov (Khrushchev)

The waning Ukrainianization came to a sudden halt with the arrival in the Ukraine's capital, Kharkiv, of Stalin's plenipotentiary, Pavel Postyšev, on 25 or 26 January 1933. Postyšev, a Russian and a prominent party man in the Ukraine in 1923 – 1930, was generally known as an adversary of Ukrainianization. He had been recalled to Moscow in 1930, probably due to opposition against him by Ukrainian Communists (Skrypnyk?). Now, in 1933, he returned in triumph, to fulfill what was probably his personal wish and was certainly his official commission: to crush his ideological (and personal) foes and to subdue Ukrainians in the party and as a nation. Returning with him was Vs. Balickij, not long before removed as chief of the secret police, and about three thousand party members from Russia. Their common assignment was to exterminate any and all Ukrainian resistance (Majstrenko 147). Appointed Second (rather than First) Secretary of the Central Committee of the CPU as well as First Secretary of the Oblast Committee of the party in Kharkiv, Postyšev had the right to give orders to anyone in the Ukraine, including the First Secretary of the Central Committee, S. Kosior. The theoretical basis for Postyšev's activity was announced a year later, at the Seventeenth Congress of the CPSU, where Stalin declared that by that time "local nationalism," i.e., Ukrainian in the Ukraine, had become the principal danger. Within this party line, Postyšev remained the absolute dictator of the Ukraine until 1937.

The violent end of the Ukrainianization policy was brought about by internal and external developments. In spite of its promoters' many declarations that the policy was not aimed at the appeasement of the peasantry, Ukrainianization was in fact planned as exactly that.

Now, by 1933, appeasement was no longer an issue. Stalin was engaged in an undeclared war with the peasants. It began with the proclamation in 1929 of the policy of (forceful) collectivization and took material form with the liquidation of the kulaks in 1930–1931 and the "minor" famine of 1932, caused by the state's heavy-handed grain collection. These were a prelude to the famine of 1933 that killed several million people and brought the Ukrainian peasantry to its knees. Achieving the capitulation of the peasantry was one of Postyšev's major tasks and he carried it out to perfection. From 1931, there was no longer any need to make overtures to the Ukrainian peasants.

In foreign policy, the hope to bring about "world communism" with Moscow at its center through colonial liberation movements, the hope that had motivated the policy of *korenizacija*, including Ukrainianization, was frustrated. Instead, a major war in Europe was becoming a tangible prospect with the Nazis' seizure of power in Germany on 30 January 1933, the same week that Postyšev arrived in Kharkiv. In that war, the Ukraine would be the main arena. Therefore the country must be ruthlessly pacified and rendered a Russian province. This was Postyšev's second assignment.

The policy of Ukrainianization was not formally abrogated either by Postyšev or by any other party or government official. The Twelfth Congress of the CPU, held in January 1934, in its resolution on the report of the Central Committee, briefly mentioned the task of "further unfolding the Bolshevik Ukrainianization" (*Rezoljuciji* 559). Only deviations from the "correct Ukrainianization" caused by "bourgeois nationalists" or "their agents," including Skrypnyk at their head, were to be excised mercilessly. Henceforth Ukrainian culture, and the Ukrainian language as an essential ingredient thereof, should follow the dictum "national in form but proletarian/socialist in content," coined by Stalin as early as 1925, although launched only at the Sixteenth Congress of the CPSU in 1930 (Luckyj 177, Stalin 367). References to the successes of Ukrainianization can be found in pronouncements of party leaders during the Postyšev era. For instance, M. Popov, in November 1933, mentioned continuity in party policy in this respect; in January 1934, a resolution of the Twelfth Congress of the CPU advised "speeding up national cultural construction and Bolshevik Ukrainianization based on industrialization and collectivization"; as late as May 1937, the Thirteenth Congress of the CPU faulted "the insufficient Ukrainianization of the Party, the Soviets, and particularly of trade-union and Komsomol organizations" (Kostiuk 73, 75, 125).

Several gestures in that direction were ordered by Postyšev: the erection of monuments to Taras Ševčenko (the poet was depicted as being guarded by a *kolxoznik*, an industrial worker, a young communist, and a red-guardist) in Kharkiv (1933–1935) and Kiev (1935–1939), the transference of the capital to Kiev (1934) and, most important, the appointment of several renowned Ukrainians to leading government (but not party) posts, including V. Zatons'kyj as commissar of education, A. Xvylja as his deputy, and P. Ljubčenko as chairman of the CPC (the latter two were former Borot'bists). Several Russian-language newspapers were established in cities of the Ukraine, but the only official outlets of the Central Committee, the newspaper *Komunist* and the journal *Bil'šovyk Ukrajiny*, continued to be published in Ukrainian alone. In the same vein, several Russian theaters were founded, without displacing Ukrainian ones; opera continued to be performed in Ukrainian.

Factually, however, the impetus for Ukrainianization had vanished. All its leading cadres in both the Commissariat of Education and in the Ukrainianization courses were arrested and either sent to labor camps or shot to death. The promotor of the whole process, M. Skrypnyk, faced with the demise of all his accomplishments and imminent personal destruction, committed suicide on 7 July 1933.

The most pernicious aspect of Postyšev's policy lay not in the prohibition of the Ukrainian language nor in the formal abolition of Ukrainianization, but in the nearly total destruction of Ukrainian intellectuals. In harmony with the new slogan of culture national only in form, anyone who ascribed to the traditions of the Ukrainian past was to be silenced or destroyed. The terror assumed previously unheard-of proportions. Thousands were arrested on false accusations; under unbearable conditions and torture, they "confessed" to belong to underground subversive "organizations" which never existed and never figured in any open trial, but which were mentioned in the public speeches of Postyšev, Kosior, and others. By referring to these contrived comments, Kostiuk (85–108) determined that there were fifteen such fabricated organizations, among which some allegedly had thousands of members. The executions of the very real "members" of those fictitious organizations were in some instances made public, especially after the murder of S. Kirov in Leningrad on 1 December 1934 (which had no trail leading to the Ukraine), but more often were conducted in silence. Not a single group of the intelligentsia in the Ukraine escaped the arrests and executions, from clergy to engineers, from workers in cooperatives to actors, from writers to agronomists. Some groups were virtually liquidated. Such was the fate of the priests of the Ukrainian Autocephalous Orthodox Church, of the usually blind singers of Ukrainian folklore (*kobzari* and *lirnyky*; Shostakovich, 214f.), of the professors of VUAMLIN (All-Ukrainian Association of Marx and Lenin Institutes, in 1933; the organization was disbanded in 1936), of historians who had studied with M. Javors'kyj (1933), of artists belonging to ARMU (Association of Revolutionary Artists of the Ukraine), and of members of the Academy of Sciences. The closure of the Academy of Sciences' institutes of Ševčenko studies, of Jewish proletarian culture, and of Polish proletarian culture during the latter half of the 1930s was probably also due in part to the decimation of their members. Other groups of the intelligentsia were affected selectively, but in none was the percentage of victims low.

For party members, arrests often came following public denunciation during the purge that raged in 1933–1934 and resulted in the party's expelling 23 percent of its members, or 27,500 people (Kostiuk 61), of whom 2,750 had held leading positions (*Narysy* 411).

The loss of the intelligentsia was all the more painful because the severely quelled and decimated peasantry was incapable of producing a new wave of intellectuals.

Also falling victim to the purge were periodicals (e.g., *Litopys revoljuciji*, discontinued in 1933; *Istoryk-bil'šovyk*, closed sometime in the mid-1930s; *Nova* [later *Socijalistyčna*] *hromada*, in 1933; *Žyttja j revoljucija* in 1933; *Červonyj šljax* in 1936), theaters (e.g., the theater group "Berezil'," disbanded in October 1933), and cinema (the famed director O. Dovženko was sent to Moscow the same year).

Struck at the same time were the national minorities of the Ukraine, with the single exception of the Russian one. Jewish, Bulgarian, Moldavian, German, Greek, and Polish administrative units were disbanded entirely or in part, and their schools and press were closed entirely or in part (Kostiuk 94).[1]

---

[1] As of the beginning of 1927, there were 21 national *rajony* in the Ukraine: 9 Rus-

The gaps in the ranks of the Ukrainian intelligentsia were as a rule left unfilled; in the party and in the state machinery, those eliminated were replaced. More often than not, the new functionaries were Russians. As already mentioned, when Postyšev came to Kharkiv from Moscow, he brought with him 3,000 party workers. In November 1933, he noted that 1,340 "comrades" had been newly appointed to district managerial jobs and that 237 (out of 525) new secretaries were serving district party committees, without disclosing their nationality. Ten thousand men were sent to administer the collective farms; most likely, the majority of them were Russians. "Political detachments" were created at tractor stations (MTS) and state farms "with the aid of the All-Union CP that supplied 4,500 party men" (Kostiuk 28, *Narysy* 402), who were undoubtedly predominantly Russian. The same was probably true of the newly formed (June 1933) group of industrial "party organizers," especially in the Donec'k basin (*Narysy* 399f.).

An important development during the Postyšev era in the Ukraine, though one not initiated by him, was the growing centralization of the administration in the Soviet Union. In overt violation of the constitutions of the USSR and its component republics, various republican commissariats were replaced, one after another, by all-Union or mixed commissariats centered in Moscow. At the time of the formation of the USSR there were five all-Union commissariats; by 1935, the number had grown to twelve (Sadovs'kyj 103). The Constitution of the Ukrainian SSR, adapted in January 1937, recognized only eight republican commissariats, such as: autotransportation, dwelling construction, municipal economy, furniture and carpentry industry, local fuel industry, education (which did not extend to institutions of higher education, art, or culture), and social security (*Konstitucii* 76). This meant that the "government" of the Ukrainian SSR had no more

---

sian, 7 German, 3 Bulgarian, 1 Polish, 1 Jewish. Several more were in the planning stage: 6 Greek, 3 German, 2 Jewish, and additional Russian ones. Apparently, the majority of planned *rajony* were indeed established in the years 1927–1931 (*Itogi raboty*, p. 23). All had schools in their national languages. No such schools survived into the 1940s. In the postwar period, official and semi-official pronouncements mention only Polish, Hungarian, and Moldavian schools, i.e., schools using the languages of the "new" national minorities incorporated into the Soviet Union at war's end (e.g., Bilodid 8). The silence about schools of other national minorities would imply their absence (this did not apply to Russian schools, for Russians were no longer considered a national minority).

functions or rights than a municipality. New laws and proclamations concerning matters specifically Ukrainian were issued in Moscow and implemented from there, in complete disregard of rights granted by the original constitution. Such were, for instance, the laws on the formation of six new districts in the Ukraine (19 November 1935; Sadovs'kyj 98) and on the improvement of coal mining in the Donec'k region (31 March 1940; *Narysy* 443), as well as annual regulations on the size of areas sown with various crops, among hundreds more. Sadovs'kyj (98) counted that in 1935 alone there were 526 such laws. After all, the constitution (§ 16) held that "the laws of the USSR are binding on the territory of the Ukrainian SSR," a provision that specified no limits to interference in the internal affairs of the Ukraine.

The effect of the anti-Ukrainian terror that followed upon Stalin's pronouncement of "local nationalism" as the major danger to the existence of the Soviet Union, and of the unscrupulous and relentless government centralization on the use and status of the Ukrainian language, was dramatic. In cities and larger towns, it went underground, except for officially sanctioned ceremonial occasions. The achievements of Ukrainianization, small as they were, in inculcating the Ukrainian language as a medium of communication in urban everyday life were struck down. Russian was fully reinstalled in that function. Even within the Academy of Sciences, Russian became the language of normal conversation (Polons'ka 2, 37), and even by official data, the percentage of Ukrainians in the Academy fell to 54.9 by 1937. The name changes of the Academy reflected its evolution: until 1935, it was "All-Ukrainian," then it became "Ukrainian," and from 1936, the Academy "of the Ukrainian SSR." Also, the immediate effect of the direct subordination of the whole state machinery to Moscow was the switch to Russian throughout the government administration.

Superficially, however, Ukrainian remained the predominant language in the Ukraine. Statistically, the number of Ukrainian schools, press organs, theaters, and published books exceeded Russian ones, although these were on the rise.

The Postyšev-Balickij terror had one more, less direct effect on the status of the Ukrainian language. Standard Ukrainian could have been enhanced by the eminence of Ukrainian culture as expressed in literature, cinema, theater, etc. But this was precluded by the terror that stalked writers, cinema and theater directors, artists, composers, etc. As a rule, its victims were the Ukraine's most outstanding cultural figures. Les' Kurbas, the leader of modern Ukrainian theater, was arrested and eventually liquidated, as were many prominent actors; Olexander Dovženko, the leading personality in cinema, was forced to leave the Ukraine; Mykola Xvyl'ovyj, perhaps the most outstanding Ukrainian prose writer of the time, was driven to suicide; hundreds of talented writers, those capable of independent thinking and experimentation, including the most gifted novelist Valerijan Pidmohyl'nyj and the leading playwright Mykola Kuliš, were shot or banished, never to return. The writers who remained were as a rule careerists with little talent or individuals willing to adapt themselves to the situation. The general level of literature and art, now squeezed into the narrow framework of socialist realism and political slogans, fell so low that it lost all appeal. Interesting works were exceptions that tended to appear only at long intervals (e.g., *Veršnyky* [The riders] by Jurij Janovs'kyj, 1935). The same general situation obtained in all Soviet literatures of the time,[2] but the percentage of writers who fell victim to the terror in the Ukraine was higher than in, say, Russia. Most critical was that Ukrainian literature virtually lost all attraction for the reader. Even Ukrainian prerevolutionary, classical literature and art were purged, and much of it was either not reissued or banned.

The Postyšev era came to an abrupt end in 1937. In mid-March he was suddenly and without any explanation recalled to Russia, where he was arrested and then disappeared. Balickij shared his fate. One reason for Stalin's action could have been Postyšev's emphatic attempts to build up his personal popularity in the Ukraine, which Stalin may have perceived as threatening. Another reason might have been the aggravation of the international situation. In 1936 Germany embarked on a course of military aggression and reoccupied the Rhineland. This reminded Stalin of the role he intended the Ukraine to have in any future war. A new pacification of the country was becoming imminent. Stalin may have contemplated the liquidation of the Ukraine as even a nominal state; Postyšev and his efforts at personal glory did not suit such a scheme.

---

[2] A decree of the Central Committee of the RCP disbanded all voluntary literary organizations and made writers state functionaries supervised by the centralized Union of Writers (23 April 1932).

If this speculation is correct, Kosior, who with the removal of Postyšev became ostensibly the number one person in the CPU, misconstrued the reasons for the removal of Postyšev. In the resolutions of the CPU's Thirteenth Congress, which convened on 27 May 1937, Postyšev's demise was used to revivify the problem of Ukrainianization. The congress, without mentioning Postyšev by name, blamed him for "the insufficient Ukrainianization of the party, of the soviets, and particularly of trade unions and Komsomol organizations" and for "the inadequate promotion of Ukrainian Bolshevik cadres to leading party, soviet, economic, and trade union posts" (cited from Kostiuk 125). This is the more significant because the Constitution of 1937 said nothing about language in the Ukraine, except for the statement that "citizens of the Ukrainian SSR have the right to an education. This right is secured. . .by school education in the native language" (*Konstitucija* 122, p. 75; it is noteworthy that the word *škola* 'school' in the Ukrainian vernacular most often refers to elementary school).

The reaction of the Kremlin and the events that followed were not publicized; to some extent they can only be conjectured here. In its issue of July 9, *Pravda* attacked the Central Committee of the CPU. In August a special commission comprising V. Molotov, N. Ežov, and N. Xruščov (Khrushchev) was sent to Kiev, and a plenary session of the Central Committee was convoked. According to unconfirmed information provided by the sovietologist Avtorxanov, by that time "several trainloads of special NKVD troops had arrived in Kiev from Moscow" (quoted from Kostiuk 127). It is a justified guess that the Moscow commission expressed no confidence in the Central Committee of the CPU and the government of the Ukrainian SSR. Whatever resistance, if any, may have followed, P. Ljubčenko, the head of the CPC, committed suicide on 30 August 1937. In the next few days two of Kosior's aides, M. Popov and M. Xatajevyč, were arrested; Kosior himself was recalled to Moscow, where he disappeared. All other members of the Politbureau, all members of the Orgbureau, all members of the Control Commission, all but two of the 62 members and 40 candidate members of the Central Committee, all the leading figures in the Ukrainian government, including the Commissar of Education Zatons'kyj and his deputy Xvylja, as well as a substantial number of oblast' and local functionaries, were liquidated. The entire machinery of rule was destroyed. It was, without question, a coup d'état. What is especially striking, and what makes one speculate that the very existence of the Ukrainian SSR was in danger, is that for five months no one was elected or appointed to replace those dismissed. Several Russian "comrades" now controlled matters in the Ukraine, the obscure individuals Starygin, Lemkov, Smirnov, Ljutavin, Špilevoj, and Telešov (listed in Kostiuk 131), but even they held no publicly defined posts.

Finally the decision to maintain the formal existence of the Ukrainian republic prevailed. On 28 January 1938, it was announced that N. Xruščov, a Russian, was "elected" the First Secretary of the Central Committee and M. Burmistenko, another Russian, its Second Secretary; on February 22, a new chairman of the CPC, D. Korotčenko, was announced; appointed commissar of education was H. Xomenko, a political nonentity of whom little was known before or after his appointment. The interregnum ended with the election of the Central Committee in June 1938, at the Fourteenth Congress of the CPU.

The impact of these events, which bordered on the liquidation of formal Ukrainian statehood and, the urban use of the Ukrainian language, can readily be imagined. The terror of 1937–1938 was much more intense than that of 1933–1934; the accompanying uncertainty and bewilderment were extremely powerful additional factors. The new tenor of things was made very clear by two new measures taken by Xruščov. Before his "election," starting on the first of January 1938, the daily organ of the Central Committee of the CPU, *Komunist*, published in Ukrainian since 1926, was augmented by a Russian-language newspaper, *Sovetskaja Ukraina*. This was tantamount to recognition that the Soviet Ukraine and its governing party gave the Russian language the same status as the Ukrainian language. If any specific event can be considered the formal end of Ukrainianization, the initiation of that newspaper was this event. It roughly coincided with the liquidation of the last old-guard Ukrainian elements in the party: the former Borot'bists, including P. Ljubčenko and A. Xvylja, and the former (prerevolutionary) Ukrainian Bolsheviks, including V. Zatons'kyj and H. Petrovs'kyj (the latter escaped arrest, but was removed to Russia and given a humble post).

The second measure of both symbolic and large practical import was the decree of the CPC of 20 April 1938 on the compulsory teaching of the Russian language in all Ukrainian ("non-Russian") schools beginning in the second grade, for four to five hours weekly (Majstrenko 160); prior to that time, teaching Russian started in the third grade, for two to four hours per week (Siropolko 48). The Fourteenth Congress of the CPU (June 1938) emphasized "the necessity to eliminate the after-effect of the hostile sabotage in the teaching of the Russian language in elementary and secondary schools as well as in institutions of higher education," and connected the necessity directly with the danger of "the separation of the Soviet Ukraine from the Union of Soviet Socialist Republics" (*Rezoljuciji* 601f.).[3]

In accordance with the new policy, some old propaganda slogans were modified and some new ones were promulgated, either directly from Moscow or via Kiev. During the Postyšev era, the prevailing slogan had called for the rejection of artificial barriers between the Ukrainian and the Russian nations and languages. Constantly reiterated now, in 1938, was the assertion that the Ukraine is an inseparable part of the Soviet Union and that the friendship of the united Soviet peoples is eternal, with emphasis placed on the greatness and leading character of Russian culture (Kostiuk 140; *Narysy* 428). This concept was also projected back into history. The contention that the Ukrainian (as well as Belorussian) nationality first arose after the Tatar invasion of the thirteenth century, whereas prior to that time there existed a monolithic "old-Russian nationality" that was the common ancestor of Russians, Ukrainians, and Belorussians, was overtly formulated only later, after World War II. But as early as August 1934, Soviet historians were instructed that "the history of Great Russia [should] not be torn apart from the history of other nations of the USSR" (J. Stalin, A. Ždanov, S. Kirov, "Zamečanija po povodu konspekta učebnika po istorii SSSR," *K izučeniju* 23). This was tantamount to abolishing the history of the Ukraine (and other non-Russian nations) and to its dissolution in the "history of the USSR," i.e., in practice, of Russia. This concept was systematically set forth in the all-Union obligatory textbook edited by Andrej Šestakov, entitled *Istorija SSSR, kratkij kurs* (first edition 1937, with many subsequent ones; cf. Shtepa 128ff.). This newly created

---

[3] The often quoted pronouncement of Xruščov, "Now all peoples will study the Russian language" (*Pravda*, 16 June 1938), is ambiguous: it is unclear whether he is referring to the new policy or to a general statement on the advantage of being in command of Russian because it is the language in which Lenin and Stalin wrote.

"history of the USSR"—which began no earlier and no later than half a million years ago—actually replaced the history of the Ukraine, especially in schools. A set purpose loomed behind the Stalin-Šestakov concept that the Ukrainian culture and language had no deep historical roots, but were due to the historical accident of the Tatar invasion and thus were fated to wither away.

In terms of practical language politics, the time of the dictatorship of Postyšev and later Xruščov brought substantial changes in education and publication.

In education, an increasing number of schools in urban and industrial centers were de-Ukrainianized; these switched in part, under Zatons'kyj, to dual Ukrainian-Russian usage and later to instruction in Russian. The development has been confirmed by numerous witnesses, but it cannot be fully substantiated by statistic data, for from ca. 1938, data on the distribution of Ukrainian and Russian schools have usually been withheld (cf., e.g., the article on education in *Ukrajins'ka radjans'ka encyklopedija* 17, 412). What information appeared in the press was episodic and cannot be verified. For instance, Xruščov reported to the Fourteenth Congress of the CPU that there were 17,736 Ukrainian schools in the republic, with a total of 4,319,000 students (*Pravda*, 16 June 1938). The semi-official publication of the Academy of Sciences of the Ukrainian SSR (*Radjans'ka Ukrajina za 20 rokiv*, Kiev, 1937, p. 98) added that Ukrainian schools constituted 82.8 percent of all schools. These data seem highly suspect. Even at the peak of Ukrainianization, in 1930, the number of Ukrainian schools was 16,162 and their percentage of all schools in the Ukraine was 77. The blackout of data on the language of education (which extended to other areas of cultural life, such as theater, film, radio, party and government pronouncements, etc.) shows that the de-Ukrainianization of education was carried out furtively and gradually, but also consistently and relentlessly. In institutions of higher education, the switch to Russian as the language of instruction was accelerated by the formation of an All-Union-Republican Committee to deal with matters pertaining to higher education (1936), to which corresponding government agencies were subordinated (the USSR's Ministry of Higher and Special Education was formally established in 1946).

Statistical data on the revival of Russian theaters in the Ukraine are also lacking. But if in 1933 "forty new theaters" were founded (*Narysy* 407), one can safely guess that most if not all of them were Russian.

Production of books in Ukrainian underwent a decline under Postyšev and Xruščov. In 1930, titles published were 6,394. The number dwindled to 3,472 in 1933; 3,232 in 1936; 2,566 in 1937; 2,159 in 1938; 1,895 in 1939 (*EU* 1, 977). Of the total number of books published in all languages, Ukrainian books, per annum, constituted 79, 69, 59, 60, 52, and 43 percent. Again, there is reason to surmise that the bulk of the non-Ukrainian production was in Russian. In addition, Russian books published in Russia were imported freely and in large quantities. The main reason for the decline in the percentage of Ukrainian books published was the policy of the government; the reasons for the decline in absolute figures were more complicated. Among them were, probably, the public's reluctance to read literature imbued with official propaganda and, generally, low in quality; another was a decrease in the number of readers, due to the extermination of the Ukrainian intelligentsia and educated peasantry.

Russian newspapers started to grow in number under the Postyšev regime; in Xruščov's time, practically every oblast' had a Russian newspaper alongside the Ukrainian one (*Narysy* 427). The general share of Russian newspapers grew from 10.1 percent in 1933 to 22.2 percent in 1940 (*EU* 1, 992). In addition, many Russian newspapers were imported, and some even had a special printing produced in the Ukraine (e.g., *Pravda*). In many cases the pre-Ukrainianization dichotomy of Ukrainian for rural use and Russian for urban and industrial use, so vigorously denied during Skrypnyk's era, was reintroduced. In certain cases this was even reflected in the titles of newspapers: e.g., published in Kharkiv were the Ukrainian *Socialistyčna Xarkivščyna* vs. the Russian *Xar'kovskij rabočij*; published in Odessa were the Ukrainian *Čornomors'ka komuna* vs. the Russian *Znamja komunizma*.

All these developments reflected, on the one hand, a political course aimed at the gradual undermining of the part played by the Ukrainian language, and, on the other hand, a certain attitude among speakers of Ukrainian. It was impractical to adhere to a language whose communicative value and social prestige were steadily falling. Under these conditions, surprising was not the retreat of the Ukrainian language, but rather its relative tenacity. This was, possibly, the explanation behind the cautious and slow pace of the de-Ukrainianization measures, as well as the furtiveness and secrecy of the Russifying ones. For one thing, the ferocious terror conducted against Ukrainian intellectuals as a rule was not noted in the press, except at the beginning of the Postyšev era. Of course, consideration of possible repercussions outside the Soviet Union must also have had some effect. Nonetheless, the main policy goal Skrypnyk had set—namely, that peasants joining the proletariat in Ukrainian-speaking cities would preserve their Ukrainian language—was destroyed. The new industrial recruits arriving from the countryside entered a Russian-speaking milieu in which the prestige of the Ukrainian language was low and its communicative function only rudimentary. These peasants were destined to be denationalized. This was even more true of those who succeeded in moving into the higher echelons of the society, to become technicians, administrators, ideologists. The traditional deficient structure of Ukrainian speakers was being reinstated: again, those who spoke the language were primarily peasants and the humanist intelligentsia.

The political course of the 1930s also deeply affected the Ukrainian language from within. It was subjected to regimentation more severe than any in its history. For the most part this was another manifestation of the centralization and regularization typical of the time; in part it had been prepared by the earlier, strict regimentation of the language's spelling (in the broad sense, including morphology and orthoepy), terminology, syntax, and vocabulary. The spirit of standardization that had been introduced by the normalizers of Skrypnyk's time was now turned against them.

During the SVU trial, S. Jefremov, accused of sabotage in his language work, reasonably stated: "I think that sabotage in language is merely impossible. When a saboteur floods a mine he does not leave his visiting card, but when one compiles a dictionary he places his name [on it]. ... Everyone who writes wants to be read by the broadest circles of readers. In my opinion, sabotage is unthinkable in that area" (quoted from Smal'-Stock'kyj 102f.). Nonetheless, the language normalizers of the 1920s were accused of sabotage, and the charge was repeated *ad nauseam*.

The campaign against these "saboteurs" would rage for more than two years. Not only linguists, but also politicians were participants, including Postyšev, Zatons'kyj and, most actively, Xvylja. The attack was initiated in 1930 with an article by Naum Kahanovyč entitled "Proty 'narodnyctva' v movoznavstvi (Kudy ide ukrajins'ka literaturna mova?)" (Against populism in linguistics [Where is the Ukrainian language going?]), which was published in *Prapor marksyzmu* (no. 1), the outlet of VUAMLIN, a party institution opposed to the subdued but still suspect Academy in Kiev. A man of Jewish descent and of Russian culture, Kahanovyč produced a useful study about the history of active participles in Russian, which remained his only scholarly work. He ventured into problems of Ukrainian when it was still protected by Skrypnyk and when the latter's sway over the Ukraine seemed secure. Kahanovyč's position in the 1930 article was essentially close to that of Synjavs'kyj and other "antiethnographers" in Ukrainian linguistics, but his sharper tone invoked the specter of Marxism in linguistics. Wrote Kahanovyč: "For a linguist, particularly for a sociologist and a Marxist, it is obvious that such a path [as recommended by Kurylo and Sulyma] is impossible. The slogan 'back to the people's speech' is essentially conservative and harmful." And he concluded: "This language [i.e., Standard Ukrainian of the future] will, of course, be created on the basis of so-called 'popular' speech, but the latter will serve only as the foundation and by no means as the entire edifice. That edifice, that real literary language, will appear as the synthesis of heterogeneous components. It shall absorb the popular components and the *jazyčyje* [the literary language developed by Galician Moscophiles, containing Church Slavonic and Russian elements] and the language of newspapers and journals, etc. This is the path of all languages. Such is also the path of the Ukrainian literary language" (63–64). Without directly referring to the Russian language (this was not yet in fashion), Kahanovyč actually called Ukrainian away from the excesses of populism to the pattern familiar to him in Standard Russian.

A few months later a new article by Kahanovyč was published, also in *Prapor marksyzmu* (1930, 3), under the innocuous title "Kil'ka sliv pro slovnyky" (A few words about dictionaries). It was directed against the Academy dictionary, noting only in passing a terminological dictionary of mechanics. Kahanovyč had grounds for two of his criticisms: that the Academy dictionary relied on prerevolutionary sources and often neglected new words of the Soviet period; and that some words invented during the Ukrainianization period were "pseudo-scholarly substitutes" (*surogaty*; 124). In comparison to subsequent articles by Kahanovyč and to those by Xvylja and his subordinates, the tone of the article is moderate, although it does contain two denunciatory statements: "this is scholarly sabotage" (124) and "Ukrainian bourgeois national [sic!] *xutorjanstvo*" (126). The latter word, derived from *xutir* 'farmstead of a wealthy farmer', is here synonymous to kulakdom, a serious political incrimination in the circumstances of the time.

In a year or two, when the "unmasking" of Skrypnyk and of the purists in Ukrainian linguistics became topical, Kahanovyč's daring sally opened the gate to a meteoric career. Suddenly he became the head of an officially approved and promoted antipurist movement, the director of the Institute of Linguistics in Kiev, the editor-in-chief of the newly founded periodical *Movoznavstvo*, and a corresponding member of the Academy (May 1934—Polons'ka 2, 32)—in a word, the arbiter in Ukrainian linguistics. After Skrypnyk's downfall, the quiet and partly scholarly tone of his political debut proved too mild. Kahanovyč underwent "self-criticism" for the "insufficiency" (but not inadequacy) of his approach in 1930. He should have spoken, he admitted, not of populism, but of aggressive bourgeois nationalism; he should not have just discussed problems but inaugurated a language pogrom.

Accordingly, a third article by Kahanovyč appeared, in the monthly *Za markso-lenins'ku krytyku* (1933, 10). It bore the title "Movna teorija ukrajins'koho buržuaznoho nacionalizmu" (The language theory of Ukrainian bourgeois nationalism). Here it was claimed that representatives of the ethnographic school in Ukrainian linguistics, i.e., Kurylo, Tymčenko, and their followers, "continued the tradition of the Union for Liberation of the Ukraine [SVU]" (37), that to them the people meant the kulaks (on which point, strangely enough, they are charged to have followed in the footsteps of Potebnja and Vossler—pp. 34, 32). A work by another linguist, Smerečyns'kyj, was described as a "frontal attack of the class enemy on the development of the Ukrainian literary language as undertaken [?] by the Communist party according to the indications of Lenin and Stalin" (39). The charge against the "bourgeois nationalists" referred specifically to the seven following points: (1) rejection of neologisms coined during the revolutionary epoch; (2) rejection of international words; (3) rejection of language components common to those in languages of the other Soviet republics, especially Russian; (4) attempts to inculcate language components having a class enemy character; (5) attempts to spread feudal and bourgeois ideology through language; (6) attempts to spread artificially created language components; and (7) distortion in the meaning of many notions, especially those political and economic.

The immediate pretext for Kahanovyč's third article was the publication, in Kiev, of a collection of articles entitled *Na movoznavčomu fronti* (1931). The volume was the first publication of the Institute of Linguistics of the Academy of Sciences. The institute was organized on 7 March 1930 to replace the Institute of the Ukrainian Scientific Language and other linguistic sections and commissions of the Academy (*Visti VUAN* 1930, 2, p. 1f.). The institute's director, and the editor of the collection, was H. Tkačenko, a party man. The bulk of the book was devoted to criticism of the Academy's previous work in linguistics in light of the new political requirements (and phraseology, as the title of the collection indicates).

The "program" of Tkačenko differed but little from that of Kahanovyč. As Tkačenko wrote (in *Visti VUAN* 1930, 4): "The proletariat, who took power into their hands in the Ukraine, also brought with them their language, their phonetics, vocabulary, and phraseology. While widely making use of the attainments of their predecessors, the proletarians adapt everything to their needs, to the needs of the broad toiling masses, beginning with spelling and the meaning of individual words" (p. 12). Hence Tkačenko's promise that the Institute of Linguistics "will periodically report on its work in factories, to the mass of workers" (p. 16).

Tkačenko's program, however, was considered faulty (and hence, in the phraseology of the time, bourgeois nationalist) because his criticism was said to have been relatively mild and, particularly, because he failed to expel all the old cadre of linguists from the Academy and to destroy all their work. Instead he declared the necessity "to select from the older staff of the linguistic institutions those who had better qualifications and who sincerely undertook to build Soviet-style research" (p. 17). Following his call, the published first three volumes of the Academy dictionary were all reviewed by V. Jakymiv, M. Kalynovyč, and O. Synjavs'kyj, and in part (vol. 2) by O. Kurylo,

who also reviewed research in dialectology. Tkačenko, while reject-
ing Smerečyns'kyj's views, still considered the latter's book on syntax
to be a useful collection of data. That approach, and the work of such
collaborators, aroused Kahanovyč's ire. He wanted, as did the party,
all work of the Academy linguists to be discredited, and the staff to be
dismissed and liquidated, which would later happen.

Kahanovyč's third article, unlike his first two, was not a daring soli-
tary call. It was part of a well-organized frontal offensive against
"nationalism" and "sabotage" in linguistics. Discounting vitriolic
attacks by Postyšev, the somewhat more professional campaign
opened with A. Xvylja's article (in *Komunist*, 4 April 1933), "Za
bil'šovyc'ku pyl'nist' na fronti tvorennja ukrajins'koji radjans'koji
kul'tury" (reprinted in *Movoznavstvo* 1, 1934). On 25 April 1933, a
commission, headed by Xvylja and charged with reexamination of
work "on the language front," was organized at the Commissariat of
Education (its two resolutions, one of a general character, the other
specifically on terminology, were published in *Movoznavstvo* 1, 1934,
pp. 15–21). Two days later, on April 27, *Pravda* published a far from
professional correspondence from Kiev by a certain B. Levin concerned with "how bourgeois nationalists bossed (*orudovali*)" that
vehemently attacked "the group of Petljurovite intelligentsia. . . Elena
Kurillo [!], Professor Timčenko, Draj-Xmara, Šelud'ko a.o.," accus-
ing them of "a zoological hatred to everything coming from the Russian language," and H. Tkačenko, "under whose wing the bourgeois
nationalists gathered." That same year, 1933, Xvylja published
another article, "Na borot'bu z nacionalizmom na movnomu fronti"
(in *Za markso-lenins'ku krytyku*, 7), and the book *Znyščyty korinnja
ukrajins'koho nacionalizmu na movnomu fronti* (Kharkiv). Beginning
in 1934, the newly organized semiannual organ of the Institute of
Linguistics, *Movoznavstvo*, at first edited by P. Mustjaca, a Moldavian, and then (from no. 5) by N. Kahanovyč, took over the campaign (H. Tkačenko simply vanished). Its first issue contained,
following an editorial note, reprints of Xvylja's article and of two
resolutions of the Commissariat of Education, and an article by S.
Vasylevs'kyj entitled "Dobyty voroha" (To deal a final blow to the
enemy), which in tone and character strongly resembled the writings
of Xvylja.

The specific measures called for by Xvylja, his commission, and Vasylevs'kyj were to purge the cadre of linguists and linguistic institutions; to withdraw all the publications of the "bourgeois linguists" in terminology, lexicography, and syntax; to revise spelling; and to prepare new general and terminological dictionaries. The principal accusation against the work already done was expressed by Xvylja thus: "Ukrainian nationalists carried out a large-scale sabotage on the linguistic front in attempting to tear away the development of the Ukrainian language from the Russian language" (*Znyščyty. . .*, 4). The main targets of the attack were the chief representatives of the ethnographic trend in Ukrainian linguistics: Kurylo, Tymčenko, Smerečyns'kyj, Kryms'kyj, and Šelud'ko, as well as Sulyma, all of whom were said to have been "assistants of the bourgeoisie in its struggle against the proletarian revolution" and to have "fostered fascist interventionalist plans" (Vasylevs'kyj 29, 36). Many others were mentioned in passing (cf. a long list, compiled by P. Horec'kyj and I. Kyryčenko, of "saboteurs" in *Movoznavstvo* 2, 41, which included such representatives of the moderate trend as O. Synjavs'kyj and L. Bulaxovs'kyj). Ludicrous as these charges were, they could not be refuted, because the accused were never allowed any public self-defense and because the works on which the incriminations were based were immediately withdrawn. In the conditions of a total blackout, the accused were fired from their jobs, arrested, and more often than not liquidated. The introductory editorial of *Movoznavstvo* called upon linguists "to break forever with the bourgeois philological tradition and to walk out into the *kolxoz* fields and factories." More to the point were reproofs for specific recommendations that were labeled as localisms, regionalisms, archaicisms, and infelicitous neologisms (Resolution of the Commissariat of Education; *Movoznavstvo* 1, 18).

The initial general articles calling for a sweeping purge in linguistic matters were followed by ones on specific issues. P. Horec'kyj defended the suffixes *-nnj* (*a*), *-ttj* (*a*) and *-k* (*a*) in substantives denoting processes, *-čyk* and *-ščyk* in substantives denoting acting persons, *-vydnyj* in adjectives denoting similarity, *-yr-* in loan verbs; except for the first two, these forms were borrowings from Russian (*Movoznavstvo* 1, 37 – 57). H. Sabaldyr rejected archaic syntactic constructions that had been recommended by Smerečyns'kyj (ibid. 1, 53 – 67). D. Drinov solicited the use of some geographical names in their Russian forms (ibid., 5, 43 – 51). O. Babenko suggested a similar approach in physical terminology (ibid., 5, 53 – 57). Some articles were essentially a critique of the language of some published work, intended either to discredit the author (e.g., V. Babak on Ostap Vyšnja, *Movoznavstvo* 3 – 4, 49 – 60; translations of Lenin's works—Kahanovyč, ibid., 9 – 24) or, in the case of "proletarian writers," to laud him (e.g., V. Masal's'kyj on I. Kyrylenko, ibid., 25 – 47). In the same vein, the Institute of Linguistics published several pamphlets "unmasking" the linguistic misdeeds of bourgeois nationalism (e.g., N. Solodkyj, *Iz sposterežen' nad syntaksoju sučasnoji ukrajins'koji hazetnoji movy*; and K. Nimčynov, *Proty nacionalistyčnoho škidnyctva v syntaksi ukrajins'koji literaturnoji movy*, both published in Kharkiv in 1934) and a small collection of articles on the language of some "proletarian" writers (Mykytenko, Kornijčuk, Holovko, writers of children's books, were criticized by Kahanovyč, O. Finkel', M. Tetijevs'kyj, O. Matvijenko, in *Za jakist' xudožn'oji movy*, Kharkiv, 1934). There were also attacks on historians of the Ukrainian language and on etymologists, as well as sallies against "bourgeois nationalism" in the Moldavian language and in the Turkic languages; a characterization of them is beyond the scope of this study.

The theoretical level of these discussions was uninspiring: they offered no contribution to general linguistics. In fact, their only essential point was to bring Ukrainian closer to Russian—a political problem, not a scholarly one. In fact, the very target of the critics, namely, the ethnographic school of the 1920s, was not strong in theory. That school's tenor and approach were romantically emotional and populistically patriotic, rather than based on a consistent philosophy or theory; its nature did not provoke theoretical discussion. The only attempt at such a discussion, the article by O. Finkel' entitled "Terminolohične škidnyctvo i joho teoretyčne korinnja" (*Movoznavstvo* 2), which was directed chiefly against T. Sekunda and M. Kalynovyč, failed on the theoretical level. Referring to Humboldt's and Potebnja's theory of a word's internal form (69), Finkel' tried to prove that terms without an obvious internal form have the advantage of being free from unnecessary associations (70), a debatable point but one never properly developed. Both etymologically lucid and etymologically opaque terms have advantages and disadvantages. But, generally speaking, when a word becomes a term, its etymological ties are broken. For instance, when in Slovene 'comet' is rendered as *repatica*, derived from *rep* 'tail', hardly any astronomer who uses this word thinks of a dog's or cat's tail. When a Hungarian calls 'ethnography' *néprajz*, based on *nép* 'people' and *rajz* 'description', so that the term literally means 'a people description,' the "concreteness" of the word hardly precludes him from being as good an ethnographer as, say, any American scholar working in that field. Finkel' made some comparisons with Czech and Polish, but these he took from Sekunda and used haphazardly. Terminological problems in the languages of Lithuania, Latvia, Finland, Yugoslavia, India, and the Arab countries were not even mentioned. Time and again Finkel' strayed from a scholarly key into cheap journalism bordering on political denunciation.

Even quantitatively, the linguistic attack was limited. Probably all its publications could be collected in a single volume. But some articles constantly reappeared in newspapers and journals published for mass circulation, and they were continually quoted and referred to. This saturation created a depressing and suffocating environment for linguistic endeavors.

Nominally the journal *Movoznavstvo* had an orientation toward Marrism. But there were no followers of Marr in the Ukraine (not even Kahanovyč espoused Marrism; the single, feeble attempt at an original work was V. Babak's report at a conference of young scholars, "Pro dejaki pytannja istoryčnoho rozvytku ukrajins'koji movy"; *Visti AN Ukr.S.R.R.*," 1936, 1, 185–95). The gap was filled with translations of works by Russian Marrists. (In 1935 the Institute also published an anthology of Marr's texts, *Narysy z osnov novoho včennja pro movu*, compiled by M. Suhak and I. Zborovs'kyj; this, too, contained no original contributions.) The generally low level of the publication can be shown (for issues 1–5) by grouping the contents into political denunciations, Marrists' writings, and scholarly materials; these three kinds of materials are represented by 333, 74, and 37 pages, respectively (discounting the chronicle and the terminological lists). Under Kahanovyč, no scholarly books were published and *Movoznavstvo* was the only outlet for scholarship in linguistics,[4]

[4] The several pamphlets (e.g., N. Solodkyj's) decrying nationalism in lingustics did not differ in tone or in scholarly level from articles in *Movoznavstvo*. One peculiar publication was the small collection of articles edited by N. Kahanovyč, *Mova robitnyka* (Kharkiv, 1934), containing contributions by Kahanovyč, L. Dohad'ko, V.

so it can be said truly that linguistic study in the Ukraine was entirely suspended.

Undoubtedly, Xvylja regarded the revision of spelling as his most urgent linguistic task. That task was accomplished in a very short time. Unlike the preceding code of spelling rules, the new one was not subject to public discussion, but only to several of Xvylja's pronouncements. Nor was it revealed who carried out the actual work—most likely it was Kahanovyč. The new spelling was introduced in newspapers and other publications suddenly, in May 1933, without any preliminaries. Unprepared readers were confronted with an accomplished linguistic coup. Teachers and students realized that the language rules they knew were now invalid, whereas the new ones were unknown to them. Soon, however, the rules were set forth in preliminary form in a little-known periodical, *Politexnična osvita* (1933, 6; see Hol'denberh and Korolevyč 180). A separate booklet of the new rules, entitled *Ukrajins'kyj pravopys*, was published at the end of 1933.

According to Xvylja (*Za markso-lenins'ku krytyku* 1933, 7, 18), 126 corrections, many of them substantial, were made to old rules, and the chapter on foreign words was rewritten in its entirety. For native words having doublet forms, preference was given to the forms resembling Russian: e.g., in the genitive singular of feminine substantives ending in a consonant, the desinence *-y* was replaced by *-i* (*radosti, soli*). Such forms occur primarily in the Southeastern dialects, so that a certain shift in the dialectal basis of the standard language ensued. In some cases, however, spellings that existed in no major dialects were introduced (e.g., the genitive singular *imeni* instead of the older form *imeny*). In the distribution of the adjectival suffixes *-s'k-* vs. *-z'k-* vs. *-c'k-*, the Russian forms were followed so closely that it was

---

Nevzorova, Z. Veselovs'ka, and I. Žurba. The articles contained observations about what was supposed to be the language of workers at the locomotive mill in Kharkiv. Inasmuch as they relate to strictly Ukrainian and not general Soviet language data, one can presume that they were actually based on the language of peasants recently driven *en masse* into industry, a case with parallels to the "mobilization" of shock-workers in literature (described by V. Hryško in *Sučasnist'* 1980, 2, pp. 70–95). Specific elements of the language of workers in the Ukraine remained unexplored, just as they were before the publication of Kahanovyč's sixty-page collection; they did not fit the scheme of Soviet ideology, which considered workers to be politically and culturally the leading class.

impossible to give any rule based on the structure of Ukrainian. The formulation that speakers should be led by language habits was reiterated, but nothing was said about these habits being Russian rather than Ukrainian.

In the choice of how to spell loan words, the reliance on Russian was nearly absolute. Use of the letter *g* was abolished wholly, so that, say, in Ukrainian *Goethe* was spelled *Hete*; the distribution of *l* vs. *l'* was copied, with all its inconsistencies, from Russian, where the usage was historically motivated (*Islandija* vs. *Finljandija*). As noted in the preceding section, East-Central Ukrainian did, as a rule, have loan words in the form mediated by Russian, so for the speakers of that—largest—part of the country, the new literary usage was a welcome innovation (or, rather, return to the old practice). For Western Ukrainians, the new spellings were a flat repudiation of their speech habits, which in the rendition of foreign words mostly followed the Polish pattern. In the Soviet Ukraine, the times called for fostering active hostility to all things Galician. The name of the Academy of Sciences was changed from "All-Ukrainian" to "Ukrainian," and its Galician members were dismissed (see above, chap. 6). Virtually all Galicians who lived in the Ukrainian SSR were arrested and liquidated. Xvylja went so far as to accuse the "Galician language" (!) of being imbued with "numerous influences of Polish bourgeois culture" (*Za markso-lenins'ku krytyku* 1933, 7, 21).

But the new spellings went farther than was justified by the speech habits of any speakers of Ukrainian. Words that had a form differing from the Russian one before the spelling reform of 1928/1929 were now relegated to the Russian usage, e.g., *xemija* 'chemistry', *ljampa* 'lamp' now became *ximija*, *lampa*. While admitting the pronunciation of *g* in some native words (onomatopoeic and naturalized medieval borrowings) Xvylja dropped the letter *g* from the Ukrainian alphabet (*Znyščyty*. . ., 69), apparently at the instigation of Postyšev. Overall, either the complete identity of Ukrainian and Russian forms or a one-to-one relation between the two was introduced wholesale, the only major exception being adherence to the traditional so-called "rule of nine letters" (the rule required that the West European *i* be rendered as *y* after nine consonants if before another consonant, and as *i* in other positions; the rule was already part of the original spelling of 1919—note its § 10). All in all, no more than perhaps half a dozen foreign words preserved their traditional Ukrainian form, e.g., *adresa*, *pošta, Evropa* vs. Russian *adres, počta, Jevropa.*

In lexicography, the new Institute of Linguistics was charged with preparing replacements for the Academy's general Russian-Ukrainian dictionary and for all the withdrawn terminological dictionaries published or cancelled in preparation. The chronicle section of *Movoznavstvo* time and again listed new dictionaries—eleven in number—as being in preparation (2, 143; 3–4, 165). Supposedly, not only Russian-Ukrainian, but also English-, French-, and German-Ukrainian dictionaries were to be published. None of these appeared. In terminology, published during Kahanovyč's time were only the so-called "terminological bulletins," i.e., lists of Ukrainian equivalents for the most common terms and abridged dictionaries for school use. Five terminological bulletins—botanical, mathematical, physical, technological, and medical—were published in 1934–1935, ranging in length from 24 to 82 pages each (of which about one-fifth was taken up by a theoretical introduction directed against "bourgeois nationalists"). Published during the same timespan were ten school dictionaries, ranging in length from 35 to 212 pages, for the fields of biology, botany, geography, mathematics (two), chemistry, anatomy, natural history, zoology. The only terminological dictionary on a somewhat higher level was *Slovnyk medyčnoji terminolohiji*, 1936 (220 pp.).

During Xvylja's time the dearth in the publication of new dictionaries—always an unmistakable sign of a language's suppression—was reinforced by the lack of new monographs in linguistics and of Ukrainian language manuals for adults. Exept for *Poradnyk z ukrajins'koho pravopysu ta punktuaciji*, by O. Bondarenko and J. Kudryc'kyj, nothing was published in those years.

The promised new general dictionary prepared by the Academy did not appear. The only completed work by the Institute of Linguistics in this domain was a Russian-Ukrainian dictionary compiled by S. Vasylevs'kyj and Je. Rudnyc'kyj, edited by Vasylevs'kyj and P. Mustjaca (Kiev, 1937). That work falls far short of all the requirements applied to academic dictionaries. It is relatively limited in size (890 small pages); in specific entries the semantic breakdown is underdeveloped, phraseology underrepresented, and the choice of vocabulary is arbitrary, with no reference to sources. Clearly, the compilers sought primarily to exclude all "class hostile" words and to include all "revolutionary" words, as well as, of course, to avoid

"Ukrainian bourgeois nationalism": wherever possible they selected (or introduced) words close to Russian and deleted synonyms that might lead the user to stray from this orthodox path. Their task was all the easier because the compilers did not delve into the realm of synonyms, lest the user gain the impression that Ukrainian was richer in words and semantic nuances than Russian. Examples of words taken directly from the Russian, with the necessary phonetic substitutions, can be quoted by the score, e.g., *hruzovyk* 'truck', *čužak* 'alien', *pryhorod* 'suburb', *rysystyj* 'trotting'. No less numerous were the semantic adaptations of Ukrainian words to the Russian ones, following the rule of one-to-one relation, e.g., Russian *dvor* 'yard' was rendered as Ukrainian *dvir*, without noting any synonyms (cf. Ukrainian *podvirja*, *obijstja*); since two Russian words, *rybak* and *rybolov*, correspond to the Ukrainian word *rybalka* 'fisherman,' the latter was assigned to Russian *rybak* while for Russian *rybolov* the same word was introduced as a Ukrainian form.

In summary, the Russian-Ukrainian dictionary published in 1937 almost ideally reflected the ideological requirements made of it. Yet it appeared at the wrong time. The dictionary's publication coincided with the fall of Postyšev and the subsequent new wave of terror, which engulfed Zatons'kyj, Xvylja, and P. Ljubčenko, as well as their followers and henchmen. Kahanovyč, too, was slated for annihilation, as were many of the "proletarian" writers he had praised, such as I. Mykytenko and I. Kyrylenko. But more scapegoats were needed. The dictionary provided them. Two correspondents of *Pravda*, T. Lil'čenko and D. Vadimov, were dispatched to Kiev with the special assignment to find Ukrainian nationalism within and around the CPU. The campaign Xvylja had promoted in 1933 was repeated in 1937, only this time Xvylja was the target. Between reports on how Ukrainian nationalism was allegedly blossoming in the museums of Kiev (*Pravda*, 25 September 1937) and in the Kiev Opera (*Pravda*, 4 January 1938), one article made a particularly frenzied attack on the Institute of Linguistics.

The issue of *Pravda* dated 4 October 1937 published the article, entitled "Kak 'očiščali' ukrainskij jazyk" (How the Ukrainian language was 'rectified'). It was signed N. N. Koševoj, probably a pseudonym (Lil'čenko and Vadimov may have been the authors). Since the scholarly production of the institute was nearly nil, and since Koševoj, or whoever the authors were, clearly understood little about linguistics, the target of the attack was the newly published Russian-Ukrainian dictionary. To quote from the report: "Ukrainian nationalists exerted every effort to tear Ukrainian culture away from the fraternal Russian culture and to direct the Ukrainian people toward the capitalist West, toward fascist Germany"; "The enemy of the people Xvylja directed all his endeavors to fighting so-called 'Russianisms,' which quite legitimate and necessary Ukrainian words were often understood to be. ... This line of Xvylja's became official because it was supported by the enemies of the people Ljubčenko, Popov, and Killerog. For four years the Ukrainian language was 'rectified' in that way." (The author[s] obviously knew very little about the campaign of 1933 and the "nationalism" of the twenties so that he presented it as beginning in 1933 with Xvylja!)

Specific facts in the *Pravda* report were few. The dictionary rendered Russian *upravljat'*, *verxovnyj*, *batrak*, *torgaš*, *blagodušnyj*, *zlonravnyj*, *gonka*, *starejšina*, *lom*, *glyba*, *sjurtuk*, *lugovoj*, and *služebnye časy* by the Ukrainian *keruvaty*, *najvyščyj*, *najmyt*, *kramar*, *bezžurnyj* and *bezturbotnyj*, *neputjaščyj*, *honytva*, *najstarišyj*, *bruxt*, *bryla*, *surdut*, *lučnyj*, and *urjadovi hodyny*, respectively. The author of the report maintained that the Russian words should be used in the Ukrainian dictionary entries. The other charge was that the dictionary (following the officially adopted spelling) admitted the declension of the words *bjuro* and *depo* and, in part (instrumental singular), *radio*—usage that was condemned as the "grossest vulgarization" (in Russian these words are indeclinable). It was for giving such usages that Xvylja and the compilers of the dictionary were said to have paved the way for German military intervention.

The accusation was so ludicrous that members of the Institute of Linguistics, headed by Mustjaca (apparently Kahanovyč had already been removed), politely repudiated them, a daring and rare act in those days. They admitted only that *verxovnyj* 'supreme' should have been used in Ukrainian, too. The root of the problem was that until 1936–1937 *verxovnyj* was used in Russian to denote the supreme court, which in Ukrainian was generally rendered by *najvyščyj sud*. The Constitution of 1936–1937 introduced the new governmental body called, in Russian, *verxovnyj sovet*, which in Ukrainian was to be rendered *verxovna rada*. In justifying their choice, Mustjaca and his colleagues stated that the dictionary was already printed when the term appeared, and they promised to rectify the situation in the next edition. Disagreement with anything *Pravda* printed was unprecedented. In the issue of 29 December 1937, D. Vadimov (yes, no longer Koševoj!) responded with the report "Russko-ukrainskij slovar' i ego sostaviteli" (The Russian-Ukrainian dictionary and its compilers). Paraphrasing the statement of Koševoj (his alter ego?), Vadimov wrote, "Following the instructions of the fascist agents Ljubčenko and Xvylja, the bourgeois nationalists expelled (*vytravlivali*) from the dictionary every word even slightly similar to Russian and international terms while filling the dictionary with hostile humbug." He labeled the compilers of the dictionary a "gang of spies that have ensconced themselves in the Institute of Linguistics." His statement "The majority of the compilers of the dictionary have been unmasked as bourgeois nationalists, as traitors of the fatherland with long-running experience" would indicate that its authors and editor had by that time been jailed. The dictionary was withdrawn from circulation.

At about this same time, *Komunist* launched an attack against Xvylja's *Ukrajins'kyj pravopys*. Finding an anti-Russian bias in that work was even harder than determining one in the dictionary. The only factual reproaches contained in the spelling manual were against *Evropa* (the word would be *Jevropa* in Russian pronunciation) and against compound words of the type *dvopoverxovyj* and *trystupnevyj*, which following the Russian pattern would begin with *dvox-* and *tr'ox-* (Russian *dvux-*, *trëx-*). The remainder of the article reiterated the familiar formulas about espionage, fascism, interventionism, etc.

The Institute of Linguistics had been routed, nearly all its workers had been arrested and either sent to forced labor camps or shot, and the publication of *Movoznavstvo* was suspended. The situation in linguistics resembled that in the political leadership of the Ukraine.

A few remarks about the staff of the linguistic institutions of the Academy are in order. After the major purge of 1929, when the trials connected with SVU were initiated, a few collaborators of the Institute of the Ukrainian Scientific Language escaped censure and became members of the Institute of Linguistics that replaced the defunct institution. None of these individuals survived the purge of 1933. The new staff of the Institute of Linguistics was swept away in 1937–1938, with only two exceptions—I. Hubarževs'kyj and I. Kyryčenko. One person whose name appeared in all three periods was P. Horec'kyj, but even this exception is deceptive: in 1932 or thereabouts he was arrested and for several years not allowed to do scholarly work. (A list of the collaborators of the institute is given by Polons'ka 2, 169ff.; unfortunately it is not fully accurate.) Any continuity in Ukrainian linguistic study was lost.

No linguists remained to revise Xvylja's spelling. Yet the language had to be "purified" from Xvylja's and Kahanovyč's "nationalistic" distortions. The initiative was taken by the style editors of party publications. There are now no written documents confirming this activity, but I, for one, saw lists of prohibited words that the style editors of *Komunist* sent to all periodicals. The lists contained two columns. The first was titled "Words not to be used," and the second bore the heading "Words to be used." The words in the second column were closer to Russian than those in the first. Although the lists were never published, they were taken as binding. Another source of information about the language norms was official publications, especially the translation of the book *Kratkij kurs istorii VKP(b)*, whose Russian original was approved and partly written by Stalin and whose Ukrainian text mirrored the original as closely as the anonymous translator(s) deemed possible. Only in exceptional cases were instructions rectifying the language printed: for instance, Hol'denberh and Korolevyč (246) register a *Movnyj bjuleten'* (1; Kiev, 1936) based on the Ukrainian translation of Lenin's work (not available to me). In most instances such instructions were hectographed.

The havoc in norms for the Ukrainian language heavily affected schools. Teachers were confused and frightened, and students were bewildered. Not to follow the new trend was criminal, but to follow it was impossible, because of the lack of information. Instability seemed to be an inherent feature of the Ukrainian language, in contrast to Russian, which suffered no upheaval of any kind. The already damaged prestige of Ukrainian sank further.

With the rise of Xruščov and the cessation of mass terror, the situation began to normalize. As if symbolically, the Institute of Linguistics got a new director, M. Kalynovyč. His fields were Sanskrit and the Romance languages, but at least he was a scholar, not a career party man—after all, Xruščov wanted to establish order, not to foster Ukrainian culture and language. Some real changes took place only later, with the occupation in September of 1939 of Galicia and Western Volhynia and their legal incorporation into the Ukrainian

SSR (except for the Berestja [Brest] area, which went to Belorussia); in June of 1940 the occupation spread to Bukovina.

Conscious of the perilous effects of the tsarist administration's policy of Russification during World War I, the government of the USSR sought to play on the patriotic, i.e., Ukrainian (and anti-Polish), feelings of the West Ukrainian population. Of the seven major newspapers that began publication (replacements for the "bourgeois" newspapers that were shut down on the day of the occupation), six were in Ukrainian and only one in Polish. (A Russian newspaper also began publication, but it was designed specifically for the military.) The university and all institutions of professional education became Ukrainian. Ukrainian replaced Polish on all signboards; it became the language of the legal system and general administration (Prokop 46ff.). To be sure, the arrest and deportation of Ukrainian civic leaders began a few days after the occupation (Prokop 45), under the direction of political police (NKVD), whose cadres were Russian; but during the first months of the occupation the heaviest blows fell on the Poles.[5] All these measures signified a necessity for some semblance of protecting, and even fostering, Ukrainian language and culture also in the "older" Soviet Ukraine. The steps taken in that direction had a symbolic and superficial character, for no cessation of Russification was intended. Nonetheless, there was some reaction to the new situation.

Some idea of the character and scope of the "new wave" in national and language policy in the Ukraine can be obtained from an enumeration of the new measures. The Galicians expelled from the Academy in 1934 were restored to their academic status. To demonstrate regard for the older generation of Ukrainian scholars and writers, academician A. Kryms'kyj, who for years had been in disfavor and in danger of annihilation, was celebrated and bestowed an order

---

[5] By the beginning of 1941, however, terror had clearly begun to be directed against Ukrainians. The incompatibility of what was labeled "bourgeois nationalism" with the new regime had become clear. This became especially evident in the case of 59 Ukrainian nationalists brought to trial in Lviv in January of 1941 (Prokop 78). Even sooner, with the arrival of Metropolitan Nikolaj (Jaruševič) early in 1940, the active Russification of the Orthodox church in Volhynia began (Prokop 58).

In Bukovina, occupied a year later, on 28 June 1940, the political sway towards Ukrainian was less ostentatious; it is said that the language of administration was to a great extent Russian (Prokop 83).

on the occasion of his seventieth birthday, in January 1941, although he was not entrusted with any editorial work (later, at the beginning of the world war, he was apparently murdered). At the Institute of Linguistics, *Movoznavstvo* was revived under a new title, *Naukovi zapysky*; volume 1 appeared in 1941. L. Bulaxovs'kyj was given the task of preparing a survey of Modern Standard Ukrainian (which was published, in two volumes, after the war). A new standardization of spelling was initiated: M. Hruns'kyj, a scholar of the older generation, was commissioned to undertake the task, and in 1939 his *Ukrajins'kyj pravopys* (fourth edition) appeared in print. In what was perhaps the most symptomatic gesture, the national (not only social) liberation of the Western Ukraine was touted. For the first time, the phrase "the great Ukrainian people" appeared in propaganda. (For example, *Pravda* gave the following account of Xruščov's report at the Fifteenth Congress of the CPU, in May 1940: "Comrade Xruščov ended his speech with a toast in honor of the *great* Ukrainian people reunited under the leadership of comrade Stalin in one Soviet Ukrainian state" [*Pravda*, 17 May 1940]; he is quoted as having said the phrase "the reunification of the *great* Ukrainian people in one Soviet Ukrainian state" (*Pravda*, 18 May 1940; emphasis mine). Until that time, the epithet was reserved for the Russian people alone, as in Xruščov's speech at the Fourteenth Congress of the CPU two years previously: "The Ukrainian people. . . is bound with blood ties to the great Russian people" (*Pravda*, 16 June 1938).

The measures were decorative in character; they introduced no substantial changes in the status of the Ukrainian language. The rules of the "Soviet Ukrainian" language set forth in 1939 were imposed on Galician writers and school students without any concessions (Wexler 153); the new edition of *Ukrajins'kyj pravopys* published in that year only eliminated some inconsistencies and incongruities. Government functionaries and other delegates sent to Galicia, Volhynia, and Bukovina used Ukrainian when speaking with or for the "natives." This had a favorable effect on the status of the Ukrainian language. By that time any remaining Ukrainian linguists were so frightened that they dared not raise their voices. By contrast, some writers did venture to do so, although they, too, had been subjected to persecution.

As has already been noted (chap. 6), during the years of Ukrainianization many writers were unhappy with the severe regularization of the standard language motivated by populist interests, and with the linguists of the ethnographic school who imposed rules on literature without regard for its unique requirements. By 1937–1938, the language situation had changed radically, but the seeds of mutual discontent were again in evidence. Ukrainian was again severely and arbitrarily regularized, this time in favor of similarities with Russian. A number of words, phrases, and syntactic constructions were outlawed.

Writers could and did protest by using prohibited language components. One writer who did so was Mykola Bažan. To give one example, the word *bryla* 'block, boulder', as already noted, was proscribed by no less an authority in questions of Ukrainian linguistics than *Pravda*, yet Bažan used it in his—otherwise officially approved—translation of Šota Rustaveli's *The Knight in Tiger's Skin*. In addition to such "silent" resistance, there was at least one instance of "loud" resistance, even prior to the occupation of Galicia and Volhynia. In 1939 *Literaturna hazeta* (no. 34, July 4) published an article by Jurij Janovs'kyj entitled "Narodna mova." Janovs'kyj overtly objected to what he called the impoverishment of the language by style editors who barred so many words and phrases in popular use. Reversing roles, Janovs'kyj made these "purificators" of the Ukrainian language from so-called nationalistic words into "nationalists" themselves: "It was in their Ukrainian nationalist interest to call native words nationalistic, to expel the national spirit (*narodnyj dux*) from the literature, so that the writer would become unable to serve his nation." He continued: "Following the example of style editors of newspapers and publishing houses, we construct something like language hencoops and hold them up as something worthwhile." Janovs'kyj went on to indulge in unabashed national romanticism: "The history of a language is the history of a nation. A nation's language is her soul, her pride, her past, present and future. . . . Let us love our people's language. If there is no language, there is no writer. Let us be frank: we are negligent in our attitude to the language. Our language is poor, lean, colorless, awkward, half-baked. . . . We do not study the language of our classical writers. We do not know the language of our people, neat and tidy." He concluded: "Let us learn from our people. Let us learn from Stalin [sic!]."

Every charge was here, expressed in Aesopian language. The "impoverishment" of the language meant its Russification, "style editors" referred to language standardizers, "language of the people" was Ukrainian free from the prescriptions of Soviet planners. Those who devoted themselves to that language, the linguists who perished in the purges of the 1920s and 1930s, Janovs'kyj did not even mention. But the Soviet reader, accustomed to all published materials being replete with an official set of clichés, was sensitive to the smallest nuances. No doubt, the article was understood by many in the meaning Janovs'kyj had intended.

Literaturna hazeta tried to organize a discussion of the article. It published (in no. 36, 16 July 1939) four responses to Janovs'kyj's initiative—by a writer (M. Ryl's'kyj, ''Davno nazrile pytannja''), by a teacher (M. Oleško), by a journalist (H. Sabata), and by a student (P. Perepelycja). Ryl's'kyj wrote: ''The system of issuing decrees, of prohibitions and restrictions, the system of administrative interference, cannot be beneficial to the development of language culture.'' He accepted what Ukrainian had in common with Russian, but he also defended ''Polonisms,'' within and without quotation marks. He wanted the dictionary being prepared at the Institute of Linguistics to be submitted to a public discussion.

No further discussion ensued, and Janovs'kyj's article has not been mentioned since. Yet neither Janovs'kyj nor the editor of *Literaturna hazeta* was punished—a novelty for the time. After so many years of relentless, cruel mass terror, an intellectual had spoken out about the Ukrainian language situation without paying dearly for the act.

An effect of the occupation of Galicia, Volhynia, and Bukovina was the exposure of the Soviet Ukrainian population, albeit limited (permissions to visit the occupied regions were issued only by the secret police), to an entirely different status of the Ukrainian language. In the Western Ukraine, speaking Ukrainian was an act of pride and defiance. During the ensuing years, a number of the Soviet (even communist) intelligentsia became ''contaminated'' with the same kind of nationalism (as well as other kinds, including political). Among them were K. Hupalo, playwright, H. Stecenko, prose writer, and J. Pozyčanjuk, correspondent of *Komsomolec' Ukrajiny*. These individuals broke with the Soviet system and ideology; some took part in the struggle against it during the war years, in reaction to the Soviet language and nationalities policy. Such changeovers were hardly a mass phenomenon, but they were not insignificant.

Twelve years earlier, in November 1927, L. Kaganovič had listed seven items in defining Russian nationalism in relation to the Ukraine. These are quoted below in full:

(1) Lessening of the significance of the Ukraine as a part of the USSR; attempts to treat the USSR as in fact a liquidation of the national republics

(2) Preaching of a neutral attitude by the party toward the development of Ukrainian culture; treatment of the latter as a backward, "peasant" [culture] in opposition to the "proletarian" Russian one

(3) Attempting to preserve at any price the predominance of the Russian language in the internal official, social, and cultural life of the Ukraine

(4) [Maintaining a] formal attitude toward Ukrainianization, often recognized only by word of mouth

(5) [Constantly] regenerating great-power chauvinistic views that Ukrainianization is artificial, that it leans on a "Galician" language incomprehensible to the people, etc.; fostering these views in the party

(6) Tending not to carry out the policy of Ukrainianization in cities and among the proletariat, but limiting it to the countryside alone

(7) Tendentiously exaggerating specific distortions in carrying out Ukrainianization, and attempting to present these as an entire system of the violation of rights of national minorities (Russians, Jews) (*Budivnyctvo* 153).

The definition reads as a characterization of the Postyšev-Xruščov era *avant la lettre*, although its composer, Kaganovič, has never been labeled a nationalist or a deviator of any sort from Stalin's "general line." In fact, the years between 1933 and 1941 was a period of systematic and frontal attack against the Ukrainian culture and language, as well as against the Ukrainian intelligentsia. The period compares with the months of the first Soviet occupation of the Ukraine in 1918, only on a much larger scale. Its effects were devastating. It brought about the Russification of many speakers of Ukrainian; it precluded the planned growth in the use of Ukrainian in cities and industrial centers; and it caused many speakers of Ukrainian to develop feelings of servility and fear.

After several years of disrepute, Russian chauvinism had triumphed. Within the Soviet Union, overtly chauvinistic anti-Ukrainian utterances were not allowed in public. Abroad, however, such censorship did not exist. The chauvinistic Russian evaluation of Xvylja's pogrom of Ukrainian culture, which many in the Soviet Union sensed, was voiced, for instance, in an article by a Russian émigré in Czecho-Slovakia, who went so far as to express his satisfaction with Xvylja and Postyšev's policy (Jakobson 335, 341) and to call the idea of the Ukrainianization of the Kuban' region "chauvinistische Abweichung." To him, Polonisms in the Ukrainian language were anathema, whereas Russianisms were laudable (ibid., 341). He greeted the new policy of "cultural rapprochement" among the "sister peoples" (ibid., 342) jubilantly, probably because it augured the future absorption of Ukrainian by Russian.

Yet if the goal of the new de-Ukrainianization policy was to deal a mortal blow to the Ukrainian language and culture, it failed—at least for the time being. That failure was evident in the reaction of at least some speakers of Ukrainian to the occupation of the Western Ukraine. During the war years it would be recognized by the government itself, as it reverted to patriotic, nearly nationalistic slogans. In other words, the conflict between Ukrainian and Russian, as the two languages in the Ukraine, was not settled. It continued into the postwar years, without resolution. What Soviet policy did achieve was to draw the conflict back to the situation before Ukrainianization was undertaken: the peasantry and the humanist intelligentsia were aligned against the workers and technological intelligentsia, although the makeup of all these groups changed radically, usually in a way that did not favor Ukrainian.

The novelty of the 1933–1941 period was that along with overt efforts to Russify speakers of Ukrainian came interference into the very substance and structure of the Ukrainian language, interference which opened it defenselessly to Russian influences and which shifted the dialectal basis of the standard language eastwards. The actual penetration of Russian elements into written Ukrainian during that time is hard to measure quantitatively, but it seems not to have been very heavy; Soviet linguistic policy legitimized Russianisms which were already common in Ukrainian, rather than introduced new ones (discounting, of course, common Sovietisms which spread via Russian to all the languages of the Soviet Union). The essential character of the Ukrainian language underwent no major changes, as can be confirmed by comparing literary or journalistic texts of, say, 1925 with those of 1935 or 1940. The major attainments of the short years of the Ukraine's independence or semi-independence were retained. A much greater change was evident in a comparison of newspapers published in 1905–1917, on the one hand, and those of 1925, on the other. (These conclusions are impressionistic and should be verified quantitatively.) Nor can one observe any drastic reduction of Galician components in the general (not technical) language of 1933–1941.

There was, however, one potentially important innovation: the opening of Ukrainian to Church-Slavonicisms introduced, naturally, via Russian. Church-Slavonicisms were used in the nineteenth century by Ševčenko and P. Kuliš, but the subsequent predominance of populistic trends eliminated most of them from Ukrainian. The development resulted in the "monolinguality" of the Ukrainian standard language as opposed to the "bilinguality" of the Russian language, in which Church Slavonic components were important and often had a specific stylistic role (Shevelov 1966, 166ff; 1977, 261f.). During the Soviet period the bilingual Ukrainian intelligentsia introduced Russian Church Slavonic, on the Russian pattern, into Ukrainian; the Ukrainians were tempted by the easy stylistic effect they produced. The main channels were newspapers; important, too, was the work of some outstanding Ukrainian poets (e.g., the words *čuždyj, obezhlavyv, smrad* in Tyčyna, 1936–1937; *syvohlavyj, vražyj* in Ryl's'kyj 1940; *zveršuje, otec', svjaščennyj, istynnyj* in Bažan 1937–1938). In poetry, Church-Slavonicisms became an ingredient of odes, a genre encouraged and imposed under Stalin. The opening of the gates to (Russian) Church-Slavonicisms threatened to change the stylistic structure of Ukrainian. The culmination of this development would come in the postwar years.

CHAPTER SEVEN

The Interwar Period (1920 – 1939) in the Western Ukraine

After World War I, the West Ukrainian lands were divided among adjacent states. In July 1918, Romania occupied Bukovina; by May 1919, the regions of Pidljašia, Xolm (Chełm), Ukrainian Polissia, and Western Volhynia were occupied by Poland; in July of the same year the Polish occupation of Galicia was completed; after the temporary division of Transcarpathia among Czech, Hungarian, and Romanian military forces, in September 1919, the region became part of Czecho-Slovakia. It is according to these divisions that the language question is discussed here.

Ukrainian Lands under Poland

A principle of Polish policy in the Ukrainian lands was to forestall unity among the Ukrainians. Therefore the policy in Galicia was different from that in those lands previously belonging to Russia. The separation of Galicia from other Ukrainian lands was especially strict. Galician publications were forbidden outside Galicia, Ukrainian Galician organizations outlawed, and any kind of collaboration was considered illegal (*EU* 1, 555). The restriction of Ukrainian activities was stronger in the other formerly Russian lands than in Volhynia. Among the former Russian lands, there were differences in policy toward Volhynia, toward Ukrainian Polissia, and toward Xolm with Pidljašia. In Pidljašia, during the 1930s, Poland instituted the complete prohibition of a Ukrainian press, publications, and public use of the language, dissolution of the society *Ridna xata* with its reading rooms, and the subordination of the Ukrainian cooperative movement to Polish surveillance. There were attempts to revivify local ethnic distinctions even within Galicia. Particularly persistent was the case of the Lemkians (Lemkos), who were often considered a separate people having nothing to do with Ukrainians. Non-Lemko teachers were eventually removed from local Lemko schools and, in 1938, the teaching of Lemkian (instead of Standard Ukrainian) was even introduced in elementary schools. Some attempts were made to keep the Huculs and the Bojkians (Bojkos) apart from the Ukrainian identity, but these were more sporadic (*EU* 1, 562).

The legal status of the Ukrainian language in Poland was determined partly by international treaties and partly by the Polish constitution and Polish laws. The earliest international treaties relevant to the issue were that concluded at Versailles between the Allied Nations and Poland, on 28 June 1919, and that concluded at Riga between Soviet Russia (with the Soviet Ukraine) and Poland, on 18 March 1921. The Versailles treaty stipulated, among other things (§ 7): "No restriction shall be imposed on the free use by any Polish national of any language in private intercourse, in commerce, in religion, in the press, or in publications of any kind, or at public meetings. Notwithstanding any establishment by the Polish Government of an official language, adequate facilities shall be given to Polish nationals of non-Polish speech for the use of their language either orally or in writing, before the courts." The subsequent sections read: (§ 8) "Polish nationals who belong to racial, religious, or linguistic minorities shall enjoy the same treatment and security in law and in fact as other Polish nationals. In particular they shall have an equal right to establish, manage, and control at their own expense charitable, religious, and social institutions, schools, and other educational establishments, with the right to use their own language and to exercise their religion freely therein"; (§ 9) "Poland will provide, in the public educational system of towns and districts in which a considerable proportion of Polish nationals of other than Polish speech are residents, adequate facilities for insuring that in the primary schools instruction shall be given to the children of such Polish nationals through the medium of their own language" (Parry 417f.).

The Riga treaty reassured Ukrainians in Poland "in conformity with the principle of the equality of peoples...free development of culture and language as well as the exercise of their religion" (§ 7, 1; Riga, p. 10). At that time, the future of Eastern Galicia was in limbo. That decision was issued two years later, on 15 March 1923, by the Conference of Ambassadors of the Allied Nations. It recognized the Ukrainian part of Galicia as a part of Poland, and reserved for it certain singularities in law (Makowski 241, Dombčevs'kyj 192).

In accordance with the obligations Poland had accepted—but without providing for the autonomy of the Ukrainian region—the first Polish constitution, of 17 March 1921, stated the following in two articles: (§ 109) "Every citizen has the right to preserve his nationality and to foster his language and national peculiarities. Special statutes shall secure to the minorities in the Polish state full and free development of their national peculiarities by means of autonomous unions of [those] minorities established by public law, in the framework of general self-governing unions. The State shall have right of control in relation to their activity as well as of replenishment of their financial means in case of need"; (§ 110) "Polish citizens that belong to minorities of nationality, faith, or language, have the right, equal with other citizens, to found, oversee, and manage, at their own expense, charitable, religious, and public schools and other educational institutions, as well as [the right to] use their language in them and to practice the prescriptions of their religion in them" (Handelsman 128).

The Constitution of 23 April 1935 reiterated these two articles word for word. Moreover, it added: (§ 7, 2) "Origin, religious confession, sex, and nationality shall not be reasons for the limitation of his [the Polish citizen's] rights"; however, these rights were limited: (§ 10) "No activity may be contrary to the goals of the State as expressed in law. In case of opposition, the State recurs to means of constraint" (*Constitution* 1935, 58f., 34f.).

Neither constitution designated Polish as the state (official) language. This notion was, however, firmly established by particular laws. According to the resolutions of the Sejm of 16 February 1923, and of the Senate of 23 March 1923, the language of these two institutions was exclusively Polish (Dombčevs'kyj 199). On 31 July 1924, a law specifically on the state (official) language was adopted: (§ 1) "The official language of the Polish Republic is Polish. All state and self-governing authorities as well as the officers of administration conduct their business in internal and external service in the official language, with the exceptions referred to in the following articles" (Dombčevs'kyj 199, Papierzyńska 220ff.). In 1927, the Ministry of Military Affairs issued a decree that began: "All military authorities on the entire territory of the Polish Republic conduct their affairs in both internal and external service only and without any exception in the state, i.e., Polish language" (Dombčevs'kyj 213).

Exceptions to the exclusive use of the Polish language were permitted in the five *województwa* of Lviv, Stanyslaviv, Ternopil', Volhynia, and Polissia. In March 1920, Eastern Galicia was renamed "Eastern Little Poland (*Małopolska Wschodnia*)." By an order of 3 December 1920, all of Galicia was divided into four województwa, with that of Cracow added to those of Lviv, Stanyslaviv and Ternopil'. The bulk of the Lemko region was included into the Cracow województwo and therefore was excluded from any guarantee of language rights. Laws concerning the predominantly Ukrainian województwa were numerous and overlapping, but their essentials can be summarized as follows. In the courts of the five województwa in question, judges should accept statements in Ukrainian and respond in that language, but all the internal documentation should proceed in Polish. A court decision can be written, if the parties so demand, in both Polish and Ukrainian. The police was obliged to record testimony in Polish alone. All appeals made to higher courts outside the five regions had to be in Polish. Promissory notes could be written in Ukrainian in the five województwa with Ukrainian population, but then they could be contested there alone. Within the regions mail could be addressed in Ukrainian, but telegrams and packages had to be addressed in Polish (Dombčevs'kyj 204f.).

School legislation was no less entangled. The semi-official publication of the Ministry of Education issued in English (1928) stated: "The mother tongue in the public and private minority schools is not only used as [the] language of instruction, but it is considered equal to the Polish language in internal administration, in conferences of the teachers' council, in correspondence between the school and parents, and in school certificates" (*Education* 128). This regulation virtually confined Ukrainian to use within school walls. To open an elementary Ukrainian state school—provided Ukrainians were not less than 20 percent (from 1932, 25 percent) of the community—it was required that parents of not less than 40 children apply to the school authorities (their signatures should all be notarized); to have Ukrainian taught as a subject in a Polish school, the signatures of 18 parents sufficed (*Education* 123f., Dombčevs'kyj 236). The law also permitted Ukrainian private schools to exist on various levels. Opening such a school was regulated by a law of 11 March 1932. In each case permission was to be granted by the Polish administration upon the submission of the school's statute and program and of the applicant's certificate of noninvolvement in any crime against morality or against the state. Private schools were subject to the surveillance of the state administration. It was understood that a school would be closed if the administration found that instruction there was disloyal to Poland or if the school failed to neutralize harmful influences upon youth (*Dziennik ustaw Rzeczypospolitej Polskiej* 1932, no. 38, p. 545f.). The same law decreed that teachers' seminaries could be either Polish or bilingual. To open a bilingual state school, the written application of the parents of at least 150 students was required (Dombčevs'kyj 246f.); to open a bilingual technical school (*szkoła fachowa*), at least 40 percent of the perspective pupils should be Ukrainian and, again, their parents should have submitted a special, signed application (ibid., 248). There were also various deadlines for such applications, some set long before the beginning of the academic year.

In sum, the opening of Ukrainian schools was made dependent on many formalities, such as certified signatures, deadlines, eligibility in terms of official census data, and loyalty to the Polish state, any of which could be manipulated as desired by authorities. The existence of any Ukrainian school was completely dependent on the local educational administration, which was entirely in Polish hands and which was often hostile to any expansion of Ukrainian education. In theory, Poland's international commitments required it to permit Ukrainian schools free ''in law and in fact''; in reality the established laws did not favor education in Ukrainian, and the actual situation was worse.

According to official data, in 1928 Poland had 804 Ukrainian public elementary schools, 2,120 bilingual ones, and 1,722 Polish ones with the Ukrainian language as a subject—altogether 4,646 schools offered some education in Ukrainian (*Education* 126). The dynamics of the educational system are revealed by a comparison of the interwar situation with that prior to 1919. For instance, in 1914, Galicia had 2,510 public elementary schools with instruction in Ukrainian, or 41 percent of all elementary schools (*EU* 1, 928). Under Poland the general number of schools grew, but that of Ukrainian schools declined drastically (from 2,510 in Galicia alone to 804 for Poland as a whole). A new type of bilingual school was established and became predominant. Soon growing in number to 2,120, the bilingual schools were a means of gradual but nearly certain Polonization.

The crucial years in the decrease of Ukrainian schools were the first half of the 1920s. In 1922/23 Galicia (more precisely the three województwa of Lviv, Stanyslaviv, and Ternopil') had 2,450 Ukrainian schools; by 1926/27, that number had dropped to 864. There were no bilingual schools in 1922/23, but by 1926/27 their number stood at 1,339. In 1926, in the three Galician województwa the ratio of Ukrainian to Polish schools had become 864 vs. 2,298 (Papierzyńska 259).

In prerevolutionary times, Volhynia and the Polissia and Xolm areas, like the rest of the Russian Ukraine, had no Ukrainian schools. These started to appear under the German occupation during World War I, when their number is estimated to have grown to about 250. In 1922/23 their number was 442, vs. 89 bilingual and 543 Polish. By 1926/27, however, it sank to 2 versus 392 bilingual and 683 Polish. In 1937/38 the figures were 8,520 and 1,459 respectively (of the latter, 853 taught the Ukrainian language as a subject). Polissia had a negligible number of Ukrainian schools: 22 in 1922/23, none of which survived into the next academic year (one private school remained in Berestja). The Xolm region had no Ukrainian schools at all. In 1922 the Lemko area had 79 Ukrainian schools; in 1937/38, by contrast, no Ukrainian schools existed there, although 58 schools were bilingual. It is surmised that throughout Poland during the late thirties 7 percent of Ukrainian children went to Ukrainian schools, 45 percent to bilingual schools, and 48 percent to Polish schools (Papierzyńska 259, *EU* 1, 945).

In Galicia the number of Ukrainian high schools (*himnaziji* and *liceji*) was, in 1931/32, 5 state and 13 private schools; in 1937/38, the numbers were 10 and 35, respectively. By contrast, Polish schools of these types numbered 120 in 1931/32 and 220 in 1937/38. The presence of Ukrainian technical schools was negligible: 4 private Ukrainian schools in 1931/32 and 4 private and 1 state school in 1937/38. Outside Galicia, there were practically no Ukrainian high schools or professional schools in the Polish state (*EU* 1, 945).

The university at Lviv was linguistically entirely Polish, including the courses on Modern and Old Ukrainian (taught by J. Janów). Chairs of Ukrainian language and literature were admitted only at the University of Cracow, outside Ukrainian ethnic territory. The University of Warsaw had a faculty of Greek Orthodox theology, but all subjects were taught in Polish. In September 1920 Polish authorities offered to open a Ukrainian university in Stanyslaviv. Whether the project would have materialized if the Ukrainians had cooperated is debatable; in any event, the offer was rejected (Mudryj 84f.). The issue was raised once more in 1926, but again without any result (Papierzyńska 266f.). In 1921–1925 a clandestine Ukrainian university existed in Lviv, but by its very nature that institution could not develop into a full-fledged, recognized educational center. The only educational institution of higher education with instruction in Ukrainian that was open to Ukrainians was the Greek Catholic Theological Academy in Lviv, founded in 1928.

Within Galicia, active support of Ukrainian schools was centered in the Ukrainian Pedagogic Society (some representatives in the Polish Sejm and Senate also supported the issue). Founded as early as 1881, the Pedagogic Society resumed its activities after World War I and the Polish occupation. In 1926 it took the name of the *Ridna škola* (Native school) society. Led by intelligentsia, the organization had a fairly broad base. By 1939, it included 2,074 chapters with 105,000 members. The Polish authorities, as mentioned, did not permit Ridna škola to operate in any Ukrainian region outside Galicia.

The history of Ukrainian representation in the Polish Sejm and the Senate is rather complex: indeed, it reflects the overall development of Ukrainian-Polish relations. The election of 1922 was boycotted in Galicia, except for a small group of *Xliboroby* who favored the Polish government (Papierzyńska 137); that year Volhynia and Polissia together with Pidljaša sent 20 deputies to the Sejm and 6 to the Senate (ibid., 149f.). The election of 1928 sent 48 Ukrainian deputies to the Sejm (8 from Volhynia) and 11 to the Senate (for comparison, that year the Sejm had a total of 444 members—which would fall to 208 in 1935—and 96 in the Senate). In the election of 1930, the corresponding numbers were 26 and 5; in the elections of 1935 and 1938, they were 14 (5 from Volhynia) and 5. The decline was brought about by the Polish policy of terror (so-called pacification) in 1930 and after 1935 by changes in the Polish constitution and electoral rules. Clearly, Ukrainian representation (often split on specific issues) was too small to influence Polish legislation substantially; nonetheless, with its declarations and interpellations, it was still an important factor in shaping public opinion, in bringing the problems of Ukrainians in Poland, including language legislation and language status, to public attention, and in precluding further potential violations of Ukrainian rights.

Another factor determining the status of the Ukrainian language was the Polish terror against Ukrainians and the Ukrainian terror against Poles. Polish action against Ukrainians had three crests: in 1919, during and after the Polish-Ukrainian war, when it is estimated (*EU* 1, 556) that up to 23,000 Ukrainians were imprisoned; in 1930, when the pacification of Ukrainians was launched, especially in the countryside, so that branches of Prosvita were sacked, the boy scout organization Plast was disbanded and prohibited, and several Ukrainian *himnaziji* were closed; and in 1938. The Polish terror against Ukrainians as a group was directed by the government, with the active participation of paramilitary organizations like *Strzelec* and some other Polish groups. By contrast, the organized Ukrainian terror, which started with the founding of the clandestine Ukrainian Military Organization (1920) and gained momentum after its entry into the Organization of Ukrainian Nationalists (1929), had an individual character, in that it was directed against Poles believed to be anti-Ukrainian and against Ukrainians believed to be traitors in the Ukrainian-Polish conflict; yet, it also targeted Polish property, means of communication, and industry. Ukrainian terror, which arose as a reaction to Polish terror, strengthened Poland's anti-Ukrainian course and, in the long run, was one factor contributing to the demise of the democratic system in Poland's gradual shift to an authoritarian state. Landmarks in that development were J. Piłsudski's coup d'état in 1926, the disbanding of the Sejm and the Senate in 1930 (preceded by the pacification), the introduction of the new constitution in 1935, and the disbanding of the Sejm and the Senate in 1938.

With these changes in the political structure of Poland, it became easier to pursue an anti-Ukrainian policy in the economic domain and to carry out such other externally non-political measures as settling an estimated 300,000 Polish farmers and city dwellers in the Ukrainian lands (*EU* 1, 580), excluding Ukrainians from state service, transferring public servants of Ukrainian nationality to Western Poland, etc. The resulting situation was a Ukrainian-Polish war overt yet without a front, fueled by spreading mutual hatred, which made a compromise virtually impossible. In such conditions, the attempt at reconciliation, the so-called policy of normalization, could yield no results.

Yet until its defeat and disintegration in September 1939, the Polish state was not openly or consistently totalitarian. Ukrainian political parties still existed, and they had some representation, however curtailed or decorative, in the legislative bodies. Ukrainian schools were in decline, but they were not entirely proscribed; the Greek Catholic church did not undergo either liquidation or the imposition of state control, but remained, instead, a bulwark of Ukrainian culture and language.[1] Restricted from pursuing careers in state institutions, Ukrainians plunged into economic activity. Some operated on private initiative, thus creating a Ukrainian merchant class. Others organized a broad cooperative movement and unions of cooperatives, among which some, such as *Centrosojuz* and *Maslosojuz*, gained sufficient economic strength to be reckoned with.

The Ukrainian press was subject to some restrictions, but it was not submitted to preliminary censorship. It could, at least in Galicia, reflect various political views and attitudes, including nationalist and communist ones. Both quantitative growth and diversification characterize the Ukrainian press in Galicia at this time. During the interwar period Galicia had 44 political organs (discounting two published by Moscophiles) and 3 illustrated biweeklies. Among Ukrainian periodicals, there were 5 designed for children, 5 for women, 8 for boyscouts, 7 for students, 6 for teachers, 5 for workers in cooperatives, 6 religious and theological, 9 literary, 1 of the arts, 2 of music, 1 of cinema, 1 of humor and satire, 4 historical and philosophical, 1 of law, 1 of bibliography, 2 popular scientific, and 2 devoted to local lore; the total number was 143. True, these figures encompass the entire twenty-year interwar period: in no one year were 143 periodicals published. But the brief lifespan typical of earlier stages in the history of the Ukrainian press expanded in those years: the average longevity of a periodical during that period was 7.7 years. (The data are tallied on the basis of lists given in *EU* 1, 933–936, and are not exhaustive.) The situation was much worse in other regions of the Polish Ukraine, with their 4 general political periodicals, 3 church and 3 cooperative

---

[1] The same cannot be said of the Orthodox church in Poland. It was subject to fairly strict state control as prescribed by the decrees of 30 January 1922 and of 10 December 1938. In the Xolm region the 389 Orthodox churches that had existed in 1914 were reduced to 51 in 1939 (*EU* 1, 564).

periodicals; also the Ukrainian press was completely silenced in Polissia and the Xolm region during the 1930s.

Book production boomed. The numbers of Ukrainian books published during the interwar period were:

1924	195
1928	450
1931	342
1932	288
1934	346
1935	223
1938	476

The average printing jumped from 2,204 to 6,524 copies. Again, however, there was a disproportion between Galicia and other Ukrainian lands. For instance, in 1930, Galicia—the regions of Lviv, Stanyslaviv, and Ternopil'—published 340 books, whereas book production in Volhynia was 10 (23 Ukrainian books were published in Poland proper) (*EU* 1, 978).

The peculiar combination of suppression with certain liberties, of legal regulations with total arbitrariness by some officials, had an impact on the status of the Ukrainian language and on the psychology of its speakers in the Polish Ukraine. Not only was the Ukrainian language a vehicle of communication among farmers, clergy, and intellectuals; it also was a means of national self-assertion and defiance against the existing political regime. In the mid-nineteenth century, it was possible to be a Ukrainian, even a Ukrainian patriot, and yet speak in Polish to one's family. In the period between the two World Wars, such duality became impossible. Excluded from official use and often rejected as a means of communication by the state administration and the co-territorial Polish population, the Ukrainian language was purposefully used at frequent large public manifestations as a badge of belonging and as a self-imposed stigma. It seemed as if to the normal language functions of communication, appeal, and expression of affectivity (as established by C. K. Bühler in his *Sprachtheorie*, 1934) the function of ostentation was added. These psychological underpinnings sometimes stifled spontaneity in speech. In the larger cities of the Russian Ukraine, a total and apparently impersonal negation of the Ukrainian language led to its diminishing use; in the cities of the Polish Ukraine, a virulent but haphazard degradation of the Ukrainian language brought about a peculiar kamikaze attitude, in which choosing to speak Ukrainian had elements of social hysteria and of the speakers' mutual quasi-hypnosis.

S. Šax, a longtime resident of Lviv and a fairly objective memoirist, recollects (232) as a heroic act how, as first-graders, he and his classmates undertook a trip by rail from Lviv. The children were instructed by two seventh-graders that each small boy should go, one by one, to the wicket at the main station in Lviv and ask for his ticket in Ukrainian. Each boy met with abuse and insult from the Polish cashiers, but the tickets were purchased and the ride took place. The deprivation of spontaneity from the speech act was certainly by no means normal. This minor episode reflects the status of the Ukrainian language under Polish domination, and the experience of Ukrainian speakers in the interwar period.

It is difficult to say whether this collective psychosis on language precluded the Polonization of the population. In terms of social strata, it was most typical of the educated classes (including the clergy), but it also affected many middle- and lower-middle class people. The defiant attitude even expanded to the countryside (where, in general, Ukrainian was used ''naturally''), especially wherever Ukrainian peasants had to confront new Polish settlers. Šax notes a clergyman's observation that, among educated lay people, in all of urban Galicia he knew only two families in which a father, son, and grandson—i.e., three generations—identified with the Ukrainian nation (and used the language; Šax 63). Even if the observation was an overgeneralization, it reflects on the language situation. No doubt, the collectively accepted use of the Ukrainian language for ostentatious purposes hampered such processes. Yet it hardly stopped them. The Polish language remained more prestigious and, in the long run, it is prestige—especially if combined with material advantages—that tips the balance in such situations. However, the interwar period was too short a time to allow any far-reaching consequences of the new attitude to manifest themselves. The whole period lasted but twenty years, and a ''new attitude'' toward the Ukrainian language became fairly widespread some time after the linguistic (and social) fronts were established, following the incorporation of Galicia into Poland. Clearly, that ''new attitude'' was shared by those outside the bounds of the humanist intelligentsia. In spite of the efforts of the Polish administration to preclude such a development, the number of non-humanist—technical, in the broad sense—intelligentsia grew considerably. Lawyers, physicians, and engineers were at the center of that group; merchants, proprietors, cooperative entrepreneurs, and the like expanded its peripheries. V. Simovyč, a thoughtful observer of Ukrainian language circles in Lviv, described the linguistic situation thus: "After the First World War... our life became much more difficult, but the framework for our life broadened substantially" (Simovyč 1934 [1], 90).

The language of the church was a special case. The Greek Catholic church, which was very influential in Galicia, continued the tradition of using a Ukrainian variant of Church Slavonic as its liturgical language and the Lviv koine or dialect of Ukrainian in sermons and in communication with parishioners. Outside Poland, the Orthodox church was subject to the Russian church authorities; in Poland, the high Orthodox hierarchy remained Russian or pro-Russian, and the liturgical language was Church Slavonic with Russian pronunciation. Many Orthodox church communities in Volhynia and Polissia were dissatisfied with the church's stand. A broad movement for the de-Russification of the Orthodox church began in the 1920s, and part of that effort became not only the Ukrainian pronunciation of Church Slavonic, but the introduction of the Ukrainian language for clerical use. After a long and often violent campaign, the Orthodox church authorities had to concede that, in principle, Ukrainian was admissible in church services, without renunciation of Church Slavonic (Statement of the Metropolitan of Warsaw Dionisij, 2 August 1928; see Papierzyńska 112).

In internal structure and form the Ukrainian language of Galicia—which influenced that in Volhynia and Polissia—remained, as in Austrian times, a regional koine typical particularly of Lviv. It was not closed to dialectal elements, which varied from district to district, but with the growth of education these dialectal features were gradually suppressed and replaced by elements of the Lviv koine. This regional character was not the outcome of a deliberate policy or attitude. On the contrary, in principle Ukrainian speakers in the Polish Ukraine wanted to eliminate many Galician peculiarities from their language and to be all-Ukrainian or, as they put it, to adhere to the Ukrainian spoken in the Dnieper region (*naddniprjans'ka mova*). The high esteem in which Standard Ukrainian as developed in the Russian Ukraine was held transpired also from another term then used for that

Ukrainian literary language, Great-Ukrainian (*velykoukrajins'ka mova*). By accepting the term Galicians implicitly agreed to consider themselves and their language to be "Little-Ukrainian" (although that designation was never used). In the mid-1930s a more careful attitude about the "purity" of the language was noted by Simovyč (1934 [1], 90). It was also he who registered some "hyper–Great Ukrainian-isms," i.e., Russian words and phrases used by Ukrainian speakers in Poland because the speakers mistook them for "pure Ukrainian" (1934 [2], 150).

This was the core of the problem. Contacts between the Polish Ukraine and the Russian Ukraine became tenuous after the Sovietiza-tion of the latter; from the mid-1930s they came practically to a standstill. As part of the campaign against "capitalist spies" and "saboteurs," the slogan "the frontier under lock and key" was launched. Certainly the war being waged by the Kremlin against the peasantry required a complete communication black-out.

The only advisers available to Ukrainians in Poland on questions of "pure Ukrainian"—i.e. the Kiev Standard—were a small number of emigrants from the Russian Ukraine who left in or about 1920. One such emigrant interested in questions of language was Modest Levyc'kyj, who wrote "Paky i paky" (*Volja* 1920) and published *Ukrajins'ka hramatyka dlja samonavčannja* (3d ed., 1923); another was Je. Čykalenko, who wrote *Pro ukrajins'ku literaturnu movu* (1920; first published in 1907). Neither was a linguist. Levyc'kyj was a writer, and Čykalenko was originally a landowner and agricultural-ist. The only professional linguist among the émigré language advi-sors was Ivan Ohijenko. Very active in the field, Ohienko published *Ukrajins'kyj stylistyčnyj slovnyk* (1924), *Čystota i pravyl'nist' ukrajins'koji movy* (1925), *Narysy z istoriji ukrajins'koji movy* (1927; not actually a history), and *Skladnja ukrajins'koji movy*, in two volumes (1937, 1938), among other works. Particularly influential was the popular monthly *Ridna mova* that Ohienko published in War-saw in 1933–1939; there he applied the approach of the Kiev ethno-graphic school of the 1920s, which was destroyed by 1933. *Ridna mova* made use of every kind of language propaganda: in addition to articles, it published reviews of the language of various publications, advice to readers, responses to their queries, fictional dialogues about language questions, linguistic jokes, etc. But the emigrants from the Russian Ukraine were prevented by the Polish administration from settling in Galicia and other Ukrainian regions; as a rule they were restricted to purely Polish territory, especially Warsaw, which made maintaining personal contacts precarious.

In Galicia a similar approach, but without going to Ohijenko's extremes, was taken by V. Simovyč. After 1923, when his *Na temy movy* appeared as a book, Simovyč published little in the field of linguistic advice and standardization, only a few articles scattered in various periodicals.

Due to these circumstances, the practical impact of the Standard Ukrainian language on the Lviv koine was limited. School grammars either stuck to the Galician tradition entirely (S. Smal'-Stoc'kyj and F. Gartner, *Hramatyka ukrajins'koji [rus'koji] movy*, fourth edition, 1928) or innovated very little (*Hramatyčni vpravy*, for various grades and types of schools, by O. Popovyč, 1924 – 1928; detailed bibliography in Simovyč 1934 [3], 39). After the Soviet occupation, in September 1939, the Kiev standard (as it existed at that time; see above, chap. 7) was imposed by the authorities on all written texts without any discussion. There was no time to influence the oral standard, however, and it remained intact until the retreat of the Soviet forces, in June 1941.

The "Great-Ukrainian" orientation of speakers in the Polish Ukraine was thus much more theoretical than real; by contrast, their exposure to Polish influences was very real indeed. Elementary phonetic substitutions apparently sufficed to make borrowings palatable. They abounded in urban life, starting with forms of social conduct such as addressing people and ending with technical notions. The former was examined at some length by Simovyč (1934 [4]). Among the forms of address he noted was *panedobrodiju* (Polish *panie dobrodzieju*) and among titles, *pane mecenase* (Polish *panie mecenasie*) in addressing a lawyer (Šax, 264 reminisces that among students of the Ukrainian *himnazija* in Lviv, Polish books on good forms of behavior circulated widely). The use of urban technical terms was reflected, for example, by colloquial names for tram lines, such as *dvijka, čvirka, pjatka*, etc. (Polish *dwójka, czwórka, piątka*). Students of a given grade in school were called: *šestak, semak, vos'mak* (Šax 233: cf. Polish *szóstak, siódmak, ósmak*). When a soccer team was organized at the Ukrainian high school (*akademična himnazija*) in Lviv it was given the name *kružok hry nižnóji pylky*; one student of that school recalls that the students called it *futbolevyj kljub* (Šax 84; the episode began as early as 1908). Both these usages were patterned on Polish (*piłka nożna, klub futbolowy*). In the phonetic substitutions, Polish accentual patterns often remained unchanged. In that way the pattern ´ - : - ´ - (*trámvaj : tramváju*), completely alien to Ukrainian, was introduced into the Lviv koine.

The general situation wrought by the interrelation between the Lviv koine and Standard Ukrainian is reflected particularly clearly in matters of spelling and, in part, of terminology.

The recommendations put forth in *Najholovniši pravyla ukrajins'koho pravopysu* published by the Ukrainian Academy of Sciences in Kiev (1919, 1920, 1921) met with some criticism in the Polish Ukraine (M. Voznjak 1921, V. Hnatjuk 1922). In 1920–1922 the Ševčenko Scientific Society (*Naukove tovarystvo im. Ševčenka*) in Lviv deliberated over matters of spelling, in an often heated debate. O. Makaruška rejected them passionately (Šax 175f.). The outcome of these deliberations was the publication, in 1922, of a booklet of *Pravopysni pravyla* formulated by K. Kysilevs'kyj (Karpova 130), which had gained the approval of the Ševčenko Scientific Society (subsequently modified by O. Panejko as member of a commission appointed by the regional inspector of secondary schools, I. Kopač— Šax 176).

Some of the traditional spelling rules used in Galician Ukrainian were set aside by the new rules (e.g., the separate spelling of the verbal postfix *sja* and of *-mu* endings in the future tense, the etymological spelling of some consonantal clusters), but others were wholly corroborated (e.g., the exclusion of apostrophes, the retention of all foreign instances of *g* as *g*, not *h*, the rendition of *l* in West European loan words as basically palatalized *l'*). Other Kiev rules were accepted in part (e.g., double *n, d, t, l* in neuter substantives, although not *s, z, š, ž, č*: therefore *zillja*, but *kolosja*) or admitted as alternatives to traditional Galician spellings (e.g., in neuter substantives *-ja* and *-je*: *žyttja* and *žyttje*; *bahato* and *bohato*, *inšyj* and *ynšyj*, *mačuxa* and *mačoxa*, dative singular in masculine substantives in *-ovi* and *-ovy*).

Upon their publication, the spelling rules of the Ševčenko Scientific Society were criticized by those who wanted stronger adherence to Kiev spelling (e.g., M. Rudnyc'kyj, 1923), as well as by those who advocated more reliance on the Galician tradition (e.g., V. Hnatjuk, 1923; I. Pan'kevyč, 1923; V. Dombrovs'kyj, 1925; bibliography, partly inaccurate, in Karpova 131f., 134, and some additional items in

Šax 175ff.). In any case, the new rules, which were published only as a proposal (*projekt*), did not become compulsory, because there existed no authority that could make them so. Consequently, the spelling rules were rarely applied consistently, and usages in publications continued to differ.

Following the Kharkiv Conference on Spelling of 1927 and the publication of its resultant *Ukrajins'kyj pravopys* in 1929, the Ševčenko Scientific Society decided to adopt that set of rules, on 25 May 1929. Commissioned by the society, M. Voznjak prepared a *Ukrajins'kyj pravopys iz slovnyčkom* (of about 6,500 words; 1929). The inconsistencies in spelling caused by the compromise of two traditions were felt no less strongly in the Polish Ukraine than they were in the Soviet Ukraine (e.g., the criticisms by S. Smal'-Stoc'kyj and M. Rudnyc'kyj, among others, referred to—inaccurately—in Karpova 136). Only the replacement of the 1929 spelling by that of Xvylja, with its strong Russianizing tendency, tempered Galician hostility to the 1929 rules. For instance, K. Kysilevs'kyj's *Pravopysni pravyla* and *Pravopysnyj slovnyček* (1934) in some cases cite (besides each other) both the spelling of 1922, by the Ševčenko Society, and that of 1929.

Even this cursory presentation of the orthographic problems in the Polish Ukraine during the interwar period illustrates the tension between two conflicting desires—that is, to maintain the spellings of the "Great Ukraine" and to preserve at least some elements of the Galician tradition—and the impasse to which the normalization of Ukrainian spelling had come.

A similar situation obtained in terminological work, though there it existed on a smaller scale, because the problems concerned smaller circles of people and because the scope of such work was very limited, due to the lack of funds and specialists in the field. Discounting K. Levyc'kyj's *Pravnyčyj slovnyk*, published in a second edition in 1920 but in structure and compilation belonging to the Austrian period, substantial new terminological works were only Volodymyr Levyc'kyj's on mathematical, physical, and chemical terminology, and Z. Lys'ko's *Muzyčnyj slovnyk* (1933). These two works constituted a compromise between the Kiev dictionaries and the Galician tradition.

In general lexicography, too, the same conflicting tendencies can be observed. Lexicographical work was very limited. Only a few practical dictionaries were published, all rather small in size: the Polish-

Ukrainian and Ukrainian-Polish dictionaries by I. Svjencic'kyj (1920) and by Je. Hrycak and K. Kysilevs'kyj (1931), and the German-Ukrainian dictionary by H. Nakonetschna (1939).

In grammar, there were no publications that presented the system of the literary language as a whole. The most important works, *Opis fonetyczny języka ukraińskiego* by I. Zilyns'kyj (1932) and *Značennja ukrajins'kyx prykmetnykiv* by R. Smal'-Stoc'kyj (1926), covered limited topics; also, they treated standard language data alongside dialectal materials, often devoting more attention to the latter than to the former.

In sum, the linguistic work carried on in the Polish Ukraine was an important counterbalance to the devastation in Ukrainian linguistics that occurred under the Soviets in the 1930s. Considered on its merits, that work was unsystematic and restricted in scope; still, it sheds light on the language situation in the Polish Ukraine and on the effort to overcome its isolation. There existed much good will for unifying the Ukrainian standard language, but there were also strong centrifugal forces at play. What is more important, there were no external circumstances that could have brought about such a unity. The political regimes and styles of life were so outspokenly different in the two parts of the country that no language unity was possible. In simplified terms, the concerns that the two parts had in common were the deprivation of the Ukrainian language's essential rights, on the one hand, and its survival in spite of that condition, on the other. Government methods against the Ukrainian language also differed in the two parts. Nominally, under Polish rule there was no government interference with the internal structure of the language. Yet in fact, in both Poland and the Soviet Union, the longterm policy goal was identical: the extermination of the Ukrainian language. Under Polish domination, Ukrainians could conduct both active and passive resistance to that policy; in the Soviet system, only passive resistance was feasible.

The similarities and the differences in the status of the Ukrainian language, and of the Ukrainians themselves, in the Soviet Ukraine versus the Polish Ukraine is epitomized by two events described below.

In Kharkiv, in 1933, when attacks against "bourgeois nationalism" in the Ukrainian language began, an instructor at the Industrial Academy surnamed Polons'kyj (his first name is unknown to me) dared to raise his voice in defense of the accused (Xvylja,

Znyščyty. . . , 112). He was arrested that same night. It is unknown whether he was shot or died in prison or in a labor camp; at any rate, he was never heard from again.

In March 1923, when the Polish government decreed that in Ukrainian high schools Polish was to be used in administration and in the teaching of history and geography, an instructor in Lviv named Myxajlo Haluščyns'kyj took the floor to protest. He, head of a family of four, was immediately fired. Ukrainian organizations came to his aid. He gained popular recognition: indeed, in the next elections to the Sejm, he ran as a candidate and was elected. In the next election he became a member of the all-Polish Senate, and subsequently the deputy speaker (Šax 141ff.).

Of course, the deeds of neither Polons'kyj nor Haluščyns'kyj curbed the anti-Ukrainian policies of the Soviet Ukraine and Poland.

Ukrainian Lands under Romania

After the occupation of Černivci on 11 November 1918 and the ensuing occupation of all Bukovina, Romanian law came into effect. In the next four years the legal status and rights of the Ukrainian language were determined by Romania's international obligations vis-à-vis its national minorities, as well as by the Romanian constitution and other laws.

Internationally, two treaties came into play: the Treaty of Saint-Germain, which Romania signed reluctantly, in Paris, after a delay of several months (on 9 December 1918; the treaty had been submitted to Romania in September in Saint-Germain), and the Treaty of Sèvres, signed on 10 August 1920.

In the Treaty of Saint-Germain the language obligations assumed by Romania are outlined in articles 8, 9, and 10: (§ 8) ''No restriction shall be imposed on the free use by any Romanian national of any language in private intercourse, in commerce, in religion, in the press, or in publications of any kind, or at public meetings. . . . Notwithstanding any establishment by the Romanian government of an official language, adequate facilities shall be given to Romanian nationals of non-Romanian speech for the use of their language, either orally or in writing, before the courts''; (§ 9) the Romanian government recognized the right of citizens ''to establish, manage, and control at their own expense charitable, religious, and social institutions, schools and other educational establishments, with the right to use their own language"; (§ 10): "Romania will provide in the public educational system of towns and districts in which a considerable proportion of Romanian nationals of other than Romanian speech are resident adequate facilities for ensuring that in the primary schools instruction shall be given to the children of such Romanian nationals through the medium of their own language" (*Treaties* iii, 3727f.).[2]

By contrast, in the Treaty of Sèvres, concluded two years later, which for the first time legalized the Romanian occupation of all of Bukovina (§ 3, 6; *Materialien*, 206f.), nothing was said about the rights of minorities or about their language.

The obligations assumed by Romania in Saint-Germain were not incorporated into the Romanian Constitution of 28 March 1923: there it was stated that (§ 126) "the Romanian language is the official language of the Romanian state" (*Constitution* 24), and in several instances it was reiterated that Romanian citizens of various languages should have the same rights [§ 8 e.g.] "All Romanians independently of their ethnic origin, language, or religion are equal in law"—p. 6). Nowhere, however, did it guarantee any rights to languages other than Romanian. The Constitution of 27 February 1938 preserved § 126 intact (where it became § 94—*Constitution* 2, p. 19), but obliterated all references to other languages, making them non-existent in the legal sense.

Of the published laws relating to the status of Bukovina or to the Ukrainian language there and in the kingdom as a whole, two should be mentioned here. The decree of 19–31 December 1918 entrusted a special minister (later called the president of the regional commission) with governing the region; in fact, this official was a dictator who stood outside the law. His dictatorial powers were extensive, for Bukovina existed in a state of siege from 1918 to 1928 and then again in 1938 to 1940, up to the Soviet occupation on 28 June 1940. (The first ministers of Bukovina were I. Nistor from the Liberal party [Romanian conservatives], and T. Savciuc-Saveanu from the National-Peasant [*ţărănist*] party.)

The second law of major importance was no. 176 (decree no. 2,571 of the Ministry of Education) dated 24 July 1924, which referred to Romanians "who forgot their mother tongue": (§ 8) "Citizens of

---

[2] These stipulations are, generally, identical to those submitted to and accepted by Poland. See above, chap. 7, section 1.

Romanian origin who forgot (*au pierdut*; literally, "have lost") their mother tongue must give their children education only in public or private schools with Romanian as the language of instruction" (*Colectiune* 530). The law, written in deliberately ambiguous language, does not specify whether its provisions obligate isolated families living outside Romania or larger population groups. It was, however, an open secret that it was intended to apply to Ukrainians. Thus the law introduced a legal division of national minorities into two groups: those entitled to preserve their languages—Hungarians and Germans (as explicitly guaranteed by § 7 of the same law)—and those denied that right—above all Ukrainians. In its application to Ukrainians the law was buttressed by some Romanian historians who "proved" that Ukrainians in Romania were but linguistically Slavicized Romanians. In any case, the law only sanctioned what was already being practiced. The resolution of each particular case was shaped in part by regional or local circulars and, probably more often, by the arbitrary decision of a particular administrator, be it an agent of the civil government or of the military, of the general police or of the notorious Romanian secret police (*siguranţa*). The law opened the way to the worst forms of terror, including unwarranted arrests, tortures, and corporal punishments, as well as to a reign of fear; on the other hand, it allowed for unexpected breeches in the general policy, including short-lived particular favors.

The history of Ukrainians and of the Ukrainian language in interwar Romania is divisible into three periods. During the first ten years (1918–1928) its government was occasionally and briefly run by the conservatives and the "people's party" (*Partitul poporului*) of General A. Averescu; as a rule, however, power was in the hands of the most conservative "liberals" headed by I. Brătianu. The times seemed to require the total negation of all things Ukrainian. Very soon after the occupation, all administrative and court offices were Romanianized. The traditional regional parliament of Bukovina ceased to exist, and local self-government was discontinued. All Ukrainian political parties were disbanded, so Ukrainians could be elected to Romanian legislative bodies solely as members of Romanian parties. Their representation in the assembly was, consequently, very small (1 in the elections of August 1919, 3 in those of May 1920, 4 in those of January 1922, in an assembly of ca. 390 deputies—Kvitkovs'kyj 340, 343; Piddubnyj 222), and there were no

Ukrainians in the Senate; those who were representatives rarely raised their voices about Ukrainian affairs. Most of the cultural and other societies that before the Romanian occupation had dotted Bukovina (there was a total of 1,763 such chapters—Piddubnyj 131) were also dissolved; some did survive, however, and a few new ones arose. The closing of the *Rus'ka besida* society, which had existed since 1869, entailed the destruction of its 125 reading rooms (lists in Piddubnyj 132ff., Kvitkovs'kyj 364).

The liquidation of Ukrainian educational institutions took several years, but that, too, was accomplished. The University of Černivci was entirely Romanianized, and its Ukrainian chairs were reorganized. Three Ukrainian high schools (*himnaziji*) were closed (in Kicman' in 1920, in Vyžnycja in 1921; in Černivci in 1925; the Ukrainian language as a subject was discontinued in 1927). In primary education the tempo was slower, but the results were the same. While in 1910/11 Bukovina had 216 Ukrainian elementary schools vs. 179 Romanian ones, by 1922/23 the number of Ukrainian schools had fallen to 155 and the number of Romanian ones had grown to 391 (Piddubnyj 144; Kvitkovs'kyj 365). The process was accelerated after the publication, in 1924, of the law on "Romanians who forgot their mother tongue"; by 1927 there were no longer any Ukrainian schools in Romania and the Ukrainian language was not taught at all. This policy was buttressed by the settlement of Romanians in Bukovina. With the agrarian reform of 30 July 1921, some lands owned by the church were confiscated for distribution among peasants. Romanians were enticed to move to Bukovina by promises of parcels of the confiscated land.

Periodical and book publication in Ukrainian were not wholly prohibited, but they were subject to severe censorship. Many periodicals were closed, including the most reputed *Nova Bukovyna* (1918); some periodicals were later revived under different names, so that in number there seem to have been more such publications than was actually the case. The real situation is revealed by a look at their duration and character. There were 17 periodicals in 1919–1928: 14 political weeklies or biweeklies, 2 satirical journals, and 1 literary journal. There was no daily newspaper. The average duration of a periodical was, however, only one and a half years, often with gaps within that span (tallied on the basis of Kvitkovs'kyj 635f. and Piddubnyj 137ff.). In hardly any one year were more than three periodicals published. They were small in size and poor in content, style, and language. The number of books published was 39 titles in nine years, for an average of 4 to 5 per year. There was one Ukrainian theater, in Černivci, which did not stage performances daily (Kvitkovs'kyj 593). Bessarabia had no Ukrainian publications or institutions.

In ecclesiastical life, the Orthodox church was completely dominated by Romanians. In 1921 the "Greek Oriental" church was renamed the "Orthodox Romanian"; in 1925 it was subordinated, as one of five metropolitanates, to the Patriarch of Bucharest. The administration of the metropolitanate consisted of the Eparchial Council, Consistory, and the advisory Eparchial Assembly, with its forty laymen and twenty priests. Ukrainians had a voice only in the Eparchial Assembly, which meant that they could not participate in any decision making; even in that body, only two Ukrainians were members (Kvitkovs'kyj 373f.). Ukrainian priests were required to carry and use Romanian documents and were encouraged to preach in Romanian (Piddubnyj 127).

In 1928 the Peasant party came to power, a development which initiated the second period in the Romanian occupation. A certain degree of liberalization was expected and some measures of the new government pointed in that direction. The state of siege was lifted, and censorship became somewhat milder—measures not revoked by the governments, coalition and liberal, that followed one after another in the years 1931–1937. This was not the case, however, with other innovations introduced by the Peasant party. Under their government, teaching of the Ukrainian language (and of religion in Ukrainian) was introduced in schools with a majority of Ukrainian pupils: eight hours weekly in the lower grades, six hours in the upper grades (decree of 31 December 1929). The actual teaching of Ukrainian continued to be hampered by a lack of teachers and schoolbooks. The decree permitting Ukrainian education was canceled by the liberal government in 1933; by a decree of 9 September 1934, twenty-four teachers who had organized Ukrainian courses were dismissed (Kvitkovs'kyj 369).

The țărănist period and the following years brought other developments favorable to Ukrainians and their language, albeit limited ones. For the first time since the Romanian occupation, a legal Ukrainian political party was founded in Bukovina, the Ukrainian National Party (1927). It campaigned for the revision of land distribution as decreed by the agrarian reform of 1921, for the admission of the Ukrainian language in education and administration, and for cessation of the treatment of Ukrainians as Romanians who "forgot their mother tongue" (Kvitkovs'kyj 347). In the elections of 1928, Ukrainians got one seat in the assembly; in the elections of 1930, they gained five in the assembly and one in the senate; in the elections of 1932, two in the assembly, and again two in the elections of 1933. Ukrainian cultural activities centered around the *Narodnyj dim* in Černivci were renewed. By 1937 Bukovina had at least fifteen Ukrainian societies of various types, e.g., cultural, feminist, student (Kvitkovs'kyj 359). In 1928, a Ukrainian daily, *Čas*, began publication in Černivci; in 1933, a monthly for children, *Lastivka*, started to appear (Kvitkovs'kyj 650). The relative relaxation in censorship prompted Ukrainian nationalists from outside Romania to found a monthly, *Samostijna dumka*, and a weekly, *Samostijnist'* in Černivci; Bukovinians were among their editors (the periodicals appeared in 1931–1937 and in 1934–1937, respectively). These periodicals survived into 1937 because they focused on non-Romanian problems; even so, they were occasionally suspended by the censorship (Kvitkovs'kyj 651). Also published were social-democratic periodicals (*Nove žyttja*, 1931–1934) and even a Sovietophile one (*Borot'ba*, 1926–1929). The number of periodicals published simultaneously grew to 7 or 8; the general number of titles fell to 10, but now their average duration was 4 to 5 years, a healthy sign. They still continued to be modest in size, and journalistically their level was often not high. Circulation was limited (*Čas* at times had only 600 subscribers, and it never had more than 3,000— Kvitkovs'kyj 645f.), so they were continually published at a loss and in need of subsidies.

There were other drawbacks and failures in Ukrainian cultural activity. Attempts to establish contacts with Ukrainians from other regions of Romania, especially Northern and Southern Bessarabia, did not succeed. The Ukrainian theater in Černivci had to accede or circumvent such orders of the local administration as a prohibition against wearing Ukrainian national attire (Kvitkovs'kyj 352). In 1929 Ukrainian cooperatives were submitted to state surveillance and soon thereafter ruined economically. Summer courses in the Ukrainian language, initiated in 1926 and gaining some popularity, were forbidden in 1933/34 (Kvitkovs'kyj 676f.). Most important, Ukrainian schools did not exist continuously, and Romanian was the language of communication in the cities. The church, too, remained basically in

Romanian hands, although in 1932 Ukrainian representation in the Eparchial Assembly grew to 14, and in 1931 a Ukrainian Orthodox fraternity was founded in Černivci (Kvitkovs'kyj 375f.).

The establishment of King Carol's military dictatorship over Romania in 1937–1938 was accompanied by the elimination of parliamentarism, the dissolution of all Ukrainian and Romanian political parties, the introduction of a new constitution, and the reintroduction of the state of siege. The "liberal course" of the preceding decade had ended. Bukovina was included in the newly formed region (*ținut*) of Suceava, which obliterated traditional boundaries. In April and June of 1937, two large-scale trials of Ukrainian nationalists took place, and their publications were closed. Of all its Ukrainian societies, Bukovina retained only five (Kvitkovs'kyj 371); of all its Ukrainian periodicals, only *Čas* remained. National minorities were supervised, from May 1938, by a special Commissariat-General for National Minorities.

In April 1940 promises of change were made to the Ukrainian representatives by the Romanian regime, now faced with the Soviet occupation of Galicia and the threat of a similar development in Bukovina and Bessarabia. On 28 June 1940 the Soviet army crossed the Romanian border. The Soviets gave the Ukrainian language in Bukovina, the Xotyn area, and Southern Bessarabia the same status it had in the Soviet Ukraine.

The gains that the Ukrainian language had made under Austria were reduced to very little during the twenty years of Romanian occupation. Its functions shrank essentially to domestic use and, to a limited extent, to use by Ukrainian societies, theater, and press. Socially, Ukrainian lost the cities and was reduced primarily to peasant use, not in its standard form but in a number of dialects. Its status in the church was precarious. Among intellectuals, Ukrainian was employed for everyday matters only by humanists—teachers, priests, journalists of the underdeveloped Ukrainian press. In spoken Ukrainian, words for new notions were as a rule cited in their Romanian form. Contacts with the Soviet Ukraine were virtually non-existent, so that neither the Ukrainianization measures nor the Russifying trends of later years touched Bukovina. Somewhat more vital were contacts with adjacent Galicia, for, after all, Poland and Romania were allied. Inasmuch as Ukrainian was used for literary matters in Bukovina, it was in the Galician (Lviv) koine, despite the Bukovinian Ukrainians' purported dislike for Galicians (Piddubnyj 99), whom they were apt to address with the phrase, ''Out of Bukovina, strangers.''

To illustrate the Ukrainian language then in use, one can point to issues of the newspaper *Xliborobs'ka pravda* (of 6 February 1938) and *Samostijnyk* (of 31 May 1936 and of 17 January 1937; the relevant passages are photographically reproduced in Kvitkovs'kyj 648, 653). Although in ideology the two periodicals differed starkly, their language is nearly identical, due clearly to patterning on the language of Galician newspapers. In spelling the two publications have in common *genij, Ljenin, Pidhirja* (in general no apostrophe is used), *ideol'ogiji*; in phonology, *narid, villjav, blesku, značinnja, vzajimno, dužannje*; in morphology, *svjatkovannja, vsi zdibnosty*; in syntax, *pjat'ox pidsudnyx. . .vidpovidatymut', nosyteljamy ideji. . .ljudy*; in vocabulary and phraseology, *kruhy* ('circles'), *zabyrajemo stanovyšče* ('we are taking a position'), *pidložennja petardy, prykaz, na dnjax, rumuns'kyj horožanyn, v cilomu sviti, pid teperišnju poru.*

Given its own state of affairs, both political and linguistic, Bukovina could not exert any influence on the Ukrainian standard language in either the Soviet or the Polish Ukraine. The only linguistic goal that it could reasonably undertake was to preserve its own Ukrainian language at a bare minimum. That it did.

Transcarpathia under Czecho-Slovakia

Following the disintegration of the Austro-Hungarian monarchy and the proclamation of an independent Hungary (16 November 1918), the new social-democratic government of M. Károlyi granted, on 24 December 1918, autonomy to Transcarpathia, now called the ''Ruthene Land'' (*Ruska Kraina*), including its own parliament and ''usage of its own language'' (Markus 13). This development did not materialize because of the quick pace of events: the communist *putsch* of 21 March 1919, with the ensuing civil war and intervention by neighboring states, which swept away the communist regime. During the short-lived Soviet episode in Transcarpathia (late March to early April 1919) one decree (no. 24) prescribed for use in schools the local language as codified in the grammar of A. Vološyn (Štec' 11). But at that time western Transcarpathia was occupied by the Czecho-Slovak army (from 15 January 1919) and the southeastern part of the country by the Romanian army, while in the central region Hungarians still prevailed. By May 1919, Czecho-Slovak forces were in possession of all of Transcarpathia (except Sighet and its environs).

On 8 May 1919, in Užhorod, a General National Congress convened. It comprised delegates from local "people's councils" (*narodni rady*), and its task was to decide upon the future of the country. The congress was to choose one of three possibilities: to remain in Hungary, to unite with Romania, or to unite with Czecho-Slovakia. A fourth possibility, of uniting with the Ukraine, was theoretical, only: besides having disparate social and political structures, Transcarpathia and the greater part of the Ukraine were separated by territories held by Poles and Romanians. In the circumstances the General National Congress unanimously decided to unite with Czecho-Slovakia. Whether that congress, whose delegates were not elected directly by the population, represented the actual will of the Transcarpathians and to what extent the decision was influenced by the presence of the Czecho-Slovak army are open questions. What is certain is that the other options had not found any active supporters. Hence Transcarpathia became incorporated into Czecho-Slovakia not through any armed conflict, as had happened in the Soviet Ukraine, in Galicia, and, on a smaller scale, in Bukovina, but either by its free will or by indifference. The incorporation of Transcarpathia into Czecho-Slovakia was sealed by the Allied Powers' recognition of the decision in their treaty with Czecho-Slovakia signed at Saint-Germain on 10 September 1919.

This Treaty of Saint-Germain also laid the foundation for the legal status of Transcarpathia and for language policy in it, defining the region (§ 10) as "The Ruthene territory" and as "an autonomous unit within the Czecho-Slovak State," granting it "the fullest degree of self-government compatible with the unity of the Czecho-Slovak State." The treaty also provided (§ 11) that "the Ruthene territory" shall have a special Diet which will "have the power of legislation in all linguistic, scholastic, and religious questions, in matters of local administration and in other questions which the laws of the Czecho-Slovak State may assign to it." The region was to have a governor appointed by the president of Czecho-Slovakia but "responsible to the Ruthene Diet." Czecho-Slovakia agreed (§ 12) that "officials of the Ruthene territory will be chosen as far as possible from the inhabitants of this territory." Finally (§ 13), "the Ruthene territory," like all other Czecho-Slovak areas, was entitled to elect deputies to the general assembly of Czecho-Slovakia (*Treaties* 3708f.).

The Czecho-Slovak constitution (adopted on 29 February 1920) dealt with language rights in two articles. One (§ 128, 3) guaranteed all citizens the right to "use freely any language they choose in private and business communications, in all matters pertaining to religion, in the press and in all publications whatsoever, or in public assemblies." Concerning the language of education: (§ 131) "In towns and districts in which there lives a considerable portion of Czecho-Slovak citizens speaking a language other than Czecho-Slovak, the children of such Czecho-Slovak citizens shall in public instruction, and within the bounds of the general regulations relating thereto, be guaranteed a due opportunity to receive instruction in their own language. The Czecho-Slovak language may at the same time be prescribed as a compulsory subject of instruction" (*Constitution* 1920, pp. 45f.; the Czech text, pp. 93f.). The constitution left open the question of an official language as well as that of the specific rights of other languages in education and administration.

These problems were addressed and resolved in the law of 29 February 1920, said to appear "in pursuance of § 129" of the constitution and popularly called the "language law." It opens (§ 1) with the proclamation of the "Czecho-Slovak language" (a politically motivated linguistic misnomer; that language is defined [§ 4] as Czech in the Czech land and Slovak in Slovakia) as the country's language, determining that it is the language: "(1) In which the work of all courts, offices, institutions, undertakings, and organs of the Republic shall be conducted. . . . (2) In which the principal texts of state and other banknotes shall be printed. (3) Which the armed forces of the country shall use for the purpose of command, and the language of the service" (*Constitution* 48f.; Czech text—Sobota iii, 140f.). It did make the provision that in localities where 20 percent or more of the population spoke another language, courts should accept statements and formulate charges in that language; another provision was that the minorities were entitled to education in their language (§ 5, p. 49).

The provisions on Transcarpathia of both the constitution and "the language law" largely paraphrase the Saint-Germain treaty. In the constitution (§ 3, 2) Transcarpathia is called "the autonomous territory of Carpathian Rus' " and it is guaranteed "the highest measure of self-government compatible with the unity of the Czecho-Slovak Republic"; accordingly, it "shall have its own Diet, which shall elect its presiding officers (*předsednictvo*) and other officials." This Diet shall "legislate in linguistic, educational, and religious matters, in matters of domestic administration and in such other matters as may be assigned to it by the laws of the Czecho-Slovak Republic" (*Constitution* 4, 22; the Czech text, p. 39f.). In the same spirit, the "language law" stated: (§ 6) "The Diet which shall be set up for Ruthenia shall have the right, reserved to it, of settling the language question for this territory in a manner consonant with the unity of the Czecho-Slovak State" (ibid., 49; Czech text—Sobota iii, 148).

There was no consensus on what to call the unexpectedly acquired land, which almost could be regarded as a birthday present to Czecho-Slovakia. Legally, the name accepted by the "General Statute" of the region was "Subcarpathian Rus'" (*Podkarpatská Rus*), yet another name, *Rusinsko*, was also admitted. The first was justified on the grounds of historical tradition, the second was probably a translation of "the Ruthene territory" from the treaty of Saint-Germain. Both names were given only "until lawful resolution" (*do právoplatné úpravy*); but there was a surety that "in schools the people's language (*lidový jazyk*) shall be the language of instruction as well as the official [language] in general"; that language was also called Ruthenian (*rusinský*). It was to be introduced as soon as possible in the first grade and gradually extended to higher grades. As a subject it was to be compulsory on all levels (Sobota i, 132).

That surety was broken from the very outset of Czech activity in Transcarpathia. Ukrainian peasants were often not sure what language they spoke. In 1918 the villagers of Pistrjalove declared: "We are unable to decide; they [the Hungarians] took from us our Ruthenian schools and tried to wipe out our language. Now we master neither Ruthenian nor Hungarian" (as quoted by Jedlins'ka 96). What was worse, the Transcarpathian intelligentsia was similarly divided. Some considered the local language to be Ruthenian (but based on which dialect?), others indignantly rejected what they considered to be a hillbilly idiom and insisted upon adopting the Church Slavonic – Russian tradition, in its many variants. Seeking objective advice, the authorities approached the Czech Academy in Prague. In a good democratic vein, that academy responded that it was up to the members of a nationality to decide what literary language they wanted to use. But it advised against the creation of a new Ruthenian language on a dialectal base and for the use of the Ukrainian language in its Galician garb, "because the local Ruthenian dialects. . .are beyond any doubt a

Little-Russian dialect,'' although in an etymological spelling that was more familiar to the Transcarpathians. As for the Russian language, the academy recommended that it be taught as a subject in the secondary school (Tichý 112f.).

In good faith, guided by both democratic principles and the opinions of scholars, the Czecho-Slovak authorities invited to Prague from Vienna the relatively young Galician linguist, Ivan Pan'kevyč (1887–1958). He was to be language adviser in the department of education in the region (Štec' 19). To his great amazement, Pan'kevyč realized that he had been given ''dictatorial rights in matters of language,'' as expressed in his letter of 25 January 1920 (Mušynka 131). But once he confronted the local situation, his enthusiasm faded quickly. About three months later he wrote: ''I am sick and tired here. One has to fight for the alphabet as we had it in the 1850s. The Russophiles would not admit the people's language and started to fight against anything that has no Russian form. I seemingly mean something here and [yet] apparently [I stand for] nothing'' (Mušynka 131). In order to promote the Ukrainian language Pan'kevyč had to make one concession after another, especially in matters relating to the alphabet and spelling. Even so, his secondary school grammar (*Hramatyka rus'koho jazŷka dlja molodšyx kljas škol serednŷx y horožan'skyx*) was not published until 1922. In the meantime A. Vološyn's unapproved grammar (*Metodičeska hrammatyka karpato-russkaho jazyka dlja narodnŷx škol*, 1901 and 1919) was used; it was written basically in Russian with an admixture of some local features, such as infinitives in *-ty* and *jak* instead of *kak*. Vološyn's grammar was designed for primary schools, where old textbooks were used exclusively.

In a luckier position was another Galician, V. Birčak, also a member of the Transcarpathian school administration. His task was to compile school anthologies of literature (*Rus'ka čytanka dlja I. kljasŷ hymnazijnoě y horožans'kyx" škol"*, 1922; the same for the fourth grade, 1924). Birčak gave literary texts without adapting them to local speech; he simply explained unfamiliar words and expressions by referring to their local equivalents in footnotes (Jedlins'ka 100).

The Czechs who were to deal with the local populace in Transcarpathia probably experienced a reaction similar to that of Pan'kevyč. The Czechs' democratic and pro-Ukrainian policy did not meet with approval among the Transcarpathians. Factions among them greeted

each Czech measure with animosity and public or private denunciations. (According to Magocsi 140, the first such denunciation was
sent to Prague in February 1920.) Newcomers to the region, both Galicians and Czechs, must have regarded such incidents as petty and
spiteful.

Given this situation, the Czechs did not fulfill some of their obligations. They did not convoke an assembly. The first governor of the
territory was to be a local man, but—perhaps for want of a native on
whom a clear majority would agree—an American of Transcarpathian
descent, Gregory Zsatkovich, was appointed in April 1920. His position was mainly ceremonial; in charge of practical matters of gover-
nance was his deputy, Petr Ehrenfeld, a Czech. This arrangement was
probably one reason for Zsatkovich's resignation after less than a year
(March 1921). The heads of the school administration were also
Czechs, first Josef Pešek (until 1924), then Josef Šimek. Faced with a
severe shortage of qualified teachers, Pešek engaged some Galicians,
Russian immigrants (who had no command of either Standard
Ukrainian or of local dialects), and Czech legionaries who had spent
several years in Russia and learned a bit of spoken Russian (Štec' 16).

All this seemed to constitute a deliberate policy by the Prague
government to absorb a colony, which Transcarpathia after all was
(Zsatkovich gave this as the official reason for his resignation); probably the appearance was to some degree true. But the lack of a local
political elite in Transcarpathia certainly exacerbated matters and, at
least in Czech eyes, justified Prague's policy. Another justification
could have been a strong Communist influence in the region at the
time (Markus 17).

It was under these circumstances that the Galicians, with limited
support among the Transcarpathians, began to promote the adoption of
standard language based on literary Ukrainian as used in Galicia.
Besides serving as advisors to schools and preparing textbooks, the
Galicians' most important undertakings were founding (on 9 May
1920) and actively promoting the cultural society Prosvita and publishing several periodicals, most on that society's behalf. These
ranged from the scholarly *Naukovyj zbirnyk* (1922 – 1938) to the popular annual *Kalendar* (1923 – 1938) to the children's monthlies *Pčôlka*
(1923 – 1934) and *Naš rodnŷj kraj* (1923 – 1939). By 1923 Prosvita
had established four branches and 82 reading rooms in addition to
those in Užhorod; by 1934, the numbers were 10 and 230,

respectively. It also ran a Ukrainian theater (*Rus'kyj narodnŷj teatr*, 1921–1929), a choir (*EU* 2, 2371), and the *Narodnŷj dom* that opened in Užhorod in 1928. Begun in 1921, the Ukrainian boy scout organization Plast became an indisputable success. The Galicians' main success, however, was that the region's intellectuals, including even the elderly and highly respected Avhustyn Vološyn (1874–1945/1946?), joined the Ukrainian orientation. Vološyn's Russophile grammar of 1919 reappeared in a revised version in 1923 as *Metodyčna hramatyka karpato-rus'koho jazŷka*. Its language was still a far cry from Standard Ukrainian, which the author never mastered, but his revisions pointed in that direction. Vološyn's linguistic evolution reflected a general trend. Thus, the situation in Transcarpathia in 1923 differed from that of 1919–1920.

Yet Pan'kevyč and like-minded people had not forgotten the lesson of earlier years. At the First Transcarpathian Congress of Teachers (16–17 April 1920) no one even raised the question of accepting Standard Ukrainian, because the general mood was in favor of the local dialects (Jedlins'ka 98, Štec' 18). The situation prompted Pan'kevyč in his grammar to disguise the Ukrainian language as an adaptation of the Carpathian (Verxovyna) and Maramureş dialects, of which he gave but a few peculiarities (what are sometimes taken by Pan'kevyč as dialectal features—e.g., Jedlins'ka 101—were but etymological spellings), and to give etymological spellings, actually pseudo-etymological, with *i* from *o* rendered as *ô*, but *i* from *e* rendered not as *ê*, but as *ě*, i.e., by "jat'." That spelling remained obligatory for the next couple of years.

The success of Pan'kevyč and the Prosvita society should not be exaggerated. The Ukrainian orientation or "party" remained one of the region's three language "parties"; by no means did it gain sway over the entire cultural scene. A good idea of how things stood is presented by the survey of the situation in the region's secondary schools circa 1924 made by Gerovskij (1934, 512): of four *himnaziji*, two offered instruction in Ukrainian, one in Russian, and one in both; of the three teachers' seminaries, two taught in Ukrainian and one in Russian, at least formally; in reality, instruction in both Ukrainian and Russian (depending, of course, on the capabilities and education of each teacher) had a strong admixture of local dialecticisms and even of Church Slavonic. As late as 1923, a teachers' congress rejected Pan'kevyč's grammar, by a vote of 544 votes to 2 (Magocsi 140).

In general, however, knowledge of Ukrainian and regard for it was on the rise, whereas use of Russian and of the local dialects was in retreat. This alarmed the Russian ''party''; it closed ranks and rushed to do battle. As a counterpoise to Prosvita, the Russophile A. Duxnovyč Society was founded in May 1923, to promote Russian language and culture. Just as in Prosvita the activists were immigrants from Galicia, so the organizers of the Duxnovyč Society were mainly Russian immigrants. This development overlapped with the installation of a new Czech administration prone to Russophilism, Governor A. Rozsypal and his deputee A. Beskid.

The Duxnovyč Society quickly organized chapters and reading rooms (274 reading rooms in 1931; cf. Gerovskij 1927, 514), founded publications (the monthlies *Karpatskij kraj*, 1923–1925, and *Karpatskij svět"* 1928–1933, 1938; yearbooks, etc.), and initiated so-called Days of Russian Culture. The society awarded a literary prize and lobbied with influential Czechs, adroitly taking advantage of traditional Czech Russophilism. In 1937 the organization claimed 21,000 members (Prosvita had 15,000). In organizing its anti-Ukrainian activity the Duxnovyč Society imitated measures Prosvita had developed. It produced a Russian grammar that successfully counterbalanced Pan'kevyč's Ukrainian one. In 1924 there appeared a *Grammatika russkago jazyka* edited by E. Sabov (who, incidentally, in 1923 defended the use of the local dialects against both Ukrainian and Russian). The new grammar's author, Aleksander Grigor'ev, was not named, because he was a native Russian who had little to do with Transcarpathia (he resided in Prešov—Tichý 114f.).

The campaign in support of the Russian language was best summarized by Gerovskij (also an outsider in Transcarpathia), to whom Standard Ukrainian was a ''language'' in quotation marks. In 1927 he wrote: ''To learn that 'language' [Ukrainian] a Carpatho-Russian student must spend no less effort than to learn the Common-Russian literary language, with the difference that in the first instance he will not be rewarded with access to any significant cultural values, whereas the Common-Russian language would immediately open to him the rich treasures of the world-renowned Russian culture'' (142).

The militant anti-Ukrainian propaganda of the Duxnovyč Society was most strongly manifested in the popular publication series ''Narodnaja biblioteka'' and related publications, totaling 115 items (Magocsi 159), among them: *Narodnyj katexizm"*, 1926; *Spor" o jazykě v" Podkarpatskoj Rusi i češskaja Akademija Nauk"* by N. Zorkij, 1926; *V" čem" glavnaja opasnost'* by A. A. Volkonskij, 1929; *Nacional'naja i jazykovaja prinadležnost' russkago naselenija Podkarpatskoj Rusi*, 1928 (more information in Nikolajenko 26, Štec' 93ff.).

Both "parties" endeavored to emphasize native roots rather than émigré connections. The Ukrainian "party" invoked the spirit of L. Csopey, the compiler of a Ruthenian-Hungarian dictionary in 1883, whereas the Russian "party" pointed to A. Mytrak, who had prepared a Russian-Hungarian dictionary in 1881.

The Russian-Ukrainian language war went on with alternate successes and failures, but generally the Russophiles were gaining and the Ukrainophiles were losing. In September 1924, Pan'kevyč and Birčak were relieved of their duties in the central school administration (Mušynka 135). The Czech administration, apparently tired of the incessant "language war" and traditionally Russophile, began gradually to shelve its original pro-Ukrainian policy. A law of 3 February 1926 stated that "the Ruthenian (Little-Russian) language is *allowed* to be used" (§ 100, 2; Sobota iii, 173; emphasis mine), not that it should be used. On 9 June 1930, the Land President of Transcarpathia, Rozsypal, decreed that since the language question had not been resolved, school inspectors were to use the Czecho-Slovak language in official correspondence. Widespread protests caused the decree to be withdrawn in August 1930 (Štec' 25), but its very appearance is significant. On 7 November 1930, the Czecho-Slovak minister of education admitted Russian textbooks for school use (ibid.) and on 1 October 1936, he recommended their use (Štec' 27). The trend culminated in the establishment of equal rights for Ukrainian and Russian, on 15 July 1937 (ibid.). Applying the very name Ukrainian to "Subcarpathia" was declared illegal (in 1933, and again in 1936; Magocsi 229).

Under these conditions the Ukrainian orientation found an unexpected ally: the Communist party, which had made use of the traditional local language (Ruthenian). In June–July 1924, the Fifth Congress of the Communist International decided that one and the same Ukrainian problem existed in Poland, Romania, and Czecho-Slovakia, and that its final solution required that all these lands join the Soviet Ukraine. A local language would hinder that plan. Communists of Transcarpathia were ordered to switch to Ukrainian and to

establish contacts with Communists of the Soviet Ukraine. In
December 1925, the editor-in-chief of the Communist daily
Karpats'ka pravda, I. Mondok, attended the Ninth Congress of the
Communist party of the Ukraine in Kharkiv (Jedlins'ka 104). At that
time Ukrainianization was in full swing, and Mondok was apparently
impressed by what he saw. (In 1927, he again went to Kharkiv, this
time for the Conference on Spelling, where he pledged acceptance of
whatever spelling would be adopted.) From 14 February 1926, the
newspaper he edited appeared not only in the Ukrainian language
(with localisms included, of course), but also in Ukrainian orthography. This was an unprecedented, revolutionary event in the region: in
December of the same year, the editors published a resolution of the
Seventh Regional Conference of the party under the title "End of the
language question" (Štec' 56). The end of the language problem it
was not, but perhaps the beginning of a final resolution was in sight.

The example of *Karpats'ka pravda* found some followers: the
social-democratic newspaper *Vpered* (in 1926), the Christian-
Nationalist *Svoboda* (in 1930), some literary publications (Štec' 58f.,
Tichý 125f.). In the third edition of his grammar Pan'kevyč introduced several changes in morphology (*vôn* instead of *ôn*, nominative
plural *syně* instead of *syny*, *čyj* instead of *čij*, etc.; Štec' 74), although
his spelling remained etymological. In the years to come a more "up
to date" textbook by Ja. Nevrli was published for school use (pt. 1 in
1937; pt. 2 in 1938); it was heavily patterned on Soviet Ukrainian
grammars (Štec' 73). Also adhering to "phonetic" spelling was
Franc Ahij's *Žyva mova* (1936). With the official recognition of the
equality of Ukrainian and Russian as local languages, the problem of
Ukrainian spelling became essentially irrelevant. In 1937–1938
"phonetic" spelling was permitted in schools (Štec' 73). The times
when the censorship crossed out any sentences calling residents of the
region Ukrainians had gone by (Štec', 58).

But habits died hard. Accustomed to an ongoing discussion of its
language, Transcarpathian society carried the debate further. In most
encounters the Russian orientation proved to be victorious. To mention only the most striking events: In May 1929, the group of teachers
who belonged to the "Teachers' Society of Subcarpathian Rus'"
(*Učitel'skoe tovariščestvo Podkarpatskoj Rusi*) split into two: when
at its convention a majority voted for using "traditional" textbooks in
the lower grades and Russian ones in the upper grades, teachers of the

Ukrainian orientation left and formed a separate "Public Teachers' Society in Užhorod" (*Narodovec'ke učytel's'ke tovarystvo v Užhorodi* (Štec' 23, 67). In 1937 pro-Russian groups founded an opposing "Russian block" (Štec' 63); in response, in October 1937, Communists attending a congress of Prosvita organized a "Ukrainian block" (ibid.). Beginning in the early 1930s "school strikes" broke out randomly in villages, either to show support for Russian as a language of instruction or to protest against it (Štec' 30). In the autumn of 1937 the Czech administration decided to relegate the question of the language of instruction in schools to the local population. Voters were to say whether they preferred the grammar by Pan'kevyč or by (pseudo-) Sabov. The Russian orientation won the school plebiscite (313 schools for Russian, against 114 for Ukrainian—Magocsi 226). The pro-Ukrainian faction contended that the Russophiles' victory was due in part to their exploitation of the ambiguity of the term *russkij/rus'kyj*, which voters took to mean "Transcarpathian Ukrainian," and in part to electoral fraud by the administration. There seems to be no way to verify this contention.

The continual state of "language war" resulted in two interesting developments. One was the revival of the orientation favoring a specific local language, whose outlet became the weekly *Nedělja* (1935–1938) supported by the Greek Catholic church. The National Theater in Užhorod began giving performances in Ruthenian (from 1936; Magocsi 223). The other development was a sharp increase in Czech schools. In 1920 there were 321 elementary "Ruthenian" schools vs. 22 Czech ones; in 1931, 425 vs. 158, respectively; in municipal schools, data for 1938 point to 21 "Ruthenian" schools vs. 23 Czech ones (Magocsi 358). The growth of Czech schools is accountable partly by the increase of Czechs in the region, from nearly zero in 1919 to 30,000 by the end of Czech rule (Markus 17), and partly by the decision of Jewish parents as well as perhaps Ukrainian parents to send their children to schools where they were not exposed to the "language war" or uncertain terminology and language norms. Also, in "Ruthenian" schools of higher education, Czech textbooks were often used: for instance, in 1934, at the Mukačevo teachers' seminary, 4 "Ruthenian" books were in use vs. 68 Czech ones (Štec' 62). These were the first steps toward Czechization of the region.

The policy of Czechization did not materialize because of the fall of Czecho-Slovakia in the late 1930s. Under the pressure of contemporary events, the Czecho-Slovak government finally initiated actual autonomy for Transcarpathia, on 26 June 1937, and granted it in October of 1938. The first regional government was formed, with A. Brodij at its head; when it proved to be pro-Hungarian, that government was dismissed, having existed for only eighteen days. On 2 November 1938 the region's southern border, including Užhorod and Mukačevo, was occupied by Hungary; Xust became the capital of the remaining territory. On 12 February 1939, in a general election, the block of Ukrainian parties was the only one submitted for consideration in voting. The Ukrainian list received 88.7 percent of the votes cast, in dramatic and unexplained contrast to the census of 1930, in which 455,000 persons declared themselves to be Ruthenians and only 2,355 said they were Ukrainians (*EU* 1, 568, Štec' 61; was the reversal a patriotic demonstration in the face of Hungarian aggression?). The proclamation of Transcarpathia's independence, on 15 March 1939, as Hungarian troops marched into the region, had a purely symbolic character. By March 20 the Hungarian occupation of Transcarpathia was complete.

The language policy of the new Hungarian regime—which existed for about five years, until 27 October 1944—was similar to that of the regime that had existed to 1919: it was hostile to the Ukrainian and Russian languages and practically prohibited their use. But now the region was given the special name of "Subcarpathian territory," a few pro-Hungarian local men were admitted to the Hungarian parliament, and the "Ruthenian" language was allowed to be a second language in the administration and in the primary and secondary schools (Markus 21). The Hungarian language program was set forth in S. Bonkáló's article "Rus'kyj lyteraturnŷj jazŷk—A Ruszin irodalmi nyelv" (published in *Zorja—Hajnal* 1–2, Užhorod 1941). The principles outlined there were the basis for the textbook *Hrammatyka uhrorusskoho jazŷka dlja serednyx učebnŷx zavedenyj*, by Ju. Maryna (Užhorod 1940; cf. Nikolajenko 27). Maryna declared that his grammar sought to restore etymological spellings and colloquial pronunciations, the former to emphasize the differences from Ukrainian, and the latter, from Russian (as related in Štec' 32). Compiled in the same spirit was I. Harajda's *Hrammatyka rus'koho jazŷka* (Užhorod 1941).

Under the Soviet occupation, beginning in October 1944, the standards of the Soviet Ukrainian language and spelling became compulsory. The "language war" had come to an end.

The period of Czech domination, during which language discussions, albeit often pointless and mostly low-level, flourished, left a deep imprint on the region. This small territory with less than a million inhabitants, many of whom had very little education, a region without any large cities, saw twelve grammars prepared and published (counting revised editions of the same grammar) in a span of twenty years. The periodical press was blossoming. The political press was differentiated by party. The non-political press included periodicals for children, for scouts, and for youth, as well as periodicals of humor, pedagogy, religion, economy, scholarship, and literature. According to Gerovskij (1934, 534), during one year (1933?) in Transcarpathia there appeared 14 publications in Ruthenian and Russian (one daily, five weeklies, two biweeklies, six monthlies) and 8 in Ukrainian (one weekly, three biweeklies, four monthlies). According to *EU* (1, 997), over the entire Czech period, the region had 62 Ukrainian periodicals, in comparison with 39 Russian, 34 Hungarian, and 13 Czech. Book production surpassed a thousand titles. These figures are stunning, especially in comparison with those of the preceding, Hungarian period. A similar upsurge can be observed in the educational system and in the "local language," be it Ukrainian, Russian, or, in particular, Ruthenian. Linguistic motleyness did not preclude the spread of education nor the reading of publications.

Indeed, the linguistic chaos, undoubtedly present, should not be exaggerated. The three hostile camps—Ruthenian, Ukrainian, and Russian—were not so distant from each other as the era's polemical articles would indicate. Publications in pure Standard Ukrainian were very hard to find, and the few in Russian were mostly by non-native (to the region) authors. All included elements of the local dialects, in differing measures. In that sense the traditional Ruthenian language variety was not being eliminated, but was being amalgamated with other languages. Transcarpathia was working its way toward accepting one of the real standard languages, that is, Ukrainian or Russian.

To illustrate, let us take a fragment from a book for children compiled by Avhustyn Vološyn after he converted to the Ukrainian orientation:

— *Što* maju robyty?

— Ydy, Yvane, *poobteraj tablu*, **stol**, lavycě, *popozeraj*, *cy* je krejda, černylo, *cy* čysta škola?

Y ja ne *lěnovavsja*, vse tak *jem* robyv, jak *mně* pan učytel' *rozkazaly*. U poludne *otvoryv jem vŷzorŷ* y koly'*m* peredav ključ panu **učytelju**, poxvalyly mene.

Ybo ja duže ljublju čystotu y porjadok. (*Azbuka* 73)

Local dialectal words and forms are in italics, whereas traditional Church Slavonic and Russian ones are in bold type.

In later publications the number of localisms diminished, but as a rule at least some continued to be present. The "language war," insofar as Ruthenian was concerned, had become pointless. As a system it was dead; yet, isolated elements of it were very much in evidence. The conflict between Ukrainian and Russian, by contrast, was on an entirely different level: they were locked in mortal combat in Transcarpathia, in a struggle for survival. In the case of Russian, the attraction of literature which Gerovskij had pointed out probably carried less weight than the appeal of its being, presumably, the language of overlords (*pans'kyj*). Like the character in Gogol's play "Marriage" who could not believe that Sicilian peasants spoke Italian (which he mistook for French), so the Transcarpathian believed, subconsciously, that Russian was the language of lords and not of plebeians, as Hungarian had been during and to some extent after the Hungarian domination. In 1924, Hnatjuk still observed a striving toward "a 'noble, lordly' language, which to some seems to be only Hungarian" (24). In that sense, traditional linguistic Russophilism dissipated after the Soviet occupation of 1944, due not only to official policy, but also to the demise of the image of Russian lords, engendered by contacts with non-aristocratic Russians.

In oral speech, Standard Ukrainian was not used by Transcarpathian natives during the Czech period, nor was its Galician variant. There is insufficient evidence to determine whether a Transcarpathian koine, based on one dialect with an admixture of Hungarian, Czech, Standard Ukrainian, Church Slavonic, and Russian words, was in the making, or whether in towns the common (local) language was a local dialect. The second option seems more likely, but that does not preclude the possibility that some words and forms became typical of a larger area. The chaotic language situation in schools and in publications may have reflected such a trend. If that was indeed the case, in this respect, even more than in the written language, the society of the region remained on a preindustrial level. The peculiarity of language development in Transcarpathia in the interwar period was rooted in the combination of this social level with the democratic measures instituted by the Czechs.

Retrospective Remarks

The attentive reader will draw his own conclusions from the material presented here. Some will see in it proof of the viability of the Ukrainian language; others, proof of its vulnerability and frailty. Perhaps both impressions are correct. In any case, there is no point here in going into further detail or in reiterating what has been said. On the other hand, some generalizations concerning the period 1900–1941 as a whole are not inappropriate.

The Ukrainian question, and the subordinate question of the Ukrainian language, acquired international dimensions. The most convincing evidence in this respect is not the question's emergence at diplomatic conferences and negotiations, but the fact that for decades three powerful governments engaged in active persecution of the Ukrainian language—those of St. Petersburg/Moscow, of Warsaw, and of Bucharest—and a fourth—of Prague—considered whether it should undertake such a policy. The forms this suppression took varied. It was a policy of total suppression in tsarist Russia, and very much so, also, in the first two occupations of the Ukraine by the Russians and in that by the White Army and by Romania. It was a policy of restriction and confrontation in Poland, and of support for the rival language in the last years of the Czecho-Slovak domination of Transcarpathia. A peculiar stand was taken by the Russians after their final occupation of the Ukraine: apparent support for the Ukrainian language with simultaneous undercutting of its social base and persecution of its bearers.

All the occupying powers applied the policy of compartmentalizing the territory where the Ukrainian language was spoken. Before World War I obstacles were erected against contacts between the Russian Ukraine and the Austro-Hungarian Ukrainian lands. After that war some frontiers became almost impenetrable (that between the Russian Ukraine and the other occupations); others, while not so rigid, hardly fostered the unity of the language. Besides the restrictions imposed by the existence of political frontiers, there were differences in legislation and in ways of life that were sometimes no less serious obstacles to unity. Moreover, under each occupation measures were taken to split the Ukrainian territory or to divest it of some peripheral areas. In the Soviet Ukraine, starting in the 1930s, such areas were the southern Kursk and western Voronež oblasts and the Kuban region. In Poland, the Lemko region was separated from Galicia, Galicia was separated from Volhynia, and both of these were divided from the Polissia and Xolm regions. In Romania a barrier was erected between the Ukrainians of Bukovina and those of Bessarabia, and in Czecho-Slovakia a wall was built between Transcarpathia and Ukrainian districts in Eastern Slovakia. All these partitions were intended to make the Ukrainian language area smaller, and in some cases they apparently succeeded.

Contacts across the frontiers and across the administrative boundaries weakened substantially, but they did not come to a complete halt. Galicia continued to influence the language of the Soviet Ukraine, although on a lesser scale than prior to the Soviet occupation (cf. examples quoted in Shevelov 1966, 124; cf. also the contacts of the Ukrainian Institute of Scientific Language in Kiev with the Ševčenko Scientific Society in Lviv). Much later, in 1970, a Ukrainian linguist in charge of the standardization of the Ukrainian literary language summarized the presence of Galicianisms in the Soviet-prescribed version of Standard Ukrainian as follows: "Eliminated from scholarly, journalistic, and official texts, Galicianisms were preserved predominantly in the spoken language and in fiction, in which they often are entirely justified" (Piliński 366). The statement is notable for its recognition of the official policy of excising Galicianisms (a policy going back to the 1930s) and in its acknowledgement of their presence as late as 1970. Whether Galicianisms have appeared only in fiction is, of course, questionable. Galician influences also spread to Bukovina (e.g., to the nationalist publications there) and to Transcarpathia (e.g., in the variegated activity of Ivan Pan'kevyč).

On the other hand, the Polish Ukraine was exposed to the impact of Kharkiv and Kiev, especially in the 1920s. In part this influence came directly, through scholarly institutions such as the Academy of Sciences; in part through party contacts between the CPU and the CPWU; and in part through the Ukrainian political emigration in

Poland and adjacent countries (I. Ohijenko a.o.).

Thus the unity of the Ukrainian language was maintained, but simultaneously, due to the limited channels of contact, regional differences were in large measure retained. The Galician koine did not merge with Standard Ukrainian, and a unique version of Standard Ukrainian was probably in the making in Transcarpathia.

These are obvious and indisputable facts. A discussion of the social basis of the Ukrainian language must stand on shakier ground. Before the beginning of the century, Ukrainian was plagued by an orientation on the peasantry, almost exclusive in the Russian Ukraine and predominant in the Austrian Ukraine. In the early twentieth century attempts were made to reorient the language, at least in part, towards the intelligentsia and the city. In literature, the attempts were successful (Kocjubyns'kyj, Lesja Ukrajinka, Vynnyčenko); in life, apparently, more often than not they failed. Infrequently did use of Ukrainian go far beyond the humanist intelligentsia, and only exceptionally did it reach the technical intelligentsia, businessmen, capitalists, and industrial workers; the attempt to involve the latter during the time of Ukrainianization was for the most part ineffective. More effective were the same attempts in the Polish Ukraine. Out of the necessity to compete with Polish and Jewish enterprises, a class of Ukrainian businessmen began to take shape. But the advance toward urbanization was slow and limited. In terms of social base, Ukrainian remained an incomplete language.

More striking was the substantial growth in the areas of life served by the Ukrainian language: from agriculture to religion, from musicology to financial bookkeeping, from poetry to economy. But in pure science and technology, where attempts to introduce the use of the Ukrainian language were made, Ukrainian did not find broad support and, after the period of Ukrainianization, shrank considerably. This reflected, of course, the gaps in the social base of the language.

In terms of prestige, the Ukrainian language won many victories; a certain number of individuals educated in Russian or Polish schools and in the Russian or Polish culture switched back to their native Ukrainian. The capacity of Ukrainian to serve on a high cultural level could no longer be denied. Yet among the non-Ukrainian urban population the reputation of the Ukrainian language remained low, and a derogatory attitude toward it was by no means exceptional. In many cases Ukrainians defected to other cultures and languages: Russian,

Polish, Romanian, and Czech. Very often the principal motivation for such defections was career or financial advancement, but behind it loomed a lack of enthusiasm, or even of esteem, for the Ukrainian language. Under all four occupations, Ukrainian failed to become the usual and common means of communication in the large urban and industrial centers.

An important shift took place in the ideological foundation for the use of Ukrainian. Before the twentieth century, the main argument fostering the use of the Ukrainian language by the educated (who, after all, were bilingual) was the need to communicate with, and enlighten, the peasants, who were not bilingual and therefore would presumably be doomed to remaining uneducated or even illiterate if not approached and instructed in Ukrainian. This argument lost its conviction and fell into disuse in the twentieth century. There were some attempts to replace it with slogans of romantic derivation, presenting language as a manifestation of national soul and as a depository of national culture, or the most important attribute of a nation.

With the caution of a scholar who preferred to stay away from ideological dictums, Vasyl' Simovyč wrote in 1934: "If one takes into account all the earmarks that make a nation a nation, language is one of the most important features of the nation's existence. Hence the extraordinary endeavors to preserve the language, because it is assumed that with the collapse of the language, the nation stops existing Such an understanding of language as the factor of utmost importance in the existence of a nation becomes part of the national political life of that nation. Such an understanding of language is rather emotional in character, but one cannot but reckon with it. We can fight that understanding as it pleases us, but we feel there is something in it" (35).

The ambivalence expressed by Simovyč, his acceptance and rejection, simultaneously, of the slogan of language as the determinant of nation, is indicative of the very situation of the Ukrainian language at the time. Under normal conditions the existence of a language does not need motivation or explanation. It would be highly unusual to start proving *la raison d'être* for, say, French in France or English in England. Those languages are simply there, as the air men breathe is there. No speaker would even imagine motivating their presence. If speakers of a language seek motivation for their language, an abnormality in the situation of the language in question is always present.

The Ukrainian language in the first half of the twentieth century was, from this point of view, in a transitional stage: from a motivated presence to an unmotivated one. When in the mid-nineteenth century the language was spoken virtually by peasants alone, the motivation of its understandability to peasants was both necessary and sufficient. The writings of a Kvitka or of a Marko Vovčok, with their stylized narrator standing in for the peasant, were in harmony with that motivation. After P. Kuliš, Franko, Kocjubyns'kyj, and Lesja Ukrajinka—that is, after the formation of a Ukrainian intelligentsia—the situation changed radically. The language of these writers and of their social group shared phonetics and morphology with that of the peasants, but lexically and syntactically it was a far cry from the language of the countryside. The writings of a Ryl's'kyj, a Semenko, a Bažan, among many others, did not meet the requirements of "rural ingenuousness." The representatives of the "ethnographic trend" in linguistics of the 1920s (Kurylo, Tymčenko, Ohijenko, Simovyč, a.o.) strived to fill the gap between the standard language and the language of the peasants. It would be futile to try to guess what would have happened if their ideas and efforts had prevailed, if they had not been crushed by the Soviet state machinery. There is some indication, however, that a number of these same linguists (Kurylo, Simovyč) moved away from the ethnographic orientation.

Language as the embodiment of the "national soul" was too romantic and poetic a notion to be acceptable as motivation in the age of science and technology. Even the thesis of language as the repository of a national tradition was not quite applicable, because archaicization played no significant role in the development of the Ukrainian language in the twentieth century. The language of, say, the seventeenth century is hardly understandable to a contemporary speaker from any social group. This "crisis in motivation" led to the non-motivated existence of the Ukrainian language, or to what is the same, motivation by mere presence. By coincidence this was the normal condition for any viable language. In the circumstances of the bi-linguality of the educated classes and of Ukrainians' bitter competition with the languages of the ruling nations—Russian, Polish, Romanian, and, in part, Czech—this normal condition, paradoxically, was abnormal. Hence came the timid but recurring attempts to stick to the romantic concept of language as the embodiment of the national soul.

The first half of the twentieth century brought the Standard Ukrainian language normalization of an unprecedented degree. A healthy phenomenon in itself, in practice it took on somewhat unhealthy forms when linguists, instead of selecting among features that did exist in the language, assumed the right to shape the language on their own, occasionally building entirely artificial, non-existent forms. True, this excess marked the "spelling" of 1928 only in the rendition of foreign words, where imposition of a system that existed nowhere in the language (*lohika* but *l'ozung*, etc.) was attempted. To some extent this also applied to vocabulary in general, and to terminological vocabulary in particular. These impositions prepared the ground, during the next reversal in Soviet policy, for another imposition of non-existent standards onto the language, this time Russian ones (Xvylja's spelling and terminology). Of course, the very fact that such experiments could take place was testimony to the permanently abnormal situation of the language, with its incomplete social bases and manifestations of internal incompleteness (the underdevelopment of technical terminology, the lack or underdevelopment of urban forms and genres of speech, including urban slang).[1]

The intrusion by the government—in these particular cases, by the Russian-run government—into a language's internal regulation was a Soviet innovation and invention. Neither the Polish nor the Romanian nor the Czech government had used such tactics: nor had they been applied by the tsarist administration in prerevolutionary Russia. In their policy toward the Ukrainian language, all of these had resorted to

---

[1] The absence of Ukrainian urban slang was in part compensated, in the speech of the intelligentsia, by insertions of Russian clichés (words and phrases) with ironic overtones. Sulyma (264) noted the phenomenon in his analysis of M. Xvyl'ovyj's language: "When Xvyl'ovyj writes in a broken language, this is really 'for the intelligentsia' because it was they who had created this 'brokenness.'" Sulyma's explanation is, however, incorrect: "Someone is unable to speak Ukrainian correctly and speaks in a distorted language, with Russianisms, whereas his appearance and tone are such to make people think that he talks facetiously, deliberately 'for laughs.' And then they get accustomed and consider that manner of speech a joke." The actual reason for that deliberate, ironic use of Russianisms by people able to speak Ukrainian perfectly (as Xvyl'ovyj did) was to fill the gap created by the absence of Ukrainian urban slang. Hidden behind this usage there was also a derogatory attitude toward the Russian language, an instance of the derision a dependent nation commonly has toward those on whom it depends.

measures of external coercion only: banning the Ukrainian language from public use, entirely or selectively; imposing the state language on speakers of Ukrainian through education, cultural developments, career opportunities, territorial resettlement; settlement of the ruling nationality on Ukrainian territory, etc. The Soviet system, in addition to applying all these "classic" methods, introduced interference into the structure of the Ukrainian language by prohibiting certain words, syntactic constructions, grammatical forms, spelling, and orthoepic standards, while promoting others patterned on Russian or directly transplanted from Russian. Through these tactics the conflict between the Ukrainian and the Russian languages in the Soviet Ukraine was extended from things external to the language into the language itself. The contamination was to affect not only speakers of Ukrainian, but the language per se in its intrinsic structure.

Under such constant assault, what augmented Ukrainian's ability to resist was the tradition (although in most cases not realized by its speakers) of the short-lived period of Ukrainian independence in the National Republic and the Hetmanate of 1917–1920. That strength came not from a political program, nor even from knowledge of the historical facts of the period (which were erased from the nation's memory by distortion and suppression), but from the actual imprint these years left on the language, in two respects: first, by extending its functions to areas where it was not admitted previously (especially state administration and education); second, by enriching it with new lexical and syntactic elements. This growth resumed, in part, at the time of Ukrainianization.

The entire range of innovations from the 1917–1920 period has never been studied thoroughly or extensively. Yet even some random examples show how many Ukrainian words—to limit ourselves here to vocabulary—that now seem quite "natural" and indispensable stem from that time. A contemporary speaker of Ukrainian would be surprised to learn that the following nine words, which belong to the neutral common stock of the language, were not listed at all or not in their present-day meaning in the most comprehensive of the prerevolutionary dictionaries, namely, Hrinčenko's: *dopovid'* 'lecture, paper', *holova* 'chairman', *hurtok* 'circle', *hurtožytok* 'hostel, dormitory', *lystivka* 'postcard', *stavytysja* 'to treat, to have an attitude toward', *urjad* 'government', *ustanova* 'office, institution', *zdibnyj* 'gifted, capable'. In his correspondence, M. Kocjubyns'kyj systematically used for 'postcard' the word *vidkrytka* (cf. Russian *otkrytka*; e.g., his letter of 24 November 1903—Kocjubyns'kyj 304). Vynnyčenko in his diary wrote "ja do vs'oho *vidnošusja*" (1911), *sposibni* (1914), and *predsidatel'* (1914, 1915; pp. 35, 119, 130, 167).[2] J. Čykalenko, in 1908, also used *predsidatel'* (II, 11c).

All these words (except *hurtožytok*, which apparently emerged after the Sovietization of the Ukraine) can reasonably be assumed to have gained their new meaning at the time of Ukrainian independence. Some of them are recorded in S. Ivanyc'kyj and F. Šumljans'kyj's 1918 *Rosijs'ko-ukrajins'kyj slovnyk* (included there are *stavytysja*, *ustanova*, *zdibnyj*; *holova* and *urjad* occur there, too, but alongside older words borrowed from or patterned on Russian: *predsidatel'*, *pravytel'stvo*, respectively, which were common in the pre-1917 Ukrainian press; others are not yet included). It is in the Academy dictionary of 1924 and thereafter that we find *dopovid'*, *hurtok*, and *lystivka*, and it is there that *urjad* is no longer accompanied by *pravytel'stvo*. Characteristically, most of these words did not enter into the "Galician koine."

These and many other words from independence times were so strongly rooted in the language by the end of the 1920s that even the "purge" of Ukrainian vocabulary in the 1930s, under Postyšev and Xvylja, was unable to delete them; moreover, such words were probably mistaken for "genuine" and native vocabulary.[3] During the comprehensive witch hunt (for "nationalistic" witches) and afterwards, numerous words from these times were incriminated and subject to elimination, especially if they had doublets common with Russian, such as *bihun - poljus* 'pole', *pidsonnja - klimat* 'climate', *ljudnist' - naselennja* 'population', *nyzka - rjad* 'many', *na tli - na foni* 'against the background' and many more. Yet the words contributed during the years of independence survived in those cases in which the "old" words fell completely out of use and, therefore, the "new"

---

[2] But in a sentence of 1914 we find *hurtok* (66). Apparently, the word came into use via the language of revolutionary parties and became common in the years of the struggle for independence.

[3] The Ukrainian names for months—*sičen'* 'January', *ljutyj* 'February', etc.— apparently also entered general usage at the time of independence. Before the revolution, Čykalenko, for instance, systematically used the "international" ones: *janvar*, *fevral'*, etc. (in the Ukrainian case, taken from the Russian).

words (now not so new) proved to be practically unidentifiable and irreplaceable. After all, the entire language purge (as well as human purge) after the 1920s was in a sense but a struggle with the spectral or real patrimony of the brief period of independence. The legacy of that period became and remained an important level in the Standard Ukrainian language.

In retrospect, in the period from 1900 to 1941, the Ukrainian language advanced rapidly in the sense that it became more rich, widespread, and regularized. Yet, existing as it did under four occupations, it remained incomplete in terms of its social base and in terms of the avenues of life it served. Furthermore it was threatened by the general bilingualism of the entire educated population on Ukrainian territory. Bilingualism always tends to become monolingualism; in each particular case, theoretically, speakers can opt for either of the two languages involved. The threat of the non-Ukrainian option in bilingualism in the Ukraine was heightened because the competing language served as a channel to all other languages, primarily the Western ones: Russian in the Russian Empire and in the Soviet system, Romanian in Romania, Hungarian or Czech in Transcarpathia and, to a lesser degree, Polish in Poland (before 1918, the Galician intelligentsia as a rule knew at least one of the major Western languages, German).

This situation was recognized repeatedly by leading personalities in Ukrainian cultural and political life, sometimes with indignation, sometimes with understanding. As early as 1891, Ivan Franko wrote about Russian Ukrainians: "They usually know only one language, the Muscovite language in which they were taught in schools This is their entire *apparatus criticus*" (Tymošenko 2, 18). In 1910, S. Jefremov stated: "The Ukrainian has borne and still bears two souls in his breast: he got and still gets access to all general human emotions from a Russian source, in a Russian attire. . . . The worst evil of our recent past was that Ukrainianophilism looked at Ukrainian life as a parochialism, as a partial variant of general Russian life" (Lotoc'kyj 2, 436). S. Petljura, in 1912, drew a conclusion from this situation: "I think that for the given moment in the development of the Ukrainian movement (*ukrajinstvo*), the influence of Russian culture is the only available means to raise our national culture, because there are so few roads to Europe that these roads look rather like very narrow paths" (Petljura 2, 191). It is for this reason that Petljura regarded Ukrainian translations of the world's literary classics as a problem with political significance (ibid., 508).

A faithful mirror of that dependence on the language of the ruling nation was the production of dictionaries. In the Russian Ukraine, whether tsarist or Soviet, Russian-Ukrainian and Ukrainian-Russian dictionaries were published almost exclusively (for the years 1918–1961, bibliographers list, discounting abridged school dictionaries, only five [five!] Ukrainian-West European dictionaries: one French, two German, and two English; Hol'denberh and Korolevyč 125ff.). In the Austrian and, later, Polish Ukraine, German-Ukrainian and Ukrainian-German, Polish-Ukrainian and Ukrainian-Polish dictionaries predominated; in pre-1918 Transcarpathia, Hungarian-Ukrainian and Ukrainian-Hungarian ones were the norm. Such dependence on the language of the ruling nation was a major handicap for the normal development of the Ukrainian language and, in fact, the growth of more than the language. It was one more manifestation of the incompleteness of the Ukrainian language in the first half of the twentieth century.

Bibliographical References

Antonovyč, V. *Tvory*. Vol. 1. Kiev: Ukrainian Academy of Sciences, 1932.

Azbuka karpato-rus'koho y cerkovno-slavjanskoho čtenyja. Compiled by Avhustyn Vološyn. 7th ed. Užhorod: Unio, 1924.

Babij, B. *Ukrajins'ka radjans'ka deržava v period vidbudovy narodnoho hospodarstva (1921–1925)*. Kiev: Ukrainian Academy of Sciences, 1958–61.

Bahmet, I., ed. *Movoznavstvo na Ukrajini za pjatdesjat rokiv*. Kiev: "Naukova dumka," 1967.

Beljaeva, L.; Zinov'eva, M.; Nikiforov, M. *Bibliografija periodičeskix izdanij Rossii, 1901–1916*. Vols. 1–4. Leningrad, 1961.

Bilodid, I. "Tvorča osnova dal'šoho rozvytku radjans'koho movoznavstva." *Movoznavstvo*, 1981, no. 3.

Bojko, I. *Ukrajins'ki literaturni al'manaxy i zbirnyky XIX–počatku XX st.: Bibliohrafičnyj pokažčyk*. Kiev: "Naukova dumka," 1967.

Borys, Jurij. *The Sovietization of Ukraine, 1917–1923*. Edmonton: Canadian Institute of Ukrainian Studies, 1980.

Budivnyctvo radjans'koji Ukrajiny: Zbirnyk. No. 1. Kharkiv: Derž. vyd. Ukrainy, s.a.

Cinqième congrès de l'internationale communiste (17 juin–8 juillet 1924): Compte rendue analytique. Paris: Humanité, 1924.

Colecţiune de legi şi regulamente. Vol. 2: *1.I.1924–31.XII.1924*. Official edition. Bucharest, 1925.

Constitution de la République de Pologne du 23 avril 1935. B. Commission Polonaise de coopération juridique internationale. Warsaw, 1935.

The Constitution of the Czechoslovak Republic. With an introduction by Jiří Hoetzl and V. Joachim. Prague: Société l'effort de la Tschécoslovaquie, 1920.

Ministère des affaires étrangères [of Romania]. *Constitution*. Bucharest, 1923.

(Constitution 2). Royaume de Roumanie. *Constitution du 2 février 1938*. Bucharest, 1938.

Curtiss, John S. *The Russian Church and the Soviet State, 1917–1950*. Boston: Little, Brown & Co., 1953.

Červins'ka, L., and Dykyj, A. *Pokažčyk z ukrajins'koji movy: Materijaly po 1929 rik*. Kharkiv: Deržavna biblioteka im. Korolenka, s.a. (1931?).

Čykalenko, Je. *Spohady (1861–1907)*. New York: Ukrainian Academy of Arts and Sciences in the U.S., 1955.

―――. "Spohady, ščodennyk ta lystuvannja (1907–1917)." Vol. 2. Manuscript. New York. Ukrainian Academy of Arts and Sciences in the U.S.

Dareste, F. R., and Dareste, P. *Les constitutions modernes: Recueil des constitutions en vigueur dans les divers états d'Europe, d'Amérique et du monde civilisé*. Vol. 1. Paris, 1910.

Desjatyj s"ezd RKP (b), Mart 1921 goda: Stenografičeskij otčet. Moscow: Gos. izdat. polit. literatury, 1963.

Dombčevs'kyj, R. "Za pravo movy." *Jubilejnyj al'manax Sojuzu ukrajins'kyx advokativ*. Lviv, 1934.

Dorošenko, Dmytro. *Istorija Ukrajiny, 1917–1923 rr*. Vols. 1 and 2. Užhorod: 1932, 1930.

―――. *Moji spomyny pro davnje mynule (1901–1914 roky)*. Winnipeg: "Tryzub," 1949.

―――. *Moji spomyny pro nedavnje-mynule (1914–1920)*. Munich: Ukrajins'ke vydavnyctvo, 1969.

Dorošenko, V. "Molod' na Poltavščyni v 90-x rokax." *Krakivs'ki visti*, 1944, no. 90.

Drahomanov, Myxajlo. *Vybrani tvory*. Vol. 1. Prague and New York, 1937.

Durdenevskij, V. N. *Ravnopravie jazykov v sovetskom stroe*. Moscow: Institut sovetskogo prava, 1927.

Dvenadcatyj s"ezd RKP (b), 17–25 aprelja 1923 goda: Stenografičeskij otčet. Moscow: Gos. izdat. polit. literatury, 1968.

Dzendzelivs'kyj, J. "Zaxody Peterburz'koji akademiji nauk ščodo vporjadkuvannja ukrajins'koho pravopysu." *Movoznavstvo*, 1971, no. 1.

Education in Poland, 1918–1928. Warsaw: Ministry of Education, 1928.

EU—Encyklopedija ukrajinoznavstva v dvox tomax. Vol. 1. Edited by V. Kubijovyč and Z. Kuzelja. Munich and New York, 1949. Vol. 2: *Slovnykova častyna.* Edited by V. Kubijovyč. Paris and New York, 1955.

Fedenko, Panas. *Dmytro Čyževs'kyj: Spomyn pro žyttja i naukovu dijal'nist'.* Munich: Naše slovo, 1979.

Franko, Ivan. *Tvory v dvadcjaty tomax.* Vol. 16. Kiev, 1955.

Gerovskij, Georgij. Review of Ivan Pan'kevyč, *Hramatyka rus'koho jazyka.* In *Slavia* 6 (1927).

Giterman, V. *Geschichte Russlands.* Vol. 3. Hamburg: Europäische Verlagsanstalt, 1949.

Gregorovich, Alex. *A List of Dictionaries, 1918–1933.* Toronto, 1957.

Handelsman, Marceli. *Konstytucje polskie, 1791–1921.* Warsaw, 1921.

Hnatevyč—Krypjakevyč, I., and Hnatevyč, V. *Istorija ukrajins'koho vijs'ka.* Lviv: Iv. Tyktor, 1936.

Hnatjuk, V. "V spravi literaturnoji movy pidkarpats'kyx rusyniv." In Muzej ukrajins'koji kul'tury v Svydnyku, *Naukovyj zbirnyk* 3. Prešov, 1967.

Hol'denberh, L., and Korolevyč, N. *Ukrajins'ka mova: Bibliohrafičnyj pokažčyk (1918–1961 rr.).* Kiev: Ukrainian Academy of Sciences, 1963.

Hrabovs'kyj, Pavlo. *Zibrannja tvoriv u tr'ox tomax.* Vol. 3. Kiev, 1960.

Hrinčenko, B. "Kil'ka sliv pro našu literaturnu movu," *Zorja* (Lviv), 1892, no. 15, 310–14.

―――. *Tjažkym šljaxom.* Kharkiv, 1907.

Hruševs'kyj, M. *Pro ukrajins'ku movu i ukrajins'ku školu.* 2d ed. Kiev, 1913.

Ihnatijenko, V. *Bibliohrafija ukrajins'koji presy, 1816–1916.* State College, Pa., 1968.

―――. *Ukrajins'ka presa (1916–1923 rr.).* Kharkiv: Derž. vyd. Ukrainy, 1926.

Itogi raboty sredi nacional'nyx men'šinstv na Ukraine: K 10–j godovščine Oktjabr'skoj revoljucii. Po materialam Central'noj kommissii nacional'nyx men'šinstv pri VUCIK. Kharkiv, 1927.

Jakobson, Roman. "Slavische Sprachfragen in der Sovjetunion." *Slavische Rundschau*, 1934, no. 6, pp. 324–49.

Jakubs'kyj, S., and Jakubs'kyj, O. *Rosijs'ko-ukrajins'kyj slovnyk vijs'kovoji terminolohiji.* Kiev: Derž. vyd. Ukrainy, 1928.

Jedlins'ka, U. "Z istoriji borot'by za jedynu literaturnu movu v Zakarpatti v 1919–1938 rr." In Akademija nauk UkrRSR, Ukrajins'kyj komitet slavistiv, *Filolohičnyj zbirnyk.* Kiev: Ukrainian Academy of Sciences, 1958.

Jefremov (Efremov), S. "Bjurokratičeskaja utopija." *Russkoe bogatstvo*, 1910, 3.

K izučeniju istorii: Sbornik. Moscow: Partizdat, 1937.

Karpova, V. "Z istoriji ukrajins'koho pravopysu v Halyčyni (1917–1939 rr.)." In Akademija nauk UkrRSR, Instytut suspil'nyx nauk, *Doslidžennja i materialy z ukrajins'koji movy*, vol. 2. Kiev: Ukrainian Academy of Sciences, 1960.

Kievskij krasnoznamennyj: Istorija krasnoznamennogo Kievskogo voennogo okruga 1919–1972. Moscow: Voennoe izdatel'stvo Ministerstva oborony SSSR, 1974.

Kistjakivs'kyj (Kostjakovskij), B. [pseud. Ukrainec]. "K voprosu o samostojatel'noj ukrainskoj kul'ture." *Russkaja mysl'*, 1911, no. 5.

Kocjubyns'kyj, M. *Tvory v semy tomax.* Vol. 5. Kiev: "Naukova dumka," 1974.

Kokorudz, Illja. "Pryčynok do sporu jazykovoho." *Zorja* (Lviv), 1891, no. 24, pp. 471–72.

Konstitucija (osnovnoj zakon) SSSR—Konstitucii (osnovnye zakony) sojuznyx sovetskix socialističeskix respublik. Moscow: Gos. Izdat. polit. literatury, 1951.

Konstytucija (osnovnyj zakon) Ukrajins'koji Radjans'koji Socijalistyčnoji Respubliky: Projekt. Kiev, 1937.

Korolenko, V. G. *Sobranie sočinenij v desjati tomax.* Vol. 8. Moscow, 1955.

Kosior, S. *Itogi nojabr'skogo plenuma CK VKP(b) i zadači kul'turnogo stroitel'stva na Ukraine.* Kiev: Gos. Izdat. Ukrainy, 1929.

Kostiuk, Hryhory. *Stalinist Rule in the Ukraine: A Study of the Decade of Mass Terror (1929–1939).* London: Atlantic Books, 1960.

Krylov, I. *Systema osvity v Ukrajini (1917–1930).* Munich: Instytut dlja vyvčennja SSSR, 1956.

Kryms'kyj, A., ed. *Rosijs'ko-ukrajins'kyj slovnyk pravnyčoji movy: Projekt.* Kiev: Ukrainian Academy of Sciences, 1926.

_____. *Tvory v pjaty tomax.* Vol. 3. Kiev: "Naukova dumka," 1973.

Kryp''jakevyč, Ivan [pseud. Ivan Xolms'kyj]. *Istorija Ukrajiny.* Munich, 1949.

Kul'turne budivnyctvo v Ukrajins'kij RSR: Važlyviši rišennja komunistyčnoji partiji i radjans'koho urjadu, 1917–1959 rr. Zbirnyk dokumentiv. Vol 1. Kiev: Deržpolitvydav, 1959.

Kurylo, O. *Uvahy do sučasnoji ukrajins'koji literaturnoji movy.* 4th ed. Cracow and Lviv: Ukrajins'ke vydavnyctvo, 1942.

Kvitkovs'kyj, D.; Bryndzan, T.; Žukovs'kyj, A. *Bukovyna, jiji mynule i sučasne.* Paris, Philadelphia, Detroit: "Zelena Bukovyna," 1956.

Lebed', D. "Vnimanie ideologičeskomu frontu." *Bol'ševik,* 1928, no. 7.

Lejtes, A., and Jašek, M. *Desjat' rokiv ukrajins'koji literatury (1917–1927).* Vols. 1 and 2. Kharkiv: Derž. vyd. Ukrainy, 1928.

Lenin, V. *Polnoe sobranie sočinenij.* Vols. 38 and 39; Moscow, 1963. Vol. 51; Moscow, 1965.

Levyc'kyj, Modest [pseud. M. Pylypovyč]. "Deščo do spravy pro ukrajins'ku pys'mennyc'ku movu." *Literaturno-naukovyj vistnyk,* 1909, no. 8.

_____. *Deščo pro sučasnu stadiju rozvytku ukrajins'koji literaturnoji movy.* Kiev, 1913, 1918.

Levyns'kyj, V. *Jedyna nedilyma Sovits'ka Rosija?: Na pravax rukopysu.* Kiev and Vienna, 1920.

Lotoc'kyj, O. *Storinky mynuloho.* Pt. 2; Warsaw, 1933. Pt. 3; Warsaw, 1934. Praci Ukrajins'koho naukovoho instytutu, 12, 21.

Luckyj, George S. N. *Literary Politics in the Soviet Ukraine, 1917–1934.* New York: Columbia University Press, 1956.

Magocsi, Paul Robert. *The Shaping of a National Identity: Subcarpathian Rus', 1848–1948.* Cambridge, Mass., and London: Harvard University Press, 1978.

Majstrenko, Ivan. *Istorija Komunistyčnoji partiji Ukrajiny.* N.p.: Sučasnist', 1979.

Makowski, Julian. *Umowy międzynarodowe Polski, 1919–1934.* Warsaw, 1935.

Markus, Vasyl. *L'incorporation de l'Ukraine Subcarpatique à l'Ukraine Soviétique, 1944–1945.* Louvain, 1956.

Materialien, betreffend die Friedensverhandlungen. Pt. 12: *Die acht Verträge von Sèvres.* Berlin: Deutsches auswärtiges Amt., 1921.

Mayo, P. J. "Byelorussian Orthography: From the 1933 Reform to the Present Day." *Journal of Byelorussian Studies* 4, no. 2 (1978).

Mazepa, I. *Ukrajina v ohni j buri revoljuciji, 1917–1921.* Pts. 1 and 2. Munich: "Prometej," 1950 and 1951.

Mazlax, Serhij, and Šaxraj, Vasyl'. *Do xvyli: Ščo dijet'sja na Ukrajini i z Ukrajinoju.* New York: "Proloh," 1967.

Mudryj, V. *Borot'ba za ohnyšče ukrajins'koji kul'tury v zaxidnyx zemljax Ukrajiny.* Lviv: Ukrajins'ka krajeva students'ka rada, 1923.

Mušynka, Mykola. "Korespondencija Volodymyra Hnatjuka z Ivanom Pan'kevyčem." *Muzej ukrajins'koji kul'tury v Svydnyku. Naukovyj zbirnyk* 3. Prešov, 1967.

Myrnyj, Panas. *Tvory v pjaty tomax.* Vol. 5. Kiev: Derž. vyd. xud. literatury, 1960.

Myxal'čuk, K. "Dejaki uvahy ščodo redaguvannja ukrajins'koho slovnyka." In B. Hrinčenko, *Slovnyk ukrajins'koji movy*, edited by S. Jefremov and A. Nikovs'kyj, vol. 3. Kiev: "Horno," 1928.

Nacionalisty v 3-ej Gosudarstvennoj dume. St. Petersburg, 1912. (No indication of author, editor, or publisher.)

Narysy istoriji Komunistyčnoji partiji Ukrajiny. Instytut istoriji partiji CK KP Ukrajiny. Kiev: Deržpolitvydav, 1961.

Nečuj-Levyc'kyj, Ivan. *Kryve dzerkalo ukrajins'koji movy.* Kiev, 1912.

———. "S'ohočasna časopysna mova." *Ukrajina*, 1907, nos. 1–3.

Nikolajenko, Z. "Borot'ba navkolo movnyx pytan' na Zakarpatti v 30-x rokax XX st." *Ukrajins'ka mova v školi*, 1959, no. 5, pp. 25–29.

Nikovs'kyj, A. "Vstupne slovo." In B. Hrinčenko, *Slovnyk ukrajins'koji movy*, vol. 1, edited by S. Jefremov and A. Nikovs'kyj. Kiev: "Horno," 1927.

Ohijenko, I. *Narysy z istoriji ukrajins'koji movy: Systema ukrajins'koho pravopysu.* Warsaw, 1927.

Papierzyńska-Turek, Mirosława. *Sprawa ukraińska w Drugiej*

Rzeczypospolitej, 1922–1926. Cracow: Wydawnictwo Literackie, 1979.

Parry, Clive. *The Consolidated Treaty Series.* Edited and annotated by C. Parry. Vol. 225. New York: Oceana Publications, 1981.

Pčilka, Olena. "Tovaryšky." In *Peršyj vinok: Žinočyj al'manax.* Lviv, 1887.

Petljura, Symon. *Statti, lysty, dokumenty.* Vol. 2. New York: Ukrainian Academy of Arts and Sciences in the U.S., 1979.

Piddubnyj, H. *Bukovyna: Jiji mynule j sučasne.* Kharkiv: Derž. vyd. Ukrajiny, 1928.

Piliński (Pylyns'kyj), M. "O kulturze języka na Ukrainie." *Poradnik językowy,* 1970, no. 6, pp. 365–75.

Pipes, Richard. "Peter Struve and Ukrainian Nationalism." *Harvard Ukrainian Studies* 3/4, pt. 2 (1979–1980): 675–83.

Politika sovetskoj vlasti po nacional'nomu voprosu za tri goda (1917/xi–1920). Moscow: Narkomat po delam nacional'-nostej, 1920.

Polons'ka-Vasylenko, N. *Ukrajins'ka akademija nauk: Narys istoriji.* Pt. 1; Munich, 1955. Pt. 2; Munich, 1958. Instytut dlja vyvčennja istoriji ta kul'tury SSSR, Doslidy i materijaly, ser. 1, pts. 21, 43.

Popov, M. *Narys istoriji Komunistyčnoji partiji (bil'šovykiv) Ukrajiny.* 5th ed. Kharkiv: "Proletar," 1931.

Presa Ukrajins'koji RSR 1918–1975. Kharkiv: Knyžkova palata UkrRSR im. I. Fedorova, 1976.

Prokop, M. "Die Ukraine und Moskaus Ukrainepolitik." Arbeits- und Forderungsgemeinschaft der Ukrainischen Wissenschaften e. V. *Jahrbuch der Ukrainekunde 1985.* Munich.

Pypin, A. Review of *Izvestija XI arxeologičeskogo s"ezda v Kieve.* In *Vestnik Evropy,* 1899, no. 11.

Rezoljuciji—Instytut istoriji partiji CK KP Ukrajiny. *Komunistyčna partija Ukrajiny v rezoljucijax i rišennjax zjizdiv i konferencij, 1918–1956.* Kiev: Deržpolitvydav, 1958.

Riga. *Traktat pokoju między Polską a Rosją i Ukrainą podpisany w Rydze dnia 18 Marca 1921 roku.* Official edition. N.p. and n.d.

Romanovyč-Tkačenko, N. "Manivcjamy." *Literaturno-naukovyj vistnyk,* 1914, no. 65.

Sadovs'kyj, V. *Nacional'na polityka sovitiv na Ukrajini.* Praci Ukrajins'koho naukovoho instytutu, 39. Warsaw, 1937.

Samijlenko, Volodymyr. *Tvory v dvox tomax.* Vol. 2. Kiev: Derž. vyd. xudož. lit., 1958.

Savčenko, F. *Zaborona ukrajinstva 1876 r.* Munich: Wilhelm Fink, 1970.

Shevelov, George Y. "Pokolinnja dvadcjatyx rokiv v ukrajins'komu movoznavstvi." *Zapysky Naukovoho tovarystva im. Ševčenka,* 173. Chicago, 1962.

――――. *Die ukrainische Schriftsprache, 1798–1965.* Wiesbaden: Harrassowitz, 1966.

――――. "Language Planning and Unplanning in the Ukrainian S.S.R." In George Thomas, ed., *The Languages and Literatures of the Non-Russian Peoples of the Soviet Union.* Hamilton, Ont.: McMaster University, 1977.

――――. "Pro pamflety Mykoly Xvyl'ovoho." *Sučasnist',* 1978, no. 2, 17–59. Reprinted in: Mykola Xvyl'ovyj, *Tvory v pjatox tomax.* Vol. 4. New York, Baltimore, Toronto: "Slovo," and "Smoloskyp," 1983.

Shostakovich, D. *Testimony.* Edited by Solomon Volkov. New York: Harper and Row, 1979.

Shtepa, Konstantin F. *Russian Historians and the Soviet State.* New Brunswick: Rutgers University Press, 1962.

Simovyč, Vasyl'. (1) "Velykoukrajins'ki vyslovy." *Žyttja i znannja* 7 (1934). Reprinted in V. Simovyč, *Ukrajins'ke movoznavstvo,* vol. 2, Ottawa: University of Ottawa Press, 1984.

――――. (2) "Deščo pro našu kupec'ku movu." *Žyttja i znannja* 7 (1934). Reprinted, as above.

――――. (3) "Ohljad lingvistyčnyx prac' ukrajins'koji emigraciji." 2. In *Ukrajins'kyj naukovyj zjizd u Prazi.* Prague, 1934. Reprinted, as above.

――――. (4) "Naša tovarys'ka mova." *Nazustrič* (Lviv), 1934, no. 5. Reprinted, as above.

――――. (5) "Ridna mova j intelektual'nyj rozvytok dytyny." *Šljax vyxovannja j navčannja* (Lviv), 8 (1934). Reprinted, as above.

――――, ed. *Lystuvannja Lesi Ukrajinky z Josypom Makovejem.* Lviv, 1938.

Siropolko, S. *Narodnja osvita na sovjets'kij Ukrajini*. Praci Ukrajins'koho naukovoho instytutu, 22. Warsaw, 1934.

Skrypnyk, Mykola. *Statti j promovy z nacional'noho pytannja*. Munich: Sučasnist', 1974.

Slavjanskoe jazykoznanie: Bibliografičeskij ukazatel' literatury, izdannoj v SSSR s 1918 po 1960 gg. Moscow: Academy of Sciences, 1963.

Smal'-Stoc'kyj, Roman. *Ukrajins'ka mova v Sovjets'kij Ukrajini*. New York: Shevchenko Scientific Society, 1969.

Sobota, Emil, ed. *Ústava republiky Československé*. Vols. 1–4. Prague: J. Otto, 1927.

Sobranie uzakonenij. . . . See Zbirnyk uzakonen'. . . .

Solovej, Dmytro. *Rozhrom Poltavy: Spohady z časiv Vyzvol'nyx zmahan' ukrajins'koho narodu, 1914–1921*. Winnipeg: "Tryzub," 1974.

Stalin, J. *Sočinenija*. Vol. 12. Moscow, 1949.

Stenogr.—Gosudarstvennaja duma, Tretij sozyv, *Stenografičeskie otčety: 1910 g.*, 4th sess., pt. 1, St. Petersburg, 1910; Gosudarstvennaja duma, Četvertyj sozyv, *1913 g.*, 1st sess., pt. 2, St. Petersburg, 1913; ibid., *1914 g.*, 2nd sess., pt. 2, St. Petersburg, 1914.

Stešenko, I. "Pro ukrajins'ku literaturnu movu." *Literaturno-naukovyj vistnyk*, 11 (1912).

Struve, P. "Na raznye temy." *Russkaja mysl'*, 1911, no. 1.

————. "Obščerusskaja kul'tura i ukrainskij partikuljarizm." *Russkaja mysl'*, 1912, no. 1.

Sulyma, M. "Frazeolohija Mykoly Xvyl'ovoho." *Červonyj šljax*, 1925, no. 1/2.

Synjavs'kyj, Oleksa. "Korotka istorija Ukrajins'koho pravopysu." In *Kul'tura ukrajins'koho slova*, vol. 1. Kharkiv and Kiev, 1931.

Šax, Stepan. *L'viv—misto mojeji molodosty*. Vol. 3: *Cisars'ko-korolivs'ka akademična himnazija*. Munich, 1956.

Ščegolev, S. *Ukrainskoe dviženie kak sovremennyj ètap južnorusskogo separatizma*. Kiev, 1912.

Štec', Mykola. *Literaturna mova ukrajinciv Zakarpattja i Sxidnoji Slovaččyny (pislja 1918)*. Bratislava: Slovac'ke pedahohične vydavnyctvo, 1969.

Tichý, František. *Vývoj současného spisovného jazyka na Podkarpatské Rusi.* Prague, 1938.

Tkačenko, H. "Perebuduvaty movoznavču robotu VUAN." *Visti Vseukrajins'koji akademiji nauk,* 1930, no. 4.

Törvénytár: Magyar törvénytár, 1907 évi törvénycikkek. Edited by Dr. Márkus Dezső. Budapest, 1908.

Treaties, Conventions, International Acts, Protocols and Agreements between the United States of America and Other Powers, 1910–1923. Vol. 3. Washington, 1923.

Tymošenko, P. *Xrestomatija materialiv z istoriji ukrajins'koji literaturnoji movy.* Pts. 1 and 2. Kiev: "Radjans'ka škola," 1959, 1961.

Ukrajinizacija radjans'kyx ustanov: Dekrety, instrukciji j materijaly. Kharkiv: Narodnij komisarijat osvity, 1926.

Ukrajinka, Lesja. *Tvory.* Vol. 12. New York: Tyščenko & Bilous, 1954.

Vasyl'čenko, Stepan. *Tvory v tr'ox tomax.* Vol. 3. Kiev: "Dnipro," 1974.

[Vasylevs'kyj, S., and Rudnyc'kyj, Je.] Akademija nauk URSR, Instytut movoznavstva. *Rosijs'ko-ukrajins'kyj slovnyk.* Kiev: Ukrainian Academy of Sciences, 1937.

Večernyc'kyj, A. "Ukrajins'ka presa." *Knyhar',* 1917 (October), 2.

Verxrats'kyj, Ivan [pseud. Losun]. "U spravi jazykovij i dekotri zamitky pro knyžky dlja ukrajins'koho ljudu." *Zorja* (Lviv), 1892, nos. 7–9.

Visti z Ukrajins'koji central'noji rady. No. 1, for 19 March 1917. No. 2, for 21 March 1917. Kiev.

Vlasovs'kyj, Ivan. *Narys istoriji Ukrajins'koji pravoslavnoji cerkvy.* Vol. 4. New York and South Bound Brook, N.J., 1961.

Vynnyčenko, V. *Ščodennyk.* Vol. 1: *1911–1920.* Edmonton and New York: Canadian Institute of Ukrainian Studies and the Ukrainian Academy of Arts and Sciences in the U.S., 1980.

———. *Tvory.* Vol. 19. Kiev: "Rux," 1928.

———. *Vidrodžennja naciji.* 3 vols. Kiev and Vienna, 1920.

Wexler, Paul N. *Purism and Language: A Study in Modern Ukrainian and Belorussian Nationalism (1840–1967).* Bloomington: Indiana University Press, 1974.

Xolodnyj, H. "Do istoriji orhanizaciji terminolohičnoji spravy na Ukrajini." *Visnyk Instytutu ukrajins'koji naukovoji movy* 1 (1928).

Xrystjuk, P. *Zamitky i materijaly do istoriji ukrajins'koji revoljuciji, 1917–1920 rr.* Vols. 1–4. Vienna, 1921–22.

Xvylja, A. "Proletarijat i praktyčne rozhortannja kul'turno-nacional'noho budivnyctva." *Bil'šovyk Ukrajiny*, 1930, no. 13/14.

_____. "Na borot'bu z nacionalizmom na movnomu fronti." *Za markso-lenins'ku krytyku*, 1933, no. 7.

_____. *Znyščyty korinnja nacionalizmu na movnomu fronti.* Kharkiv, 1933.

Zbirnyk uzakonen' ta rozporjadžen' robitnyčo-seljans'koho urjadu Ukrajiny. (=*Sobranie uzakonenij i rasporjaženij raboče-krest'janskogo pravitel'stva Ukrainy*). [Kharkiv] 1919–1932.

Zvidomlennja pro dijal'nist' Ukrajins'koji akademiji nauk u Kyjevi za 1920 rik, Kiev, 1921; . . . *za 1921 rik*, Kiev, 1923; . . . *za 1922 rik*, Prague, 1925; . . . *za 1923 rik*, Kiev, 1924; . . . *za 1924 rik*, Kiev, 1925; . . . *za 1925 rik*, Kiev, 1926; . . . *za 1926 rik*, Kiev, 1927; . . .*za 1927 rik*, Kiev, 1928. (Slight variations in the titles.)

Žovtobrjux, M. *Mova ukrajins'koji periodyčnoji presy: Kinec' XIX – počatok XX st.* Kiev: "Naukova dumka," 1970.

_____. "Jedyna literaturna. . . ." *Ukrajins'ka mova i literatura v školi*, 1964, no. 10.

Žučenko, M. "Pro ukrajins'ku literaturnu movu." *Dniprovi xvyli*, 1912, nos. 22–24; 1913, 1.

Žyvotko, A. *Istorija ukrajins'koji presy.* N.p.: Ukr. tex.-hospod. inst., 1946 ("Na pravax rukopysu").

Index